Rehabilitating

Government

*Pay and Employment Reform
in Africa*

WORLD BANK

REGIONAL AND

SECTORAL STUDIES

Rehabilitating Government

Government

Pay and Employment Reform in Africa

EDITED BY

DAVID L. LINDAUER

BARBARA NUNBERG

The World Bank
Washington, D.C.

The World Bank Regional and Sectoral Studies series provides an outlet for work that is relatively limited in its subject matter or geographical coverage but that contributes to the intellectual foundations of development operations and policy formulation. Some sources cited in this paper may be informal documents that are not readily available.

The findings, interpretations, and conclusions expressed in this publication are those of the authors and should not be attributed in any manner to the World Bank, to its affiliated organizations, or to the members of its Board of Executive Directors or the countries they represent.

The material in this publication is copyrighted. Requests for permission to reproduce portions of it should be sent to the Office of the Publisher at the address shown in the copyright notice above. The World Bank encourages dissemination of its work and will normally give permission promptly and, when the reproduction is for noncommercial purposes, without asking a fee. Permission to copy portions for classroom use is granted through the Copyright Clearance Center, Inc., Suite 910, 222 Rosewood Dr., Danvers, Massachusetts 01923, U.S.A.

The complete backlist of publications from the World Bank is shown in the annual *Index of Publications,* which contains an alphabetical title list and indexes of subjects, authors, and countries and regions. The latest edition is available free of charge from Distribution Unit, Office of the Publisher, The World Bank, 1818 H Street, N.W., Washington, D.C. 20433, U.S.A., or from Publications, The World Bank, 66, avenue d'Iéna, 75116 Paris, France.

Cover design by Sam Ferro

Library of Congress Cataloging-in-Publication Data

Rehabilitating government: pay and employment reform in Africa/
    edited by David L. Lindauer and Barbara Nunberg.
        p. cm. — (World Bank regional and sectoral studies)
    Includes bibliographical references.
    ISBN 0-8213-3000-4
        1. Developing countries—Officials and employees—Salaries, etc.
    2. Civil service reform—Developing countries. I. Lindauer, David
    L., 1952- . II. Nunberg, Barbara, 1948- . III. Series.
    JF1661.R45   1994
    331.2'8135'000091724—dc20   94-26924
                                                                          CIP

Contents

Part II: Attempts at Reform

Contributors

Harold Alderman is a senior economist in the Policy Research Department, World Bank.

Sudharshan Canagarajah is an economist in the Population and Human Resources Operations Division, Western Africa Department, World Bank.

Louis de Merode is a principal management consultant in the Organization and Business Practices Department, World Bank.

Peter R. Fallon is a senior economist in the Southern Africa Department, World Bank.

Peter Gregory is a professor of economics, emeritus, at the University of New Mexico.

David L. Lindauer is a professor of economics at Wellesley College and a faculty associate of the Harvard Institute for International Development.

Barbara S. Nunberg is a senior public management specialist in the Europe, Middle East, and North Africa Technical Department, World Bank.

Luiz A. Pereira da Silva is an economist in the Southern Africa Department, World Bank.

Mike Stevens is a public sector management adviser in the Operations Policy Department, World Bank.

Charles S. Thomas is a private sector development specialist in the Private Sector Development Department, World Bank.

Stephen Younger is a senior research associate for the Food and Nutrition Policy Program, Cornell University.

Preface

The idea behind this book was to assemble a group of essays that accurately reflected the real-life trials and tribulations of designing civil service pay and employment reforms. These reforms seem to be spreading as if by contagion from one continent to another of the developing world. We hope to reach an audience that is an amalgam of scholars, development practitioners, and government policymakers who are interested in both the analytics and the operations and who want to understand firsthand how these fit together. To achieve this objective, we sought out practical work on this topic, most of which comes from World Bank country and economic sector work, and evaluations or reviews of Bank lending operations.

The essays selected reflect the interdisciplinary approaches that characterize work on this topic, drawing on economics, political science, and management perspectives. The challenge was to transform these analyses—intended for quite different purposes—into a cohesive set of articles that could compose a unified volume. To meet this challenge, the editors took extraordinary liberties in revising and reshaping original materials submitted by contributing authors. The process has been iterative, involving what must have seemed like endless back-and-forths. Contributors were patient and cooperative, although all were burdened with full-time work agendas unrelated to our task at hand. We appreciate their labor of dedication and ask their indulgence for a finished product that, although taken a distance from the initial effort, embodies, it is hoped, the essence of their excellent work.

Support for this research was received from several sources within the World Bank, including the Research Advisory Staff, the Public

Economics Division of the Policy Research Department, the Operations Policy Group in the Operations Policy Department, and the former Public Sector Management and Private Sector Development Division of the Country Economics Department. We would also like to acknowledge the useful comments provided by the anonymous referees who reviewed the manuscript for the World Bank's Editorial Committee.

David L. Lindauer
Barbara Nunberg

1

Introduction: Pay and employment reform of the civil service

David L. Lindauer and Barbara Nunberg

For more than a decade, new currents in development theory have disputed the previously accepted wisdom of an interventionist state in developing countries. Buttressed by ideological winds in the developed world and a dismal record of bureaucratic failure in many developing countries, policymakers, academics, and international donors have promoted a reduced role for government in economic affairs. The prevailing view: divestiture in preference to state ownership; privatization rather than public provision; market forces rather than regulations. In the aftermath of this revisionism, predictions about shifting winds and swinging pendulums abound. Witnessing the success of state-guided development models in East Asia and the proliferation of market failures in many countries, some now foresee a late-century correction. What is presaged is a more tempered advocacy of the private sector along with the realization that certain essential functions remain the unique purview of government.[1]

The case for pay and employment reform of the civil service

Although this volume focuses on the government sector, it does not position itself in the debate on the proper role or dimensions of the state in fostering development. Instead, we take as given that government, whatever its role, will have to improve its performance and do so in a more cost-effective manner than in the past. Reforms with this end in mind are essential if the many low- and middle-income countries that have stagnated in recent years are to achieve sustainable growth. The process of rehabilitating government so that it can undertake its crucial responsibilities is the subject of this volume.

Rehabilitation begins with strengthening the capacity of government employees to do their jobs. This implies sometimes marginal but more often profound reform of the civil service. Procedures by which staff are recruited, rewarded, and managed must all be improved, as all too frequently these functions have collapsed into disarray. Fundamental to the task of civil service reform is the overhaul of government pay and employment practices that in so many countries have become severely dysfunctional over the past few decades. Although more intricate analysis of government pay and employment is provided in subsequent chapters, the basic outline of the problem involves surplus employees, eroded wages, compressed salary structures, and aggregate wage bills commanding an increasing share of public revenues. The consequences for civil service performance have been disastrous: low morale, high absenteeism and moonlighting, difficulties in attracting and retaining skilled professionals, a breakdown in supervision and discipline, and the unavailability of complementary inputs to carry out routine tasks.

Reforming government pay and employment has become an important item on the development agenda, attested to by the considerable and growing number of developing country programs designed to redress the syndrome just described. These reforms have priority for several reasons. Reining in the wage bill has obvious fiscal implications in the context of structural economic adjustments that emphasize public expenditure reductions. Indeed, the prominence of pay and employment issues in stabilization and adjustment underscores the need for good analysis of the problem; heretofore, mistaken notions of inappropriately high government wages and a narrow emphasis on fiscal stringency led international donors to pursue solutions that failed to apprehend the link between government pay and employment policies and government performance. Thus, conditionality froze aggregate wage bills without proper examination of the micro consequences for the structure of employment and remuneration. The result often was further wage erosion and compression, exacerbating all the problems alluded to above.

Beyond purely fiscal considerations, government pay and employment problems merit attention because their resolution will determine prospects for further improvements in civil service performance. Such improvements begin *but do not end* with the establishment of an affordable, appropriately staffed, well-equipped, reasonably remunerated, civil service cadre—the intended outcome of pay and employment reforms.

Critiques of civil service reform programs frequently assail the inordinate emphasis placed on pay and employment issues at the expense of longer-term management concerns. Such critiques are often well-founded, particularly when initial reforms are not followed by sustained institutional development efforts. Some recent approaches to civil service strengthening stress the need to attack the root causes of "bad government," including patrimonial politics and entrenched clientelism, rather than to target efforts at pay and employment practices, which, it is argued, are merely symptoms of a larger disease. The development of practical interventions to ameliorate these types of fundamental structural problems certainly merits attention.[2]

Tackling these comprehensive issues for the long haul is a task of undisputed importance. An equally forceful case can be made, however, that appropriate pay and employment policies constitute a necessary, though insufficient, element in building government administrative capacity. Indeed, it is difficult to imagine how other types of administrative reforms might succeed amid poorly paid or overstaffed civil services forced to operate with severely constrained resources.

The success of pay and employment reforms requires addressing not only the political determinants just discussed, but also the economic conditions that led to the problems in the first place. Pay erosion, for example, often has been due to rapid price inflation brought on by financing large budget deficits; similarly, redundancy has been a consequence of the expansion of public employment in response to rising unemployment. If the macroeconomic difficulties that fostered pay and employment problems persist, and the policy response to these difficulties does not change, pay and employment initiatives will prove short-lived.

This is not to say that successful civil service pay and employment reform necessarily requires an economic upturn or even attainment of some measure of fiscal balance. It is necessary, however, that governments not respond to macroeconomic problems with the types of dysfunctional pay and employment adjustments that led to the current state of disarray.

"First generation" studies

Recognition of the need for civil service pay and employment reform is already widespread, but analytical perspectives providing practical policy insights are only now catching up. The absence of analysis reflects the frequent lag between real events and research findings. In addition, the applicability of developed country research and experience has been limited.[3] But attention to civil service pay and employment reform in developing nations has probably been handicapped even more by suspicions that the underlying problem was straightforward: *there are too many government workers who get paid too much.* With this misconception in place, serious consideration of reforms was unlikely. But by the early 1980s, reality, especially in Africa, had dealt the prevailing view a major blow. The macroeconomic crises of the 1970s and early 1980s, with their subsequent impact on civil service pay and employment, spawned a "first generation" of literature on pay and employment reforms that reported on emerging problems and turned conventional wisdom, at least about government pay policy, on its head.

Early work on government pay and employment in developing countries exists, but it had raised few warning flags. Martin Segal's 1971 volume on Ceylon, for example, predates the dramatic changes of the 1970s and was concerned mainly with the mechanics of wage administration in the public sector. Ragia Abdin and others reported on emerging trends in Africa but were content with considering the institutional context and historical legacy of their cross-country observations.[4]

The published research of David Lindauer, Oey Meesook, and Parita Suebsaeng ushered in a first generation of studies on civil service reform, confirming what African officials already suspected. Their paper drew on unpublished studies, some conducted by the authors themselves and most related to World Bank country economic work, to highlight disturbing trends in government pay and employment and their implications.[5] Detailed studies of wage erosion in Sudan, pay compression in Zambia, and redundancy in Liberia rejected the previously held notion of "high" government pay and helped to open the door for civil service pay and employment to be considered an area for policy reform.

Similar studies on more countries followed, much of it, including the first analyses of Latin American cases (Bolivia and Brazil), in unpublished reports. Recently, the International Labour Organization (ILO) added to the published record with three volumes: Gus Edgren, editor, *The Growing Sector: Studies of Public Sector Employment in Asia*; Wouter van Ginneken, editor, *Government and Its Employees*; and Derek Robinson, *Civil Service Pay in Africa*. The first two of these volumes add to our general knowledge of pay and employment trends in the public sector and reveal, not surprisingly, that Southeast Asia has generally avoided the worst-case scenarios witnessed in Africa. Robinson's work, which harks back to earlier ILO studies on the subject by concentrating on the details of wage administration in Africa, concludes that certain situations are in dire need of reform.[6]

The contribution of these first generation studies of civil service pay and employment was to identify the problems and offer initial empirical assessments. But this body of work is short on prescription and has nothing to report in the way of concrete examples of attempts at reform.

The task of the "second generation" of analysis is to offer prescriptions and to evaluate experience with reforms.

"Second generation" studies

This volume is divided into two parts. Part I, "Diagnosing the problem," inaugurates the second generation of studies of civil service pay and employment in low-income economies by further developing the methodology for assessing pay and employment problems, and documenting the nature and extent of prevailing difficulties. The chapters on Somalia and Tanzania, in particular, go on to offer detailed strategies for reform based on empirical findings.

Part II, "Attempts at reform," examines what we have learned to date from the implementation of civil service pay and employment reform programs. Evidence is drawn both broadly and narrowly. Chapter 7 offers a survey of evidence from the World Bank's decade-long experience in supporting civil service reform programs. The remaining chapters in part II adopt a narrower focus, primarily on civil service pay and employment reform in Ghana. Ghana has received so much attention because, in relative terms, its reform program is both deep and far along.

Before turning to an introduction of individual chapters, two dimensions of this volume should be noted. First, with the exception of the conceptual chapters and some of the survey material, individual case studies are exclusively from Africa. This is not because of the singular relevance of civil service pay and employment issues to African circumstances. On the contrary, and by way of examples, problems are reported of precipitous real wage erosion in Laos, crippling salary compression in Jamaica, and widespread redundancies in Bolivia. Public employee pay and employment crises appear endemic in Eastern Europe and the republics that have emerged from the collapse of the Soviet Union. The need for civil service pay and employment reform certainly spans the globe.

But what distinguishes Africa is how deep and sustained have been the region's economic decline and the subsequent collapse of the government sector. Probably nowhere else have the problems of government performance been so pervasive and so long-lived. This situation has created in Africa more of an opportunity for reform and, perhaps, more initial receptivity to it than exists in other regions. This is not to say that all of Africa faces the same government pay and employment problems. Countries in the Communauté Financière Africaine (CFA), for example, with the particular constraints imposed by their system of monetary management, have not experienced the precipitous real wage erosion of some of the Anglophone countries, although redundancies and low expenditures on nonwage inputs are common in the CFA zone as well.

From a practical standpoint, we found in Africa more reform programs and more evaluations of them than elsewhere. In compiling this volume we wanted to present the best examples of pay and employment analysis, and were thus forced to trade off the extent of regional coverage for more intensive scholarship. Future work on civil service reform programs undoubtedly will reflect more fully the worldwide nature of the problems.

A second decision was to constrain our focus to the central government sector, eliminating all but the briefest discussion of pay and employment issues in local government and public enterprises. The availability of data on local and regional government is woefully inadequate. In any case, most African countries employ unitary rather than federal systems, with local government subsumed under central budgets. (Nigeria is the most significant counterexample.) A focus on central government, therefore, captures a large percentage of total civil service employment.

We appreciate, and several papers make reference to, the linkages between civil service and public enterprise pay and employment policies, but space limitations dictated our coverage. Others are working on pay and employment reform in the public enterprise sector and interested readers are directed to these studies.[7]

Part I: Diagnosing the problem

This volume is fundamentally empirical, but chapter 2, "Government pay and employment policies and economic performance," offers a more conceptual treatment. David Lindauer traces the evolution of policy advice on pay and employment in the government sector over the past three decades. He describes how concern has shifted from negative "spillover" effects on private wages, to expanding fiscal deficits, to the failures of government performance. Lindauer emphasizes how macroeconomic circumstances, and responses to them, have generated inappropriate pay and employment policies that in turn have contributed to a decline in government performance.

In chapter 3, "Diagnosis with limited information: government pay and employment reform in Somalia," Peter Gregory provides a "field guide" for others wishing to diagnose the state of pay and employment in the civil service. Somalia offers stark evidence of a government that faced the full range of problems associated with a grossly distorted civil service pay and employment regime. Because of the tragedy of civil war we would be remiss in not placing the Gregory paper in some perspective to recent events. Gregory was asked to appraise the pay and employment situation in the Somali civil service in 1989, prior to the outbreak of the crisis. The problems he documents suggest a government that had ceased to perform even the most basic tasks; that such a government would fall was not unexpected.

The task that Gregory confronted was to estimate the extent of redundancy in employment and the distortions in the pay structure of the Somali civil service, and to propose reforms in employment and compensation in a context of extreme scarcity of reliable information essential to the task. He demonstrates that by drawing on diverse sources of information it is possible to establish a reasonably robust picture of the situation and to propose a consistent set of targets for reform. The lessons of Gregory's analysis go well beyond Somalia's borders. What Gregory offers is a methodological approach for any setting in which civil service pay and employment require dramatic reforms.

Chapter 4, "Public expenditure and civil service reform in Tanzania" by Mike Stevens, provides a chronological narrative of pay and employment practices—how and why they became so distorted and what preliminary steps have been taken to reverse their direction. His approach involves determining the increases that are needed if a motivating wage structure for the public service is to be put in place. Once this is established, tradeoffs between pay increases, salary decompression, staff reductions, and the time required to reach these goals are presented. For example, to what extent, and how quickly, can revenue growth alone achieve desired pay and compression targets? What sort of pay adjustments can be realized from differential rates of retrenchment? Although the details apply to Tanzania, the basic script is classic to pay and employment problems and could easily have been written for any number of nations, especially in the Sub-Saharan region. The inescapable conclusion is that in countries where public sector employment has long outstripped revenue growth, deep cuts in existing staff are required to restore pay and set the conditions for a turnaround in productivity.

Chapter 5, "Recognizing labor market constraints: government-donor competition for manpower in Mozambique" by Peter Fallon and Luiz Pereira da Silva, illustrates how pay and employment outcomes in the civil service are ultimately conditioned by labor market as well as fiscal constraints. In Mozambique tight fiscal pressures on civil service pay and employment have been but one of the many negative consequences of rising defense expenditures, increasing debt service, and a near-bankrupt public enterprise sector. However, after reviewing the profile of civil service pay and employment, the authors conclude that even modest increases in government resources can do little to offset pressures emanating from the labor market. In particular, donor competition, by bidding up prevailing wages, has created a significant negative externality as highly skilled individuals have been attracted away from public administration. This in turn weakens the implementation capacity of government, which the donor community itself depends on to achieve its aims of national development. Fallon and da Silva call for a more cooperative and less competitive approach among members of the donor community in the hope of taking some pressure off of a government trying to restore civil service compensation to levels consistent with both fiscal and labor market constraints.

The last chapter in part I, "Preparing for civil service pay and employment reform: a primer" by Mike Stevens, provides explicit "how-to" instructions for those needing to conduct their own pay and employment analysis. Stevens lays out the nuts and bolts of data collection on pay and employment in the public sector. He describes the universe of public sector employment, distinguishing between the civil service narrowly defined, local government, teachers and health workers, police, military, budget-dependent agencies, public enterprises, and daily paid staff. These divisions are essential since all are linked to the government budget and many, if not all, are tied to the salary structure of the central civil service. Stevens cautions that all these branches of public employment should not be tackled simultaneously; however, their linkages must be understood in assessing the consequences of any reform program. He also provides tips on where to find information on public employment and compensation, indicating how to capture the direct and hidden reward structure of allowances, payments in kind, off-budget expenditures, pensions, and severance payments.

Part II: Attempts at reform

Part II of this volume draws its prescriptions for civil service pay and employment reform based on the experience of actual reform programs. Chapter 7, "Experience with civil service pay and employment reform: an overview" by Barbara Nunberg, examines lessons learned in the context of World Bank lending activity between 1981 and 1991. During the 1980s few countries pursued reform programs on their own, although some were willing to accept loan conditions in return for needed injections of external assistance. The World Bank, more so than the International Monetary Fund or bilateral donors, quickly became the primary international agency promoting government pay and employment reforms. Over the decade, such reforms were a prominent feature of ninety World Bank loans to more than forty different nations.

Nunberg distills the experience gained from these varied operations and reports on the practical aspects of implementing pay and employment reforms.[8] She organizes alternative methods of containing the costs of personnel expenditures—a necessary feature of programs aimed at rationalizing pay and employment practices—by ranking them along a continuum of political difficulty and, within each category of cost containment, reviews experience in implementation. Nunberg also assesses the impact of reforms to date. Reductions in the aggregate wage bill of the government sector have been the exception rather than the rule, and employment reductions have at best been modest. Nunberg concludes that these somewhat disappointing results do not suggest that civil service reform programs should be abandoned, but rather that future initiatives must build from the lessons of a first decade of trial and error.

The chapter 7 survey of reform experience makes frequent reference to those civil service reform programs that are long-lived and deep. Chapter 8, "Implementing civil service pay and employment reform in Africa: the experiences of Ghana, the Gambia, and Guinea" by Louis de Merode with Charles Thomas, narrowly focuses on three such programs. De Merode and Thomas offer a case-by-case review of reform measures followed by a comparative assessment of the impact of these reforms in terms of employment reduction, rationalization of compensation, fiscal benefits, and improvements in government performance.

All three West African countries considered in chapter 8 faced differing degrees of macroeconomic and institutional crisis that precipitated civil service reform initiatives. In all three the problems were severe enough to call for retrenchment of government workers and significant pay and regrading measures. However, although the problems shared much in common, policy instruments varied. The chapter provides considerable detail on the use of alternative policy instruments, experiences that should prove invaluable to reform program planners contemplating similar approaches.

Chapter 8 introduces Ghana's civil service reform program, the subject of the analyses offered by Peter Gregory in chapter 9, "Dealing with redundancies in government employment in Ghana," and by Harold Alderman, Sudharshan Canagarajah, and Stephen Younger in chapter 10, "Consequences of permanent layoff from the civil service: results from a survey of retrenched workers in Ghana." Taken together, these two chapters offer an ex ante and ex post analysis, respectively, of the dismissal of serving civil servants. In other words, they inform us, at a household level, of the consequences of a key ingredient of any civil service reform program.

Gregory's analysis of civil service retrenchment was conducted during the summer of 1988, roughly one year into the Ghanaian Civil

Service Reform Program. Although the government had agreed to reduce the size of the civil service as part of a larger package of economic reforms, it was proceeding with considerable reservations and doubts. In particular, the government expressed fears about the unemployment consequences and poverty implications of releasing so many former civil servants into a labor market that already seemed incapable of generating many productive job opportunities.

Gregory argues that although one can sympathize with the concerns of the Ghanaian government, an ex ante evaluation suggests that they were unduly pessimistic. The evidence he summons is, first, previous experience with civil service retrenchments as well as with the 1983 and 1985 repatriation of vast numbers of Ghanaians from Nigeria; second, survey data on both the characteristics and job aspirations of government employees slated for redeployment; and third, an analysis of the aggregate employment consequences of all elements of the economic reform program.

Gregory concludes that the government has underestimated the absorptive capacity of the labor market. It should be expected that, rather than face open unemployment, many retrenched civil servants will instead continue in the subsidiary activities, including trading and agriculture, that they already pursue to supplement their low government wages. Gregory does not suggest that retrenchment will be painless. On the contrary, many government workers already suffer from low standards of living and the loss of their positions will not improve their situations. However, the general lesson for Ghana, or many other governments needing to retrench, is that neither individual workers nor the labor market is so rigid as to generate the worst-case scenario of massive unemployment and the wholesale transfer of former government employees into dire poverty.

The work by Alderman, Canagarajah, and Younger in chapter 10 refers to field research undertaken in the second half of 1991 and offers an ex post assessment of Ghana's retrenchment program. In so doing it verifies some of the points Gregory raises in the previous chapter. The Alderman and others study is unique, employing the first survey conducted expressly for the purpose of tracking retrenched government workers.

Chapter 10 reviews the Ghanaian redeployment program and provides an updated report on progress in meeting reform targets. However, most of the chapter is devoted to an analysis of the survey data collected on a random sample of redeployed workers. The authors provide considerable detail on the profile of the redeployed, including gender, age, and migration behavior; unemployment experience and labor force participation; income levels and sources; and amount and uses of severance payments. Where appropriate, characteristics of the redeployed are compared with those of the population at large by using results from another household survey, the 1987–88 Ghana Living Standards Survey.

Fears of widespread open unemployment of redeployees in Ghana have proved unfounded. Forty percent of former civil servants are now engaged in agriculture as a primary activity, another 40 percent are self-employed, and the remaining 20 percent have found wage work. In addition, the median household incomes of the redeployed as against the general population are roughly the same, although the distribution of income among the redeployed is more skewed. Forty percent now fall in the bottom three income deciles, including many who are now engaged in some type of farming activity. Alderman and others emphasize that a nontrivial proportion of redeployee households are poor. To the extent that this is the result of redeployment, Gregory's more optimistic ex ante predictions of the consequences of redeployment require some qualification.

The final chapter, "Conclusion: The political economy of civil service pay and employment reform" by Barbara Nunberg and David Lindauer, raises the question that logically follows from the evidence presented throughout this volume: Are deeper reforms desirable and feasible? To answer this question requires consideration of the political economy of reform efforts.

What is perhaps most striking about attempts at reform over the past decade is the relatively low domestic opposition they have confronted. Although governments have been reluctant to pursue pay and employment reforms, and international agencies have been loath to require them, the predicted dire consequences of reforms do not seem to have come to pass. Regime destabilization has not been a characteristic of the reform initiatives reported on in previous chapters. Even milder forms of opposition, for example, strikes by civil servants, have been rare. Although all reforms entail political and economic costs, the limited evidence to date suggests that pay and employment reforms appear to exact a lower political price than have other types of liberalization, such as removing grain subsidies or raising bus fares.

Nunberg and Lindauer offer a range of explanations for the lack of political reaction to retrenchments and other reform measures: the shallowness of reform efforts to date; the weak political profile of the targets of retrenchment; the limited value of government employment in light of a decade or more of pay erosion and compression; and the implementation strategies themselves. Based on this very preliminary assessment of the political economy of civil service reforms, they conclude that deeper reforms may be less politically costly than thus far has been assumed.

Goals of this volume

The present volume extends the literature on civil service pay and employment by building on first generation studies that identified problems and by introducing a second generation of work that offers prescriptions based on better information, deeper analysis, and more extensive experience with reform implementation. The volume is drawn from analysis conducted in the context of proposed or ongoing reform operations, mainly in connection with World Bank lending or analytic studies. The applied character of these contributions suits the reader who, whether policymaker, scholar, or student, is seeking pragmatic, hands-on understanding of the subject.

It is hoped that this book will leave the reader with a few basic concepts about rehabilitating government pay and employment. These include how to analyze and diagnose the problem, what relationships to examine, what comparisons to make, which data to procure, and, in the all too frequent absence of those data, what substitutions to make or proxies to use. It is hoped that the collection of case studies conveys the enormous difficulties confronted in carrying out this analysis, again in the face of partial or unreliable information and under the very real pressures of tight reform program schedules and resource constraints.

Grounded in a history of trial and error, the work we present should also impart a sense of cautious optimism about the feasibility of reforming government pay and employment practice. Where data permit, the analyses take a hard look at program implementation and outcomes, often depicting the glass as half empty. But on balance, even flawed programs appear to have had some positive effects, and certain obstacles, especially political ones, that were once thought to be insuperable, have been overcome. Perhaps the richest finding to be gleaned from the collection is an appreciation of the growing body of best practice with regard to implementing reforms. Taken together, the contributions document a sizable technical package that, when adapted to specific country conditions, can be applied to civil service pay and employment reform programs elsewhere.

Notes

1. This change in direction is evident in remarks by Lawrence Summers, then-Chief Economist of the World Bank, at the 1991 World Bank Annual Conference on Development Economics.

The great lesson of the 1970s and the 1980s was that governments that tried to occupy the commanding heights of their economies found themselves looking a long way down, to stagnating growth and deteriorating performance. The policy lesson was and is clear. Governments must get out of activities that competitive markets do best: producing and allocating goods and services....

The market message was new and true, but it is only part of the story. There are indeed things that governments must not do. But taking the brakes off is not enough to make your car go, and crash diets do not ensure continuing health. Government involvement to make the tangible and intangible infrastructure investments that underpin rapid growth and a healthy private sector—and that ensure social and economic justice—is critical to growth.

...We have worked very hard in recent years on governments' errors of commission; it is time for work on the errors of omission. The research agenda I see for the next few years addresses the pivotal issue of helping governments identify and perform the central functions that only they can do.

2. See Mamadou Dia ("Position Paper for Improving Civil Service Efficiency in Sub-Saharan Africa," Africa Technical Department Working Paper, World Bank, Washington, D.C., 1993) for an example of this approach.

3. See Barbara Nunberg, "Managing the Civil Service: What LDCs Can Learn from Developed Country Reforms," Policy Research Working Paper 945, World Bank, Washington, D.C., 1992.

4. Martin Segal, *Government Pay Policies in Ceylon* (Geneva: International Labour Organization, 1971) and Ragia Abdin, Paul Bennell, Olufemi Fajana, Martin Godfrey, and Bachir Hamdouch, *A World of Differentials* (London: Hodder and Stoughton, 1983).

5. David Lindauer, Oey Meesook, and Parita Suebsaeng, "Government Wage Policy in Africa," *World Bank Research Observer,* vol. 3, no. 1 (January 1988). Peter S. Heller and Alan A. Tait (*Government Employment and Pay: Some International Comparisons,* IMF, OP 24, 1983) also offer an early empirical assessment but their study is more focused on establishing cross-country patterns than on establishing the emerging pay and employment crisis of the government sector.

6. Gus Edgren, ed., *The Growing Sector* (New Dehli: ILO, 1988); Wouter van Ginneken, ed., *Government and Its Employees* (Aldershot, England: Avebury, 1991); Derek Robinson, *Civil Service Pay in Africa* (Geneva: ILO, 1990).

7. See, for example, Alice Galenson, "Labor Redundancy in the Transport Sector," Policy Research Working Paper 158, World Bank, Washington, D.C., 1989.

8. Earlier reviews can be found in Barbara Nunberg, *Public Sector Pay and Employment Reform*, Discussion Paper 68, World Bank, Washington, D.C., 1989; and Barbara Nunberg and John Nellis, "Civil Service Reform and the World Bank," Policy Research Working Paper 422, World Bank, Washington, D.C., 1990.

PART I

DIAGNOSING THE PROBLEM

2

Government pay and employment policies and economic performance

David L. Lindauer

To understand current advice on government pay and employment policy it is useful to trace the evolution of thinking about levels of pay and employment in the public sector. To do so, we must look back some thirty to forty years.

Excessive urban wages

During the 1950s and 1960s it was observed that a subset of urban residents in many developing economies—those who worked for wages in the so-called formal or modern sector—enjoyed considerably higher incomes than their rural counterparts. Such income disparities, it was argued, generated a steady flow of rural migrants to urban areas, especially capital cities. However, contrary to what standard economic theory would predict, no noticeable reduction in the earnings of those fortunate enough to land an urban job followed. With the gap in relative pay between urban and rural areas remaining high, it was argued that external competitiveness waned while urban slums proliferated. The failure of wages to adjust suggested that either a misguided wage policy or imperfect labor markets, or both, contributed to increasing unemployment, underemployment, and poverty among the swelling number of urban inhabitants.

This view of urban-rural interactions was embodied in various models of dualism that would strongly influence development theorizing and policy advice. A key element of these models was the existence and persistence of relatively high wages in urban areas despite the expanding pool of available labor.[1] Most attention was devoted to the consequences of this situation as explanations for both migration behavior and levels of urban unemployment. But attention was also paid to explaining why wages were so high in the first place. Three institutions in particular were cited as contributing to the wage differential:

- Trade unions, which were able to control the supply of labor to urban firms and earn a monopoly rent for their workers.
- Multinationals, which had deep enough pockets to pay wages above market clearing levels and which were inclined to do so to minimize any perception of exploiting local labor.
- Government wages, which were alleged to exceed market rates for reasons of political expediency and which then "spilled over" to inflate private sector pay as well.

Models of dualism and migration, popular in the 1950s, 1960s, and early 1970s, have been subject to varied critiques, but it is their conclusions concerning government pay that are most important to our discussion. Did governments pay in excess of market rates? Did they act as "wage leaders" and distort wages elsewhere in the economy? Have these advantages persisted, especially over the decades of economic stagnation and structural adjustment that followed?

"Spillover" effects

As many of the chapters in this volume document, finding evidence on public-private pay differentials in developing economies is far from easy. Evidence on pay levels that adjusts for the skill, education, and experience of workers generally is not available, and historical studies that report on relative government-to-private earnings twenty or more years ago are even scarcer. The limited number of studies that have been undertaken do support the stylized facts of the early concern over government pay levels. Government workers often earned a premium over their counterparts in the urban private wage sector. In Tanzania in 1971 a government worker is estimated to have earned 14 percent more than did a private sector employee with the same amount of schooling and work experience, while in Kenya in 1970 the estimated differential ranged from 11 percent to 16 percent.[2]

Explanations for these premiums often focus on political factors. Especially in the newly independent nations of the 1950s and 1960s, it became politically expedient, if not outright necessary, to transfer the salaries of formerly expatriate officials to the newly indigenous civil service.[3] Such practices readily generated compensation well out of line with local labor market conditions. Similarly, the social agenda of some African governments (for example, Tanzania and Zambia) often called for generous payments to the least skilled and least educated, with government pay scales designed "to demonstrate" the standards expected of all employers.

It is relatively easy to understand why a government would want to reward its civil servants generously, but it is a different matter for a government to be able to finance such expenditures. At least in the early decades under consideration, resource rents and aid flows may have provided the means. The obvious consequence of such policies was a misuse of government resources. By paying workers in excess of the market clearing wage, resources were diverted from expanding needed government services. Alternatively, instead of paying a wage premium to civil servants, tax burdens might have been reduced.

These resource allocation issues, however, were not the source of early concern over inappropriate levels of government pay. Instead, attention was called to the spillover effects of excessive government salaries on wage levels in the private sector. The suggestion was that the government acted as a wage leader, setting high wages that would become the standard for other modern sector employers. As already noted, such spillover effects could then generate a host of economic and social ills ranging from lost competitiveness to excessive rural-to-urban migration.

The "wage leadership" model of government pay setting has considerable appeal, particularly in settings—common to many developing countries, especially in Africa—where the public sector is a dominant employer of wage labor. But what is missing in the wage leadership scenario is the counterbalancing influence of the labor market. In many of the economies under consideration, high government pay coexisted with an excess supply of labor, especially of the unskilled. Under such conditions private employers would be influenced both by the level of government pay and by the lower wages dictated by the relative abundance of workers. Larger, more visible, private employers might effectively be pressured to follow the government's lead. But other employers, notably those running small establishments, probably would be less subject to pressure and enforcement measures, especially when employment needs could be satisfied at the lower wages determined by the market. In other words, the spillover effects of high government pay on private wages may have been less than was assumed.[4]

With the collapse of government pay in the 1980s—both in real terms and, for many occupations, relative to private sector compensation—wage leadership and spillover effects are not the significant issues they once were. But the legacy of this earlier preoccupation with excessive government pay levels continues to influence perceptions of government pay and employment well after the initial conditions have changed.

Fiscal crisis

For most economies now in need of government pay and employment reforms, the 1970s and 1980s were a period of severe fiscal pressure. On the revenue side, low-income economies are often heavily dependent on taxes levied on exports and imports,[5] and with the price shocks of the 1970s government receipts fell precipitously. On the expenditure side, competing demands on government revenues escalated. Subsidies to consumers and state enterprises grew, new and often large-scale investment projects were initiated, school and health services for rapidly growing populations were expanded, and previous borrowing resulted in growing debt service payments. In retrospect, the government sector should have adjusted more quickly to the decline in resources available to compensate the civil service. But often it did not. Rather than choosing policies to maintain the performance of the existing government work force, decisions were made that had the opposite effect. All too often governments became less able to fulfill their missions.

Just as the source of increasing fiscal pressure varied across countries, individual government pay and employment responses to the budgetary crisis also varied. But in general, governments tended to expand public employment, erode real government pay, compress government salary structure, and reduce expenditures on complementary inputs. Evidence and explanations for these tendencies follow.

Employment expansion

With mounting resource constraints, governments should have retrenched public employment or, at least, engaged in alternative types of hiring freezes until the fiscal situation improved. Instead, government employment frequently continued to grow. Chapter 3 of this volume reports, for example, on the rapid increase in Somalia's government employment rolls. Gregory estimates that the number of Somali civil servants grew from about 20,000 in 1970 to 56,500 in 1990. This translates into a growth rate of 5.3 percent a year as compared to a negative GNP per capita growth rate over the same time period. And in Ghana, government revenues fell from 15 percent of GDP in 1970 to 6 percent in 1983, while some estimates place government employment growth in double digits for the same period.[6]

Why did government employment expand when the fiscal situation dictated the exact opposite? Many explanations can be offered. Some governments maintained long-standing employment guarantees in the public sector for university graduates and those discharged from military service. In other countries, job guarantees extended to all secondary school graduates or, more narrowly, to graduates of specific training institutions, for example, teacher training schools.

The worsening macroeconomic situation from the mid-1970s onward, coupled with demographic trends, also contributed to the expansion of the government sector. With low and even negative growth rates plus rapidly growing labor forces, governments worried about rising urban unemployment and felt pressured to absorb new entrants by providing government jobs. At the same time, even though fiscal resources dwindled, rapid population growth increased public demand for basic health and education services. Once again, governments felt compelled to respond by increasing the numbers employed, ostensibly, to provide these services.

Political pressures compounded the economic problems. Administrations, whether elected or not, rely on their power of appointment to reward supporters. Such actions often lead to an expansion of government employment because of both the excesses of political patronage and the legal and institutional barriers to removing standing civil servants. An example of the latter is Senegal where in the early 1980s a presidential decree was required to remove any permanent government employee, regardless of rank. And in other settings, public sector unions opposed retrenchments.

Not all nations worsened the problem of dwindling resources by expanding employment. Estimates suggest that Zambia, for one, held the line on staffing, increasing government employment by less than 1 percent a year from 1975 to 1983.[7] But even fiscally prudent hiring decisions could not prevent further adjustments in the conditions of government employment that further weakened government performance.

Salary erosion

With revenues dwindling and government employment expanding, or at least not falling, earnings expressed in real terms had to decline. In most economies wage indexing arrangements did not exist and the adjustment mechanism for pay erosion was in place. Frozen nominal pay scales confronted growing price inflation and real pay fell quickly. Government workers could not easily recoup these losses because, unlike most private employees, government workers do not renegotiate wage agreements on a periodic basis. Instead, pay adjustments are often realized by assembling high-level commissions to review government compensation. By leaving official salary scales intact, double-digit inflation rates rapidly took their toll on the purchasing power of government wages.

Precipitously falling real salaries of government workers have been a worldwide phenomenon in developing economies with severe macroeconomic difficulties. In Zambia the salary of an under-secretary in 1986 was worth only 22 percent of its 1976 purchasing power. In El Salvador during the 1980s real salaries of civil servants declined by 48 to 80 percent, depending on rank, as compared with only a 14 percent decline in GDP per capita. By 1990 the official monthly salary of a Laotian school teacher was worth US$4.20, assuming it was paid at all. In Sudan even unskilled government workers witnessed rapid erosion in their pay; by 1983 they were receiving only one-third of their 1975 real wage.[8]

Those who subscribe to the notion of government as a high wage employer see these trends, if not wholly warranted, at least as a necessary elimination of the economic rents that had accrued to government workers. Although some adjustment of government pay was undoubtedly warranted, due to both the existence of such rents and the overall macroeconomic adjustment of the nation's economy, the precipitous declines noted above seem well in excess of government workers' "fair" or warranted share of the costs of structural adjustment.

Others see the erosion in official salaries as poor indicators of the true compensation from government work. Benefits, both legal and illicit, are not fully reflected in the official salary structure. Official allowances, including housing and health benefits, transportation and travel privileges, and the more nebulous "access" of government officials to goods and services, are often not monetized, are rarely captured by the salary scales, and are alleged to be poorly correlated with salary movements. These criticisms of real wage trends in government jobs are legitimate. Undoubtedly, allowances, especially those paid in kind, cushion the blow of declining real wages. Annual awards and progression up the salary scale for existing civil servants—including premature promotions—have a similar effect. But the conclusion regarding the overall magnitude of change in the government's salary structure stands up to further analysis.

The major official fringe benefit for some civil servants, especially in Anglophone Africa, is housing, either in the form of actual housing or a housing allowance. If, as is often assumed, households spend 25 to 35 percent of their income on housing, then, for those who receive housing, 65 to 75 percent of total compensation is still subject to the precipitous decline in purchasing power brought on by the combination of frozen nominal salaries and rising consumer prices. In Zambia, for example, between 1975 and 1983, civil servants of grade S12 (entering university graduate) experienced an estimated 59 percent decrease in their real base starting salary; the effective decline was only 41 percent if they were provided government housing, but was 58 percent if, as was more likely, a cash housing allowance was provided in lieu of an in-kind housing benefit.[9] But more important, the fiscal crisis that forced govern-

ments to freeze salary scales in Zambia and elsewhere equally constrained the government's ability to provide all civil servants, especially
new hires, with the housing benefits they were technically entitled to
receive. Housing benefits have protected some of the real income of relatively senior and high-seniority civil servants, but such benefits were not
widespread enough to alter the course of declining real compensation.[10]

Other official benefits, including transport, health, and family
allowances, are difficult to quantify. Impressionistic evidence suggests
that they often do not cover the majority of government workers, are
often small relative to basic wages, and generally have not been
increased in response to falling wages.[11] As for unofficial perquisites of
office, there is no denying that government jobs may provide access to
scarce commodities, valuable contacts, or the opportunity for illicit
incomes through bribes and kickbacks. While such incomes cannot be
measured, how many government workers are in a position to benefit
substantially from these opportunities? Officials in key positions or
activities (for example, customs) may have the opportunity as well as
the means to collect significant illicit gains, but the bulk of the civil service occupies the lower occupational grades, especially in agriculture,
education, health, and public works. For these government employees
the opportunities for illicit incomes also present themselves, with examples including teachers who expect payments on the side and government drivers who use their vehicles for nonofficial and remunerative
activities. Although such benefits of government employment probably
help explain why poorly paid government workers do not simply aban-
don their posts, they reinforce rather than negate the proposition of the
inadequacy of official compensation.

Without reliable panel data on individual earnings and benefits of
government workers, it is difficult to predict accurately the precise fall
in the real compensation of civil servants. However, the fiscal realities
suggest that just as salary increases were constrained by dwindling revenues, other nonwage adjustments also would be constrained. Similarly,
the revealed tendency of civil servants at all ranks to engage increasingly in moonlighting and "daylighting" activities (the pursuit of remunerative work while present at one's government job) suggests that the real
value not only of basic wages, but also of total government compensation, was in decline, often rapid decline.

Salary compression

The preceding statements about erosion in real government pay refer to
average tendencies. When viewed at a disaggregated level, that is, by
occupation or salary grade, it becomes clear that civil servants have

fared differently from one another. Governments often responded to the fiscal crisis by permitting the real salaries of better-paid civil servants to fall more quickly than the earnings of those at lower salary levels. In other words, compression in the government salary structure was another adjustment mechanism to accommodate the growth in employment and the decline in revenues available to compensate the government's work force.

Tanzania provides an example of significant salary compression throughout the 1970s and 1980s. In chapter 4, Mike Stevens indicates that in 1969 a top public sector salary commanded thirty times the minimum wage in government employment. By the mid-1980s this differential had collapsed to a ratio of 6:1. In Zambia in 1971 an assistant director (S7 salary grade) received seventeen times the lowest-paid salaried employee (S21). In 1986 the ratio stood at a mere 3.7:1.[12] It is difficult to imagine that such drastic changes in relative pay did not generate equally significant consequences for the retention and performance of more senior civil servants and, hence, the productivity of those under their supervision.

Salary compression resulted from two alternative mechanisms for revising government pay scales. In the face of rising prices, governments often adjusted civil service wages by granting across-the-board increases in nominal pay. Absolute increases, by definition, account for larger percentages of the wages of lower-paid workers and result in compression of the wage structure. Governments also granted larger percentage increases to those at lower grades. In Zambia between January 1980 and September 1985 the bottom half of the twenty-one salary grades received pay increments on three separate occasions. As a result, the entry point of the lowest-paid salaried employee realized only a 7 percent drop in purchasing power. In comparison, during this same period (which averaged price inflation of 17 percent a year) the top seven grades received no increment at all. This strategy resulted in the real earnings, for example, of messengers being relatively protected, while the real starting salary of an under-secretary plummeted to one-third of its 1980 value.[13]

In evaluating salary compressions, one should not automatically assume that the wage differentials prevailing in an earlier period were the right ones, in the sense of reflecting market-determined premiums to education and experience, compensating differentials, and the like. Economic rents undoubtedly were built into many civil service pay scales. However, the dramatic compression of the pay structure in Tanzania, Zambia, and other countries suggests adjustments well at odds with prevailing labor market circumstances. In the 1960s and early 1970s government pay, especially for educated workers, dominated wages paid by private employers, but by the 1980s the situation had been reversed. Widespread evidence on pay compression as a response to fiscal constraints challenges the conventional wisdom of government pay that is "too high." More disaggregated treatment of government pay levels reveals that while some wages (usually of the least skilled) may still be "too high," other wages are now "too low."

Complementary inputs

One other response to fiscal difficulties was to trade off expenditures on materials and supplies (or on operations and maintenance) for spending on wages and salaries. Empirical evidence to substantiate these trends in the reallocation of government expenditures is spotty and anecdotal. Aziz Khan estimates that between 1977 and 1981 the wage bill's share of government revenue in Liberia jumped from 36 percent to 66 percent. By 1981, reports of widespread shortages of materials throughout the government were commonplace. Similarly, John Harris and others report the findings of an independent study of the Ministry of Rural Development in the Central African Republic. By the mid-1980s, 95 percent of the ministry's budget is reported to have gone to wages and salaries.[14]

A variety of data and measurement problems, including the familiar index number problems of distinguishing between changes in relative prices versus quantities, confronts more robust determination of trends in wage to nonwage expenditure allocations. But the widespread impression is that payments to workers often take precedence over spending on even essential nonlabor inputs. The consequence of these actions is to increase the number of redundant government workers, that is, those government workers without the necessary complementary inputs to perform their duties even when inclined to do so.

Government performance

Civil service pay and employment policies undertaken in response to the fiscal constraints that emerged in the 1970s left many governments unable to respond to the pressing needs of their economies. In many cases the civil service expanded well beyond the level dictated by aggregate growth; factor complementarities in the government sector became grossly distorted by pay, employment, and spending decisions; and incentives to motivate government employees were sorely diminished. Rehabilitation of the government sector will require policies that address these problems—specifically, policies that eliminate redundancy in the civil service and restore the linkage between compensation and effort.

Redundancy

A redundant employee is one who is not required to fulfill the tasks of a particular agency or department. In some cases this may mean a worker who does no work at all. A more likely situation is one in which several workers share work that a smaller number could easily perform. In either case, redundant government workers effectively have a marginal product of zero—if removed from government service there is no appreciable decrease in government output.

Redundant employees are the outcome of policies that expanded government employment, especially of the unskilled, in response to macroeconomic contraction and of spending decisions that traded off expenditures on materials and supplies in return for maintaining payments of wages and salaries. To the extent that redundancies are the result of an inefficient mix of labor skills in government jobs, they can also be linked to policies of pay compression.[15]

Precise technological coefficients for the amount and skills of labor needed to efficiently produce various government outputs are not readily available. Nonetheless, recent trends toward an increasing labor intensity of the public sector, especially of unskilled labor, suggest growing problems of redundancy. The burden of redundant workers lies in the opportunity cost of resources that maintain an "overstaffed" civil service. A reallocation of revenues could be used either to provide more or improved government services or to increase private consumption via lower tax rates.[16] Alternatively, redundancy can be tackled by increasing government revenues. This alternative calls for injecting sufficient new revenues into government to restore factor complementarities and make existing workers productive. Such a strategy can reduce redundancy, but is unlikely to be feasible under current fiscal conditions.

The problem of redundant employees needs to be separated from the more ideological debate over the proper role of the state in the economy. It would be convenient, to say the least, if we had a positive theory of government that could prescribe the "optimal amount" of public employment. But we are far from having such a theory and even empirical evidence, devoid of theory, offers little guidance. If the largest governments, measured in terms of the ratio of government expenditure to GDP—or of government employment as a share of the overall labor force—also possessed the most redundant workers, then one should observe a strong negative correlation between the size of government and GDP growth rates. No such relationship is readily apparent.[17]

The problem of redundancy can be seen as independent of the size of government. Eliminating redundancy and improving government performance, whatever the role of government in the economy, should stimulate growth.

The wage-effort nexus

Political opposition to large-scale retrenchments persists, but few would disagree that improvements in a government's fiscal situation and overall performance require removal of redundant public employees. By comparison, less agreement exists about the relationship between compensation levels and the performance of civil servants. Skeptics contend that significant increases in government pay levels or substantial decompression in government salary scales will cost the government money but can guarantee little in the way of a better-functioning government sector.

The impact on worker motivation of a civil service pay structure that is more consistent with market wages depends on the elasticity of effort in response to wages. This elasticity is difficult to observe, let alone quantify. However, a variety of arguments can be raised in support of a realignment of civil servant salaries to offset the recent and precipitous decline in real pay.

First are the consequences of real wage decline observed in many countries. As government compensation falls, both in absolute terms and relative to alternative remunerative activities, civil servants adjust to the new situation. Turnover rates and absenteeism increase; moonlighting and daylighting become more frequent, and the latter, more blatant;[18] recruitment and retention, especially of professionals, become more difficult. It has also been argued that petty corruption rises, including the sale of government services themselves, for example, under-the-table charges for livestock vaccinations or the extortion of payments by teachers to instruct schoolchildren.

The effects of falling real compensation on government performance are summed up in a passage from the 1982 Ugandan publication, "Report of the Public Services Salaries Review Commission":

> ...The civil servant had either to survive by lowering his standard of ethics, performance and dutifulness or remain upright and perish. He chose to survive.[19]

Do these sentiments imply that a sudden increase in pay will restore a virtuous and productive civil service? Of course not. Many previously redundant civil servants will remain redundant even while those who are productive receive more appropriate compensation. Also, the pay-effort relationship is complex and not necessarily symmetric. Especially after a prolonged period of low morale, limited expectations, and weak discipline, pay increases may do little to change behavior. However, in the longer run, as discipline from above is restored and government positions are viewed as both valuable and scarce, adequate compensation will be necessary to ensure improved performance.

Confidence in the productivity benefits of an improved pay structure can be found in two further observations. First, those nations that have maintained relatively high pay for public servants are generally recognized as having superior civil services. In the Sub-Saharan region, Malawi is often cited for the competence and professionalism of its civil service. It is probably not a coincidence that Malawi also possesses one of Africa's highest ratios of senior civil service pay to GDP per capita.[20] Second, the issue at hand is one of incentives, not of the intrinsic quality of workers. How often is it observed that the civil servant who appears lackadaisical and unproductive in his government job can the very same day become an aggressive and spirited entrepreneur or trader in his moonlighting or daylighting engagements?

Just as there are those who deny that peasant farmers will respond to changes in agricultural prices, others deny that government workers will improve their performance in response to wage changes. Both groups are wrong. Effort is elastic to wage levels. But this does not imply that the lags and complexities involved in improving performance via pay scale adjustments can be minimized. A nostalgic view of earlier decades, when real and relative government pay were higher, should not be adopted. Government performance may have been superior to today's standard, but by no means was it superlative. Similarly, as discussed in chapter 7, recent attempts at civil service reform are not replete with examples of improved performance of government workers in response to pay decompression or marginal increases in real pay.[21] It is for these reasons that improvements in government pay levels and structures, advocated in this volume, are presented as necessary but not sufficient conditions for rehabilitating the government sector. Administrative and management reforms are equally critical to a successful rehabilitation of the government sector.

Conclusion

The civil services of many developing economies today are too large, too expensive, and too unproductive. They are *too large* in the broad sense that in many nations the government sector is overextended, possessing too many agencies and departments charged with too broad a span of responsibilities. Civil services are also *too large* in the narrower sense of employing workers in excess of the requirements of designated tasks. Government employment is *too expensive* in the sense that the government's wage bill constitutes too high a percentage of government revenues for sound fiscal management. The civil service is *too unproductive* because government workers do not fulfill the tasks assigned to them or do so only partially, with great delays and at high cost.

Pay and employment reform of the civil service is one of the steps required to ameliorate these problems. The remainder of this volume, especially part II, "Attempts at reform," outlines the options and surveys the evidence on specific policy alternatives. This chapter's conclusions are more general, calling for a recognition that reforms must be directed at improving the microeconomic performance of the government sector itself.

What must be overcome are the legacies of past approaches to pay and employment reforms. The notion that government is a "high wage island," distorting wage-setting elsewhere in the urban economy, is in many cases no longer a plausible argument. For many occupations, government compensation is well below rates prevailing in the private sector. For those positions in which civil servants continue to receive a premium—for example, positions in the unskilled ranks—spillover effects are negligible as market forces dominate private sector wage determination. Another commonly held belief—that government workers are overpaid no matter what they earn—also must be abandoned.

In addition, government pay and employment policy must get beyond its preoccupation with the short run. The problems of fiscal deficits cannot be minimized, but if pay and employment reforms are to contribute to a rehabilitation of the public sector they must be driven by more than the immediacy of budget crises. One of the consequences of the short-run myopia of stabilization measures during the 1980s was too much attention paid to curbing the wage bill and too little attention to how reductions or cost containments would be realized. If, in addition to the size of the wage bill, conditionality had targeted issues of government wage and employment structures, then redundancy, wage erosion, and salary compression might now be less severe. In other words, earlier attention to the microeconomic implications of pay and employment policies might have enhanced not only fiscal objectives but the performance of the government sector as well.

Rehabilitation of the civil service requires a recognition that a well-performing government sector is an important ingredient in restoring economic growth. A more rational system of pay and employment of government employees is critical to achieving these goals.

Notes

1. The literature on wage determination and dualism in developing nations is vast. Useful surveys and discussions of the issues most relevant to this volume can be found in A. Berry and R. H. Sabot, "Labor Market Performance in

Developing Countries: A Survey," *World Development*, vol. 6, no. 11/12 (1978); Subbiah Kannappan, *Employment Problems and the Urban Labor Market in Developing Nations* (Ann Arbor, Mich.: University of Michigan, Graduate School of Business Administration, Division of Research, 1983); R. Webb, "Wage Policy and Income Distribution in Developing Countries," in Charles Frank and Richard Webb, eds., *Income Distribution and Growth in the Less Developed Countries* (Washington, D.C.: The Brookings Institution, 1977); and Jeffrey Williamson, "Migration and Urbanization," in H. Chenery and T. N. Srinivasan, eds., *Handbook of Development Economics*, vol. I (Amsterdam: North Holland, 1988).

2. The results for Tanzania are from David L. Lindauer and Richard H. Sabot, "The Public/Private Wage Differential in a Poor Urban Economy," *Journal of Development Economics*, vol. 12 (1983); and for Kenya from G. E. Johnson, "The Determination of Individual Hourly Earnings in Urban Kenya," Institute for Development Studies Discussion Paper 115, University of Nairobi, 1971. Evidence on public enterprise workers receiving a premium over both private sector and government employees is presented in the Tanzania study. More recent estimates of public-private pay differentials in developing economies can be found in: for Tanzania, J. B. Knight and R. H. Sabot, "Educational Expansion, Government Policy and Wage Compression," *Journal of Development Economics*, vol. 26 (1987); Katherine Terrell, "Public-Private Wage Differentials in Haiti: Do Public Servants Earn a Rent?," *Journal of Development Economics*, vol. 42 (1993); and J. Van der Gaag, M. Stelcher, and W. Vijverberg, "Wage Differentials and Moonlighting by Civil Servants: Evidence from Côte d'Ivoire and Peru," *World Bank Economic Review*, vol. 3, no. 1 (1989). These more recent studies reveal both positive and negative pay differentials for government workers.

3. On this point see J. Weeks, "Wage Policy and the Colonial Legacy—A Comparative Study," *Journal of Modern African Studies*, vol. 9 (October 1971), and David B. Abernethy, "Bureaucratic Growth and Economic Stagnation in Sub-Saharan Africa," a paper delivered at the 1984 Annual Meeting of the American Political Science Association, Washington, D.C. (August 1984).

4. An altogether different mechanism by which government pay and employment decisions could have spilled over to the private sector is via "crowding out" rather than wage leadership. Decisions to expand the public sector could have raised labor demand for a broad range of labor skills, especially for school graduates. The desire to increase the provision of public goods and services, combined with the proliferation of state enterprises, may have significantly increased public employment and, hence, influenced the wage levels facing private employers. But in this instance it is employment policy and the labor market, not any institutional form of wage determination that explains high wages prevailing in the private sector. These alternative scenarios of public-private pay determination are spelled out in more analytical detail in David L. Lindauer, chapter 6, "Government Pay and Employment Policy: A Parallel Market in Labor," in Michael Roemer and Christine Jones, eds., *Markets in Developing Countries, Parallel, Fragmented and Black* (San Francisco, Calif.: International Center for Economic Growth and Harvard Institute for International Development, 1991).

5. According to the *World Development Report 1988* (Washington, D.C.: World Bank), low-income countries derive 38 percent of government revenues

from international trade taxes as compared to 19 percent for middle-income economies (p. 75).

6. Revenue shares of GDP in Ghana are reported in chapter 10 of this volume; estimates of employment growth in the Ghanaian government are presented in David L. Lindauer, Oey A. Meesook, and Parita Suebsaeng, "Government Wage Policy in Africa: Some Findings and Policy Issues," *World Bank Research Observer*, vol. 3, no. 1 (1988), table 1.

7. Ibid. It should be noted that while government employment growth was less than 1.0 percent, public enterprise employment in Zambia grew by 3.3 percent a year over the same time period.

8. Pay trends in Zambia are reported by Christopher Colclough, "The Labor Market and Economic Stabilization in Zambia," WPS 222, World Bank, Country Economics Department, Washington, D.C., 1989, table 15. Trends in El Salvador are reported in Peter Gregory, "Increasing the Efficiency of the Public Sector," a report prepared for USAID/El Salvador (September 1991), p. 13. The Laotian estimate is from Jinny St. Goar, "Half-Hearted Liberalization in Laos," *The Asian Wall Street Journal Weekly*, March 12, 1990. Trends in Sudan are reported in Lindauer and others, op. cit., table 3.

9. From Oey A. Meesook, David L. Lindauer, and Parita Suebsaeng, "Wage Policy and the Structure of Wages and Employment in Zambia," CPD Discussion Paper 1986-1, World Bank, Washington, D.C., 1986, table 4.2.

10. Excessive reliance on housing benefits can also lead to an overconsumption of housing, that is, rather than being able to choose their preferred consumption bundle, civil servants are compensated by "too much" housing, since if this benefit is in kind, it cannot be converted into other goods. Malawi has been cited as a case in point.

11. At the top echelons of the civil service the situation can be entirely different. An internal World Bank report (1991) on the compensation of cabinet ministers in Uganda notes that although the minister's monthly salary was about 12,000 Uganda shillings (U Sh) in early 1989, he would also receive either government housing or a housing allowance worth U Sh 500,000 a month, along with a chauffeur-driven car valued at U Sh 200,000 a month. In addition, ministers are entitled to four domestic servants, a value of U Sh 10,000 a month. Thus, a minister's salary, augmented by these benefits alone (and there are many others), amounts to U Sh 722,000 a month *or 60 times his basic salary*.

12. Zambian data are from Colclough, op. cit., table 14. More evidence on wage compression is presented by Barbara Nunberg in chapter 7 of this volume, table 7.6.

13. Colclough, op. cit. Housing benefits, which, as already noted, disproportionately accrue to more senior government officials, mitigate some of this compression in salary levels.

14. Aziz Khan, "Employment and Wages in Liberia: Some Preliminary Notes with Special Reference to the Public Sector," World Bank, Country Policy Department, Washington, D.C., 1983, p. 11; John Harris, E. Andoh, K. Evlo, and M. Starr, "Experiments in Wage-Bill Containment in Africa," World Bank, Special Office for Africa, Washington, D.C., 1987, pp. 34–40. In chapter 7 of this volume, Barbara Nunberg provides estimates of the share of wages and salaries

out of current expenditures for fourteen African and Latin American countries. The ratio ranges from 65 percent (Central African Republic, 1982; Mali, 1982) to less than 20 percent (Ghana, 1983; Uganda, 1981). The cross-sectional evidence itself is not proof of declining expenditures on complementary inputs, but does suggest vastly different budgetary allocations across countries.

15. Technically, if there is a high degree of substitution of unskilled labor for skilled labor or of labor for nonlabor inputs, or both, redundancy need not occur. However, in practice, the possibilities for factor substitutions in the provision of public goods and services appear more limited.

16. A. Gelb, J. B. Knight, and R. H. Sabot ("Public Sector Employment Rent Seeking and Economic Growth," *The Economic Journal*, vol. 101, 1991) employ a simulation model of an economy to illustrate how the hiring of redundant public workers can drive economywide growth rates down. In their model, marginal government workers have zero marginal products. As government employment, driven by rent-seeking, expands, domestic savings are syphoned away from more productive private uses to finance redundant public employment. The emphasis of this model, however, is not on the problems of poor government performance but on a public sector whose growth is intrinsically unproductive. For Gelb and others, supplying additional government workers with complementary inputs represents a further waste of resources and may even lead to *negative* marginal products for redundant workers.

17. For a review of the literature relating government size and economic growth, see David L. Lindauer and Ann D. Velenchik, "Government Spending in Developing Countries: Trends, Causes, and Consequences," *World Bank Research Observer*, vol. 7, no. 1 (1992).

18. Van der Gaag and others, op. cit., provides a sophisticated econometric treatment correlating government pay with moonlighting behavior.

19. Cited in Lindauer and others, op. cit., n. 12.

20. See ibid., table 2.

21. In addition to the discussion in chapter 7, see also Barbara Nunberg, "Managing the Civil Service: What LDCs Can Learn from Developed Country Reforms," Policy Research Working Paper, WPS 945, World Bank, Washington, D.C., 1992, pp. 33–36. Nunberg reviews the experience with performance-based pay rewards in the civil services of developed countries. She finds little evidence to substantiate a linkage between pay and performance. However, the industrially advanced country case concerns financial rewards at the margin and may not be entirely relevant. The developing nation situation is often one of motivating performance by meeting the minimal thresholds of "living wages" for government workers.

3

Diagnosis with limited information: government pay and employment reform in Somalia

Peter Gregory

Broadly stated, the purpose of this paper is to examine the employment and remuneration practices of the Somali civil service and to make recommendations for reforms. The evolution of staffing levels and pay scales over time have become central issues since the civil service ranks, as well as those of autonomous government agencies, have expanded excessively and compensation levels have deteriorated precipitously with unfortunate consequences for the operating efficiency of the government sector. The objective of this review is the determination both of a staffing level adequate to the needs of the government and of remuneration adjustments required to restore the public sector to a competitive position in the labor market.

The assigned task proved to be a difficult one. The absence of any systematic procedures for monitoring employment in the public sector poses an enormous obstacle to the development of reliable measures of employment. More detailed information with respect to the current characteristics of the work force is even more remote; one must rely for this kind of detail on the employment census of the public sector completed in 1985.[1] A review of a number of previous studies of the civil service with resources and time far exceeding ours confirms the paucity of reliable information for this sector. In addition, visits to individual

This paper was prepared in 1990 with the aim of formulating a civil service reform program for Somalia for the 1990s. Although the five-year reform program was never implemented because of the civil war in Somalia, the author's analysis offers a methodological approach applicable to any setting in which civil service pay and employment require dramatic reforms.

ministries did not prove as helpful as one might wish. Although the data base leaves a great deal to be desired, the deficiencies and distortions within the civil service are of such magnitude that many useful observations can be made and broad recommendations formulated.

Definition of the problem

The problems to be addressed can be characterized as follows:
- An oversized work force.
- Extremely low levels of remuneration.
- No clear definition of employee functions and responsibilities.
- An inadequate supply of cooperating factor inputs.
- Employment arrangements devoid of incentives or motivation to perform.
- Widespread demoralization of personnel.
- An extremely low level of overall efficiency.

A low level of efficiency is only the visible consequence of the demoralization of the work force. Less visible, but equally serious, are the responses of personnel needful of more adequate incomes. Some fortunate civil servants are able to augment their incomes in legitimate fashion through employment on donor-funded "projects." Although this represents a legitimate response, it is not free of undesirable consequences. The most visible is a widespread absenteeism that is justified by employees' need for other remunerative employments. More reprehensible and dangerous to the long-run integrity of government is the petty and gross corruption to which employees resort in order to augment their pitiful salaries.

Unfortunately, the challenge of reform cannot be met by adjustments at the margin. Rather, a whole new institutional structure is required within which reform of employment and remuneration practices can be addressed. Although the institutional requirements of reform cannot be discussed in any detail here, it is important to emphasize that institutional reforms are a fundamental prerequisite to the problems of overstaffing and the wholesale revision of salary levels and practices.

If meaningful reform is to be achieved, it must enjoy a powerful commitment to reform at the highest level of the government, a commitment that has not yet been evinced. Significant increases in the efficiency of the civil service will also be costly. For a government seriously lacking in resources, the costs of reform are likely to pose a formidable obstacle to its enactment. This report suggests ways in which the reforms may be implemented within the resource constraints defined by economic projections for the economy and the public sector.

The next section traces the evolution of employment in the public sector and offers rough estimates of the extent of redundancy. The process by which appropriate staffing requirements can be established is then outlined. Compensation issues are subsequently reviewed: the course of real wages is traced, and comparisons of civil service remunerations with those in other parts of the economy are offered as indicative of the levels the former will have to reach in order to be competitive and to permit the reestablishment of effective and enforceable performance requirements. Finally, the costs of reform are estimated and a strategy and timetable for implementation offered.

Employment levels and staffing requirements

The first comprehensive analysis of the existing conditions of Somali employment in both the private and public sector was undertaken in 1971.[2] A detailed survey of central government ministries and autonomous agencies revealed 14,014 employees in the former and 17,511 in the latter. In addition, 9,600 were employed in other public programs and in municipal governments. At the time, a rapid increase in public sector employment was forecast as the government assumed the leading role as the "engine of growth" of the Somali economy. Indeed, expanding government employment was viewed as a positive development, responding to the need for both greater employment opportunities and economic progress. In anticipation of this expansion, positions, or the establishment of positions, were authorized well in excess of current requirements. Furthermore, the government assumed a legal obligation to hire any secondary school or university graduates who requested employment.

It should come as no surprise that public employment expanded at a rapid pace (table 3.1). Establishment surveys of the ministries conducted by the Ministry of Labour and Social Affairs in 1969 and 1975 reported roughly 18,000 and 20,600 authorized positions. However, while these numbers included vacancies, they excluded temporary and casual employees, and thus most likely understated actual employment levels. According to a manpower survey in 1978, central government employment had reached a level estimated at about 32,300. Expansion continued during the 1980s. Another survey of ministries yielded an estimate of more than 45,000 employees for 1983. However, the latest survey completed in 1985 reported only 43,134 employees. A large part of the growth is attributable to the expansion of the educational system during the 1970s. Whereas in 1971 employees of the Ministry of Education numbered only 3,087, or 23 percent of total central government employment, by 1983 their number had increased to 22,654, roughly half of the total.

The course of employment since 1985 is largely speculative. Table 3.1 offers estimates for subsequent years. Column 2 data originate in the finance ministry and show employment to have peaked in 1985 at about 53,600, or at a level 10,000 above that of the 1985 census. Since then, there appears to have been an irregular downward trend in employment to a little more than 50,000 in 1989. However, these numbers appear so erratic that it is difficult to place much confidence in them. Attempts to determine from the ministry precisely how these estimates were derived were fruitless. The estimates attributed to the Somali Training and Development Program in column 3 for years subsequent to 1985 are derived by adjusting the 1985 census level by the numbers of accessions and separations recorded by the Ministry of Labour. However, there is ample evidence that the ministry fails to capture all of the personnel changes that occur.

In short, it is impossible to establish with any degree of certainty the actual level of employment in the civil service. While estimates of employment abound, the precise meaning to be attached to the term "employment" is subject to a number of qualifications. It cannot be taken to refer to the number of persons occupied on a full-time basis at a set of well-defined tasks. It may most closely approximate the number of individuals appearing on the public payroll. The rolls thus include individuals who make only token appearances at their place of government employment, others who never appear yet draw a salary, still others who report to their places of employment but have nothing to do, as

Table 3.1 Estimates of central government employment, Somalia, selected years, 1969–89

Year	I	II	III
1969	17,951	18,000	18,000
1971	13,203	—	13,000
1975	20,619	20,600	20,600
1978	32,282	32,269	33,100
1983	44,094	45,100	45,100
1984	—	47,536	—
1985	—	53,614	43,134
1986	—	48,085	42,910
1987	—	40,961	43,988
1989	—	50,128	43,841

— Not available.

Source: I: Government of Somalia, Ministry of Labour and Social Affairs, *Somali Civil Service Study*, September 1984, table 3.3, pp. 3–15; II: Ercis Kurtulus, "Personnel Emoluments and Civil Service Employment," prepared for World Bank expenditure review mission to Somalia, December 1989, pp. 44–45; III: Somali Training and Development Program (SOMTAD), *Report on Civil Service Reform*, September 1989, pp. 12, 14, and 22. The estimates for years subsequent to 1985 were derived by adjusting the census levels by the Ministry of Labour's record of the number of accessions to and separations from the civil service.

well as those who put in a substantial portion of the normally defined workday at reasonably productive activity. It is this large discrepancy between the number of persons now on the payroll and the number that would be required to produce the current level of output if diligently employed full-time that gives rise to the phenomenon of overstaffing or employee redundancy.

Estimating current employment

Because it is difficult to place much confidence in the various measures of employment in the central government, we have tried to arrive at an estimate of current (1990) government employment by indirect means. Our procedure involves the estimation of an average salary net of allowances accruing to civil service personnel in 1990 and the division of the total budgeted salaries (again net of allowances) by this average. Since more reliable employment data for 1989–90 are available for the education ministry, we omitted that ministry's salary payments and employment for the purposes of this exercise. The average salary level for the remaining ministries and central government agencies was derived as follows.

We started with the distribution of public servants by civil service grade as reported for 1985. To each grade in 1990 we applied a salary corresponding to something less than the average for the grade's salary range. For example, there are three divisions in B grade—B3, B2, and B1—with minimum, or entry-level, monthly salaries (in Somali shillings, Sh) of Sh 5,049, Sh 6,512, and Sh 8,157 net of allowances as of January 1990. The simple arithmetic average of the three salaries is Sh 6,573. Because there are likely to be fewer individuals at higher grade levels, we adopted a slightly lower value of Sh 6,500 for grade B. The estimated monthly salary for each grade is then multiplied by the number of individuals reported in that grade in 1985 to derive the total monthly salary payments. The weighted average salary is then computed by dividing this total wage bill by the number of employees in the 1985 survey of public sector employment. This yields a weighted average monthly salary (net of allowances) of Sh 6,366, or an average annual salary of Sh 76,392. This average annual salary is then divided into the budgeted basic wage bill for 1990 (table 3.2). Since the total amount provided for basic salary payments in the Somali government ordinary budget for 1990 is Sh 3,173.46 million, this yields an employment level of 41,542 for noneducation ministries and agencies. If to this we add the 15,000 employees on the payroll of the education ministry at the end of 1989, we derive a grand total of 56,542, a number significantly larger than any of those provided in the above estimates.

Admittedly, this figure does not rest on as solid a foundation as we would like, but an assessment of potential sources of bias leads us to treat the estimate as robust. For example, the distribution of the work force through the various occupational grades recorded in the 1985 census was assumed to be representative of the actual distribution in 1985, and it was further assumed that the proportional distribution has remained unchanged since then. There is no way to determine whether in fact that distribution was representative of the actual in 1985.

However, if any reporting errors were randomly distributed over the various classifications, the recorded distribution would be unbiased for our purposes. We can think of no obvious reason for believing that the reporting agencies would choose to bias the outcomes in any particular way. Indeed, since holders of positions at the upper end of the occupational structure are more visible, they are less likely to be overlooked in an accounting of personnel. If this is so, and any understatement of employment is concentrated in the lower ranges of the occupational

Table 3.2 Estimates of central government employment and salary, Somalia, 1990

(shillings)

Grade classification[a]	1985 employment	1990 salary range (monthly)	Estimated average salary (monthly)	Total monthly wage bill (thousands)
A	1,569	6,512–13,881	9,500	14,905.5
AY	49	8,157–8,673	8,400	411.6
B	2,891	5,049–8,157	6,500	18,791.5
F	2,354	6,512–8,673	7,450	17,537.3
C	7,501	4,215–8,157	6,200	46,506.2
X	3,740	4,215–8,157	6,000	22,440.0
D	1,805	2,550–4,215	3,300	5,956.5
Unknown	1,373	n.a.	6,500	8,924.5
Total	21,282	n.a.	n.a.	135,473.1

n.a. Not applicable.
Note: Estimates exclude the Ministry of Education.
a. A detailed comparison of grade classifications with occupations requires a matching of individual steps within grades to representative jobs. A general association of grades with occupations follows (more detail is provided in table 3.7):

Grade	Occupation
A, AY	Professional (senior accountant)
B	Mid-level white collar (cashier)
F	Administrative (maintenance supervisor)
C	Clerical (typist)
X	Tradesman (mechanic)
D	Unskilled (laborer)

Source: Government of Somalia, Ministry of Labour and Sports, *The Characteristics of Public Sector Employment and Key Issues of Manpower Development*, Mogadishu, June 1985; Government of Somalia budget for 1980.

structure, our estimated average salary figure would represent an over-statement of the actual and would result in an underestimation of current employment levels.

Operating in the same fashion would be our estimating procedure for the average salary of each civil service grade. We made only a very minor downward adjustment to the simple arithmetic average of the minimum salaries of each subclassification within a grade even though one would expect the lower grades to have larger numbers of occupants and, therefore, to exercise a greater downward weight on the grade average.

Whether the occupational structure of the work force of 1985 is an accurate reflection of the current one remains an issue. We believe that it is unlikely that the current structure is more heavily weighted with skilled employees than that recorded for 1985. Given the wider set of alternative employment opportunities open to skilled individuals, there is little reason to believe that the growth in government employment since 1985 has been disproportionately greater in the high-skill categories. Indeed, many ministries report a shortage of skilled personnel due to uncompetitive levels of remuneration. To the extent that this assessment is correct, our estimated average salary is unlikely to represent an understatement of the actual current salary level and thus an overestimate of the current level of employment. Therefore, in the remainder of this chapter we will proceed on the assumption that total central government employment in Somalia at the beginning of 1990 numbered about 56,500.

Estimating redundancy

In view of the decline in the real expenditures of the central government over the past decade, the expansion of employment that has since occurred must have led to the creation of a large number of redundant workers on the public payroll. If central government expenditure for the provision of services and development is defined as the total expenditures in the ordinary budget less defense and interest expenses plus the domestically financed expenditures in the development budget, then central government expenditure reached a peak in 1979 at a level of Sh 928 million (in 1977 shillings).[3] In 1989 these expenditures amounted to Sh 349 million in constant purchasing power, or 38 percent of the 1979 level. The 1989 level was well below even the 1975 level, which measured Sh 664 million. Considering that 1975 and 1979 employment levels have been estimated at 20,600 and 35,000, respectively, the 1989 estimated level of 56,500 clearly suggests a substantial degree of overstaffing.

How large a civil service would be required to adequately fulfill the functions of government at current levels of expenditure? There is no simple way to determine that level. The approach adopted here is one that employs the concept of a production function. A production function is a mechanism for relating quantities of productive factors, or inputs, to the quantity of goods and services produced. In the case of government, we can visualize its output of services as a product of two classes of inputs, labor and nonlabor.

Applying the concept of a production function to the Somali case, we would proceed on the assumption that, in order for a civil servant to "produce" any given level of services, his labor must be accompanied by some volume of other inputs, such as office equipment, supplies, transportation services, and the like. The optimal quantity of such cooperating factors of production is not obvious. However, we can determine the volume of nonlabor inputs that were combined with each worker to produce different levels of services in the past. This experience then serves as a benchmark for estimating current labor requirements.

We have adopted two measures of nonlabor inputs per worker. One is derived as the sum of nondefense ordinary budget expenditures plus the domestically financed development budget less interest charges and wage and salary payments. Table 3.3A provides these data for each year since 1975. While the pre-1981 and post-1980 data are not fully comparable, they are sufficiently so to permit the derivation of rough measures of the relevant variables. As can be seen, real aggregate nonlabor expenditure increased substantially from 1975 to a peak in 1979 and then declined in irregular fashion throughout the 1980s, although a small recovery is discernable at the end of the decade. However, in terms of expenditure per employee (table 3.3B), the decline has been very substantial, from Sh 23,107 per employee in 1975 to Sh 19,971, Sh 6,725, and Sh 5,558 in 1979, 1981, and 1989, respectively, all in constant 1977 shillings.

If 1975's nonlabor inputs of Sh 23,107 per employee are taken as a benchmark of the requirement for efficient production by a civil servant, then the 1989 level of expenditure would have sufficed to provide that quantity of cooperating inputs for only 13,589 employees. Use of the 1979 inputs yields labor requirements in 1989 of 15,723. These estimates of labor requirements would imply redundancy of about 40,000 employees.

An alternative approach restricts the nonlabor inputs to only those encompassed in the operations and maintenance items in the ordinary budget. These expenditures were available on a consistent basis for only the 1981–89 interval (table 3.4). By interpolation, we estimate 1981 employment at approximately 40,000, and the per worker expenditure at around Sh 2,202 (1977 shillings). For 1989 we have a per worker expenditure of Sh 1,055, only 48 percent of the 1981 level. If the 1981 per worker expenditure is applied to the 1989 operations and maintenance expenditure, only 27,071 workers could have been provided with the 1981 bundle of nonlabor inputs. However, recall that 1981 must have already suffered a high degree of redundancy since total central government civilian expenditure in that year was less than half that in 1979 while employment had increased. Therefore, 1979 operations and maintenance expenditure per employee was likely to have been at least twice as great as that in 1981, or more than Sh 4,400. If the 1989 operations and maintenance budget is divided by this value, only 13,548 employees could have

Table 3.3A Central government nondefense expenditure, Somalia, 1975–90

(millions of 1977 shillings)

Year	Nominal expenditure	Wage bill	Difference (column 1 minus column 2)	Consumer price index (1977=100)	Real expenditure
1975	527	150	378	79.4	476
1976	649	173	477	91.1	524
1977	814	207	607	100.0	607
1978	1,047	312	735	110.0	668
1979	1,264	312	953	136.2	700
1980	1,244	385	859	217.1	396
1981	1,281	437	844	313.4	269
1982	1,497	464	1,033	384.2	269
1983	1,914	579	1,335	524.0	255
1984	2,397	646	1,751	1,007.4	174
1985	3,018	684	2,334	1,388.4	168
1986	4,877	662	4,215	1,829.4	230
1987	8,571	869	7,702	2,416.3	319
1988	11,997	1,308	10,689	4,391.4	243
1989	32,260	3,223	29,037	9,240.8	314
1990	77,123	8,318	68,805	19,500.7(est.)	352

Source: Expenditure: World Bank estimates; consumer price index: Government of Somalia, Ministry of National Planning, Central Statistical Department.

Table 3.3B Central government nondefense expenditure per employee, Somalia, selected years, 1975–89

(1977 shillings)

Year	Expenditure (millions)	Employment	Expenditure per employee[a]
1975	476	20,600	23,107
1979	700	35,000	19,971
1981	269	40,000	6,725
1989	314	56,500	5,558

a. Expenditure includes total ordinary expenditures less defense and interest expenses plus domestically financed development expenditures.
Source: Expenditure: World Bank estimates; employment: table 3.1 and author's estimates.

been provided with the 1979 bundle of inputs, a number virtually identical to that derived in the preceding paragraph.

A procedure for estimating an appropriate staffing level for the central government that holds constant the volume of nonlabor inputs is, of course, an extreme one. It implies that no increases in output would be achievable if the ratio of nonlabor to labor inputs were to decline, that is, that the marginal product of labor is zero. This is patently an unrealistic assumption. However, it would be equally unrealistic to assume that significant increases in output are realizable indefinitely as more labor is combined with a shrinking volume of cooperating factors of production. Thus, we would opt for a target volume of employment that allows for the unreasonableness of the assumption of fixed factor proportions. In addition, we would allow for the likelihood that employment figures for the earlier years were understated; understatement would have the effect of overstating the quantity of nonlabor inputs per worker in the earlier years and thus understating the current labor requirements. Finally, we would make allowance for the likelihood that there is a minimum number of employees required to staff an agency even if they cannot all be fully employed.

As an interim objective, we propose an employment objective of 17,000 for the ministries and agencies other than education plus 8,000 for the latter for a total of 25,000 to be achieved by 1995. Note that this represents a level almost twice that yielded by the crude procedure employed above. Not only does it compensate for the factors leading to a possible understatement of staffing requirements in the preceding paragraph, it also allows for a growth in real government expenditure in

Table 3.4 Central government expenditure on operations and maintenance, total and per civil servant, Somalia, 1981–90

| Year | Consumer price index | Operations and maintenance budget (millions of shillings) | | Estimated employment | Operations and maintenance per civil servant (1977 shillings) |
		Nominal	Real		
1981	313.4	276	88.07	40,000	2,202
1982	384.2	316	82.24		
1983	521.0	421	80.34		
1984	1,007.4	487	48.34		
1985	1,387.9	575	41.43	44,000	941
1986	1,884.4	837	44.42		
1987	2,413.5	1,092	45.24		
1988	4,386.3	1,618	36.86		
1989	9,240.8	5,508	59.61	56,500	1,055
1990	19,500.7(est.)	11,624	59.61		1,055

Source: Expenditure: World Bank estimates; consumer price index: Government of Somalia, Ministry of Planning, Central Statistical Department; employment: table 3.1 and author's estimates.

the interim. For example, the Ministry of Education's employment goal of 8,000 already contains considerable slack that will permit the expansion of student enrollments without increasing the number of teachers. At an average of only 23.5 students per teacher in the 1987/88 school year, class size is well below that of the 1970s when the ratio stood in the range of 31–35 students to each teacher.[4] Since teachers currently are commonly working only half-time, a condition necessitated by low salary levels, the education system clearly has considerable excess capacity even before the ministry's current employment goal is met. Alternatively, if enrollments do not increase, the number of teachers required could be substantially reduced as salaries are increased and teachers return to full-time employment.

In short, the interim objective of 25,000 central government employees does not seem unreasonable. Since a reduction in force of the magnitude projected by this goal will have to be spread over several years, there will be time to adjust this figure so that it corresponds to the actual needs of the central government.[5]

Remuneration trends

Recent years have seen severe erosion in employee remunerations and a compression of salary scales—a picture somewhat complicated by allowances and benefits awarded at the upper levels of the civil service.

Pay erosion and compression

There can be little dispute about the actual course of civil service remunerations over the past fifteen years. In real terms, pay levels have suffered a devastating decline. Real basic salary scales declined by the end of 1989 to less than 5 percent of their 1975 levels (table 3.5). Because wage adjustments made in the interim have tended to grant larger proportional increases to the lower salary grades, the decline in real salaries has been sharper in the upper ranges of the structure, producing a considerable degree of compression in the salary structure. The ratio of the nominal salary of the highest grade (A1) to that of the lowest grade (D14) was 9.1:1 in 1975, and shrank to 5.7:1 by the end of 1989.

Allowances and benefits

It should be pointed out that the formal structure of basic salaries does not include all of the compensation received by civil servants. There are a variety of allowances that accrue to individuals occupying certain positions. For example, most university graduates are automatically eligible for a professional allowance of Sh 700 a month. Responsibility allowances are paid to individuals occupying certain managerial, supervisory, or technical positions. Their monthly values cover a wide range, from Sh 2,000 a month for the general manager of a Class A agency to Sh 50 for a fire fighter. Cash housing allowances are paid to selected senior managerial and professional personnel, ranging from Sh 100 to Sh 500 a month. A variety of other allowances are paid to teachers and school administrators, artists in the performing arts, medical personnel, and legal professionals, none of which yields more than Sh 400 a month. Finally, the cost-of-living adjustments that have been made periodically since 1975 have been granted in the form of allowances rather than as adjustments in the formal salary structure. (In tables 3.5 and 3.6 these cost-of-living supplements have been included in the definition of the

Table 3.5 Civil service salary structure, Somalia, 1975 and 1989

Grade[a]	Step	Salaries in 1975	Salaries in 1989 (current shillings)	Real salaries in 1989 (1975 shillings)	1989 as a percentage of 1975
Apprentice		132	665	6	4.3
D14	1	220	1,109	10	4.3
	5	264	1,294	11	4.2
D13	1	275	1,348	12	4.2
	5	319	1,563	13	4.2
D12	1	330	1,617	14	4.2
	5	374	1,780	15	4.1
D11/C11/X4	1	375	1,833	16	4.2
	5	452	2,185	19	4.2
C10/B10/X3	1	473	2,195	19	4.0
	5	557	2,501	21	3.9
C9/B9/A8/X2/F3	1	630	2,831	24	3.9
	5	720	3,192	27	3.8
C8/B8/A7/X1/F2/AY3	1	800	3,546	30	3.8
	5	920	3,732	32	3.5
A6/F1/AY2-1	1	1,000	3,771	32	3.2
	3	1,060	3,918	34	3.2
A5	1	1,090	4,029	35	3.2
	4	1,150	4,250	36	3.1
A4		1,160	4,287	37	3.2
A3/AY1	1	1,200	4,435	38	3.2
	3	1,300	4,805	41	3.2
A2/AY1	1	1,400	5,174	44	3.2
	3	1,600	5,787	50	3.1
A1	1	1,800	6,035	52	2.9
	2	2,001	6,339	54	2.7

Note: All salaries are monthly. Salaries include cost-of-living adjustments made to the original salary structure since 1969.

a. Occupations representative of salary grades are presented in table 3.7.

Source: Government of Somalia, Ministry of Labour and Sports, Department of Manpower Research.

base salary.) Since none of the salary supplements has been adjusted over time for inflation, their real values have declined to the point of insignificance. At the official exchange rate of early 1990 of approximately 1,000 shillings to the U.S. dollar, the professional allowance amounted to only 70 cents a month, and the largest responsibility allowance to 2 dollars.

Actually, a comparison of the current real level of the basic salary structure with that of 1975 leads to an overstatement of the decline. In the earlier year, all civil service salaries were subject to a graduated "development tax," which for higher-level civil servants amounted to a significant reduction in net pay. However, since allowances have not been adjusted for inflation over time, it may well be that the sum of after-tax pay plus allowances has declined as sharply as suggested by table 3.5.

Ministers and some top administrators are also eligible for payments in kind in the form of housing plus utilities and the use of an automobile provided with a weekly fuel allowance. The market value of these in-kind payments is very large relative to the cash salaries received. Since the quality of housing provided varies widely among recipients, it is impossible to place a single monetary value on this benefit. The estimated market values of housing cited in interviews ranged between Sh 50,000 and Sh 200,000 a month, with an additional Sh 50,000–Sh 100,000 cited for the value of utilities. The use of an automobile represents a salary supplement at least as valuable as housing. Thus, for top government officials the market value of supplements alone is on the order of Sh 200,000–Sh 300,000.

Official salary scales are also supplemented by allowances that become available from that portion of the development budget that is financed by foreign donors. Somali civil servants who are directly engaged on such projects receive, in addition to their official salaries, salary supplements as well as allowances in cash or in kind, or both. The finance ministry has promulgated guidelines that are supposed to govern the size of these supplements for each class of participants in project activities. The size of the supplements is a function of the dollar value of the project rather than of the characteristics or demands of the duties performed. Thus, the general manager of a project with a total budget of Sh 40 billion (US$40 million) or more is eligible for a Sh 5,000 responsibility allowance and an equal housing allowance, for a total of Sh 10,000 a month. In contrast, the general manager of a project with a budget of less than Sh 5 million (US$5,000) is eligible for allowances of Sh 3,000 (responsibility) and Sh 2,500 (housing), for a total of Sh 5,500. Other allowances are also available to project personnel. The most significant of these has been directed at narrowing the gap between the market salaries of highly educated employees and the official civil service salary levels. Thus, monthly allowances of Sh 5,000, Sh 10,000, and Sh 20,000 have been authorized for project personnel with bachelor, master, or doctoral degrees. Finally, all project managers and many employees of professional rank are also provided with the use of an automobile, free gasoline, and maintenance. Although these are the provisions under the finance ministry's directive, it appears that individual projects have exercised considerable discretion in determining the size and distribution of allowances. The ministry must authorize any departures from its directive, but apparently it generally grants approval to such requests. In sum, Somali civil servants have suffered significant erosion in real pay and compression of earnings differentials; however, for top administrators nonwage benefits and new sources of allowances have offset at least some of this decline.

Establishing competitive remunerations

The reestablishment of an efficient civil service will require very substantial increases in salary scales as well as extensive reforms in the administration of the service. Therefore, it is most important to determine what level of remuneration would be adequate to realize this end. As one approach, we asked senior civil servants whether there had existed in the past a level of real salaries that was consistent with the maintenance of a full-time and dedicated work force. The responses all pointed to the real salaries of the mid-1970s as adequate. Thus, one might begin by adjusting the salary scales of 1975 by increases in the consumer price index in order to define the current equivalent nominal salaries. However, it should be recalled that in 1975 civil servants were not receiving the full amounts as defined in the salary structure, for in 1970 their salaries had become subject to a "development tax," with marginal rates ranging from 5 percent on the first 200 shillings to 30 percent on earnings of more than 1,500 shillings. Therefore, to allow for these deductions we chose to bring forward to the present the real salary levels of 1977 (table 3.6). We assume the moderate inflation between 1975 and 1977 would have reduced the value of the gross 1977 salary to a rough equivalence with the 1975 salary net of the development tax.

Prevailing wages

Although this adjustment provides a starting point for the consideration of an appropriate salary level, it is not the only criterion that is relevant. Salaries paid by the government need to bear some consistent relationship to those offered in nongovernment employments. We have made an attempt to bring together information about local payment practices in order to establish some benchmarks against which to compare the salaries yielded by the procedure applied in table 3.6. As sources of information about payment practices we had access to two wage surveys conducted by the U.S. Agency for International Development (USAID) in September–October 1988 and July–August 1989.

The earlier survey included eight private firms, two international agencies, and three autonomous government agencies. The latter was sharply reduced in number to only six observations for reasons that are relevant to an appreciation of the obstacles facing any inquiry into prevailing wages. Six of the private firms had to be dropped because of sharp reductions in staff attributed to shortages of foreign exchange for

Table 3.6 Current and adjusted civil service salary structure, Somalia, 1977 and 1990

Grade[a]	Step	Current salary, January 1990[b]	1977 salary in January 1990 shillings	Proposed salary in January 1990 shillings
Apprentice		1,530	18,977	18,000
D14	1	2,550	31,629	28,000
	5	2,975	37,955	33,000
D13	1	3,099	39,537	30,000
	5	3,595	45,863	35,000
D12	1	3,719	47,444	33,000
	5	4,095	53,770	38,500
D11/C11/X4	1	4,215	53,914	40,000
	5	5,026	64,912	48,000
C10/B10/X3	1	5,049	67,931	46,000
	5	5,752	80,008	56,000
C9/B9/A8/X2/F3	1	6,512	90,575	60,000
	5	7,341	103,514	74,000
C8/B8/A7/X1/F2/AY3	1	8,157	115,016	70,000
	5	8,584	132,268	90,000
A6/F1/AY2-1	1	8,673	143,770	105,000
	3	9,011	152,396	126,000
A5	1	9,266	156,709	130,000
	4	9,776	165,336	150,000
A4		9,861	166,773	170,000
A3/AY1	1	10,201	172,524	178,000
	3	11,051	186,901	192,000
A2/AY1	1	11,901	201,278	210,000
	3	13,310	230,032	245,000
A1	1	13,881	258,786	260,000
	2	14,580	287,683	300,000

Note: All salaries are monthly.
a. Occupations representative of salary grades are presented in table 3.7.
b. The current salary reflects the full adjustments made to basic salaries as of January 1, 1990. In the column on 1977 salary levels, the nominal salaries of that year (from table 3.5) were inflated by the consumer price index for December 1989.
Source: Author's calculations.

the purchase of inputs as well as other economic difficulties. Information received from government agencies proved unusable because reported payment practices bore no relationship to the actual receipts of employees. The result was a much heavier reliance on the findings of diplomatic missions and international organizations, a data set that cannot be assumed to depict accurately the local labor market conditions for most of the labor grades of the civil service.

A second category of information was derived from interviews with three private sector businesses—two manufacturing firms and one hotel. These interviews and the USAID wage surveys (especially the earlier of the two) provided the principal source of information on market salaries. We would have liked to include more private sector firms, but there are few such firms employing a substantial number of workers distributed over a wide range of occupations, and we were unable to establish contact with any others.

A major challenge in interpreting the available data is posed by the inflationary context from which these have been drawn. During a period of rapid inflation, a survey that records salary scales for a fixed moment in time may be expected to show a large variance in payments. Some employers will have recently made wage adjustments that elevate their salary levels substantially above wages that have not been recently adjusted. Thus, it is impossible to distinguish between those salary differentials that are induced by inflationary leads and lags, and those that would be present in the market under more stable conditions. Ideally, one would like to have several observations drawn over an extended period so that a more representative average wage could be calculated. A further complication arises when adjustments to inflation are made in different ways. For example, one private firm had not adjusted basic wage rates since July 1988 in spite of an intervening increase of 230 percent in the cost of living. At the time of our interview in January 1990, the management reported it was planning a lump sum payment to employees in lieu of an adjustment of basic salaries. In such a case, the formal pay scales prove to be misleading. In addition, we found extensive payments in kind for which reliable monetary equivalents are difficult to obtain.

In view of these difficulties, we have had to exercise considerable discretion in choosing and interpreting the information gathered. Because the USAID survey of 1988 included more private firms, we were inclined to give greater weight to their pay scales. Therefore, we adjusted those salaries to reflect their purchasing power as of January 1990. These and selected observations from our and USAID's second surveys are presented in table 3.7 and compared with the salary levels yielded by the adjustments made to the 1977 civil service wage levels in table 3.6.

The number of comparisons that it is possible to make is limited to only ten occupational groupings. It should be emphasized that the occupations reported for the private sector have been assigned to a civil service category on the basis of incomplete information. We do not have a detailed schedule of job classifications. Rather, we have had to resort to a rough classification contained in the 1984 civil service study report.[6] The survey data we have are deficient in observations of managerial and professional categories. Their salaries appear to have various components in cash and in kind, some of which, like profit sharing, are not fixed in size. However, it can be stated categorically that private sector payments for such positions rank far above even the adjusted 1977 civil service salary structure at its upper reaches.

In making the salary comparisons that were possible, we included the median as well as the range of salaries. It should be noted that most firms in the private sector offered fringe benefits that have no counter-

Table 3.7 Labor market salary observations, selected occupations, Mogadishu, Somalia

Civil service grade	Number of observations	Equivalent occupation	Salary range (shillings)	Median salary (shillings)	Adjusted civil service salary[a]
D14/ D13	14	Janitor, laborer, unskilled entry level	4,500–60,000	23,500	31,629–37,955 39,537–45,863
D12	13	Gardener, driver	11,568–60,000	26,400	47,444–53,770
D11/ C11/ X4	6	Assistant craftsman, entry level clerical, mail clerk, messenger	14,520–60,000	54,219	53,914–64,912
C10	12	Routine office, clerk, typist, timekeeper	20,000–161,832	39,600	67,931–80,000
C9	7	Secretary	24,000–458,000	55,440	90,575–103,514
X1	7	Skilled tradesman, mechanic	57,816–305,000	69,432	115,016–132,268
C8/ B8	15	Accountant, personnel or purchasing clerk	17,820–305,000	70,250	115,016–132,268
B8	9	Cashier	48,312–305,000	67,500	115,016–132,268
F1	8	Maintenance supervisor	60,000–458,000	107,016	143,770–152,396
AY1	8	Senior accountant	35,112–528,000	130,225	172,524–186,901

Note: Salaries are paid monthly.
a. This column presents the 1977 salary structure in January 1990 shillings as it appears in table 3.6.
Source: USAID wage surveys, September–October 1988 and July–August 1989; author's interviews.

parts in the public sector. Transportation or transportation allowances, food, and bonuses were frequently encountered. A few cases of housing existed for highly skilled or responsible positions. Where possible, we have incorporated estimates of the value of some of these fringes, except for housing and irregular bonuses, into the salaries recorded in the table. In the last column we provide the 1977 civil service salary structure in terms of January 1990 shillings. As expected, the recorded market observations display a wide range of values. Four of the occupational groups record a multiple of more than thirteen between the highest and lowest salary. The narrowest range still records a ratio of high to low wages of more than four.

How well would a restoration of the 1977 salary structure serve for establishing salary levels comparable to those in the private sector? It appears that, at the lower ranks of the civil service, grades D14 through C10, the adjusted 1977 scale would pay salaries well above market levels. For all the middle-ranking occupations that make up the rest of our listing, the adjusted civil service salary structures would yield earnings above the median but well within the private sector salary range.

An alternative benchmark may be provided by the salary levels of teachers in countries at levels of development comparable to Somalia's. Such a comparison reveals that teachers' salaries average about five times the per capita income of poorer African countries.[7] If one accepts the estimate of Somali annual per capita income at about Sh 166,800 (January 1990 shillings), the expected annual teacher's salary would be about Sh 834,000. Reduced to a monthly basis, this yields a salary of Sh 77,083. This can then be compared with the salary of the A7 grade, which defines the basic salary of teachers with a university degree. As can be seen, the 1977 adjusted salary for that grade, Sh 115,016 to Sh 132,268, lies well above that salary. Indeed, a salary of about Sh 70,000 for teachers with a university degree is very close to the market median for other occupations that occupy the same civil service grade. Thus, it would seem that the restoration of the 1977 real levels of salary in both the lower and middle ranges of occupations would result in overpayment of civil servants.

Assessing the comparisons

Is it reasonable to expect to find the 1977 real salary levels excessive for these low- to middle-level occupations, particularly in view of the opinions expressed that 1975 net levels would appear to be the appropriate goal? First, let us address the relevance of the 1975 salaries. The opinions with respect to the relevance of those levels came largely from civil servants at the highest professional or managerial levels. For such individuals, a case may be made for the higher levels as represented by the 1977 or even the 1975 salary levels; we will return to a more careful consideration of these higher occupational groups shortly.

Returning to the low- and middle-level occupational groups, however, there are two possible reasons for considering the real salaries of thirteen years ago inappropriate. In the first place, there is no reason to accept the 1977 salary levels as representative of those paid outside the public sector at that time. Indeed, since the country was pursuing a socialist path to development the observations outside the public sector were very reduced. It has been observed that it was not uncommon for newly independent African countries to establish public sector wage scales that were well in excess of workers' opportunity costs. If Somalia followed the example of some of its neighbors, it could very well be that the salary levels of the 1970s were higher than needed to attract a stable and efficient work force. In that case, the 1977 wage levels may not represent appropriate targets for a salary reform.

A second factor that may contribute to the gap between past and current levels is the course of the economy over the past decade. In the face of stagnant economic growth and an expanding labor force, it would not be surprising to note a decline in market wages. With the substantial expansion of middle school leavers during the 1970s and early 1980s, one might expect the increase in the number of literate workers in the labor force to reduce the wage premium that was paid when they were fewer in number.

Although, as a general rule, it might make sense to set salary goals for the lower and middle grades of the civil service below 1977 real levels, there might be specific technical occupational groups that are currently classified in these grades that will prove to be misplaced relative to their market wage. Thus, as part of any civil service reform, a reconsideration of the classification of all occupational groups should be undertaken. Alternatively, the range of in-grade step increases could be widened to permit greater flexibility in response to changing market conditions, particularly for technical skills.

In the case of the professional and administrative categories of the civil service, it is more difficult to determine with precision the salary levels that would attract and retain an able cadre. The private sector in Somalia is very small, and there are few enterprises with positions with responsibilities commensurate to those of the upper levels of the civil service. Furthermore, we found that compensation schemes in the private sector tend to be complex and not easily defined. Wide use is made of payments in kind and payments tied to a firm's economic performance.

The other reference points available to us are the salaries offered to professionals and administrators employed on projects or on the staffs of international organizations. As we noted above, however, even project emoluments show great dispersion. Project directors frequently receive salaries and allowances in cash and in kind (for example, housing and automobile) that exceed the adjusted salary in grade A3, the highest administrative grade short of that of director general of a ministry. On the other hand, the remunerations of project professional staff on straight salary do not appear to exceed the levels corresponding to the lower AY grades.

Skilled Somalis also have the option of seeking employment in external markets. Although one would normally expect that most Somalis would accept a lower real salary in their own country than is required to induce them to work in a foreign land, there are obviously limits to the degree to which the differential may depart from foreign pay scales. As a first approximation, it would not seem unreasonable to accept the 1977 real salaries as a target for the A and AY grades. As salary levels are adjusted upward, reclassification of occupational titles and adjustments in salary grade levels can be made as experience proves necessary.

Proposals for a new salary structure

Before proposing a new salary structure for the civil service, a few additional comments on the desirable shape of a reformed government pay system are in order. First, we have sought to establish a civil service pay scale by referring to compensations offered in the private sector. It should be kept in mind that there are nonmonetary considerations that are also important in determining the availability of labor to government. For example, if public employment is viewed as more secure, more prestigious, or as satisfying a patriotic duty, it will be valued more highly than private employment. Under these circumstances, salaries below those paid in the private sector would be expected to attract all classes of employees.

Second, the current pay structure is characterized by a basic wage and various allowances. It would be advisable to integrate allowances into a basic salary structure. If an occupation carries with it a high degree of responsibility, the job salary rate should reflect that and be appropriately placed in the corresponding grade. Similarly, education allowances bear no relation to the task to which an individual is assigned. If a defined set of duties requires certain educational qualifications, this should be reflected in the salary assigned the job. There are substantial advantages to collapsing allowances into salary rates. It would greatly simplify the salary structure and make clear the total remunerations accruing to each position. Furthermore, it would mean that the entire salary would be subject to adjustment as the salary structure is revised. And it should be almost painless to effect the change, given the insignificant real value of most of the cash allowances. In our proposed salary structure we have included a margin to account for existing allowances.

Third, a similar argument can be advanced for the conversion of payments made in kind into cash payments. The present practice of providing housing to senior personnel can give rise to considerable inequities, since there is no standardization of the value of housing assigned. The real value of utilities consumed by each household also varies. Indeed, the present practice of blanket coverage of utility use as well as of housing encourages wasteful consumption of both. It would be preferable to raise the cash salaries of such civil servants to compensate them at a level commensurate with their alternative opportunities and allow them to allocate their expenditures on housing and other goods as they see fit. We realize, however, that such a reform may be difficult to effect. Payments in kind appear to be widely generalized throughout the private economy. Furthermore, in view of rapid inflation and the great lags in adjusting cash wages, a preference for large payments in kind on the part of current recipients can be fully appreciated. If the Somali economy could return to a condition of prolonged price stability, it might then be possible to consider a transition to a salary structure defined wholly in terms of cash payments.

Beyond the issues of allowances and in-kind benefits, it is clear that all salary levels will have to be increased substantially but that a reestablishment of real salaries, at all grades, to levels equivalent to the 1977 salary structure will not be required. The 1977 structure as revalued in table 3.6 is pegged too high at the bottom and rises too rapidly through the lower and middle ranges. We suggest an entry level salary for grade D14 (laborer) on the order of Sh 28,000. That would actually set the lowest salary at a marginally higher ratio to per capita GDP than it occupied in 1977—about 2:1 compared with 1.83:1 in 1977.[8] Our suggestions for in-grade steps in the D grades range between 115 and 118 percent of the first step. The range of in-grade steps widens as one moves up from the lowest to the higher grades. The last column of table 3.6 suggests the configuration that a wage structure in line with current market conditions might assume. The civil service salaries are related to the observed market rates with adjustments for the unaccounted value of fringe benefits granted in private employments. However, we emphasize again that the actual final form of the wage structure should be shaped by labor market conditions as these are established more clearly. The government should plan to effect a careful labor market survey several years into the reform to establish salaries paid in the market. If the government acts on its commitment to freer enterprise and privatization, by that time there may be a much larger number of observations than is now available.

Some observers will be critical of the levels at which unskilled labor salary rates have been keyed in our suggested structure. There is a school that argues that no wage should be considered as adequate or "just" if it is not high enough to afford a basket of goods adequate for the support of an average family unit. We do not accept such a criterion for determining wage levels as practical or even as "just." In the first place, it should not be assumed that a family unit depends on only a single wage earner for its sustenance. For example, a recent World Bank household budget survey of civil servants found that the civil servant's salary amounted to only a small fraction of family income, even for employees in the lowest grades. To argue that civil servants should be guaranteed a salary that covers the needs of the entire family unit is to ignore the costs that would be imposed on other wage earners in the economy—perhaps with incomes far below those of the meanest government employee—who are taxed to meet the government's payroll. If the society deems some level of family income as minimal, then it should devise a system of subsidies keyed to family incomes to fulfill that objective, not guarantee the wage levels of individuals. Otherwise, households with multiple wage earners, all employed at the family-sustaining wage, will also enjoy a multiple of that income. Wages are best determined by the contribution to output that labor makes. Redistribution of income, on the other hand, can be achieved more efficiently by other means.

Effecting civil service reform

In the preceding two sections we have been concerned with establishing the current levels of employment and prevailing payment practices. We also have suggested some objectives a reform might seek to achieve in both areas. To those charged with effecting reforms, these objectives might appear difficult to achieve or even undesirable. Therefore, in this concluding section we examine the implications of the prescribed reforms and suggest ways in which they might be implemented.

Employment objective

Let us first consider the employment objective set forth earlier. It was suggested that a considerable scope exists for reducing the size of the civil service. The Ministry of Education has already established the goal of reducing its work force by almost 50 percent over a two-year period. Our attention here will be focused on the reductions suggested for the remaining ministries and agencies of the central government.

Our analysis of staffing produced an estimate of the current number of employees on the civil service payroll at approximately 41,000 (net of education). We also suggested as an appropriate target an employment level of 17,000, implying the elimination of 24,000 positions. Most senior ministry officials object to the release of civil servants because government employment provides a safety net for their families and because releases would aggravate an already severe unemployment problem. Clearly, these concerns must be allayed if officials are to implement willingly the proposed reforms.

First, consider the safety net that government employment provides. The World Bank's survey of civil servants' budgets cited earlier reports that government pay constitutes only a very small proportion of households' expenditures, 7.9 percent. Respondents report a variety of other sources of income, including earnings from nongovernmental activities as well as the earnings of other members of the household. If the income reported as attributable to public employment accurately reflects total receipts accruing to that activity, then separation from public service would not have serious consequences for family consumption levels, for most employees reported earnings from other employments far in excess of their government salaries. However, the survey may not have captured all the nonsalary income derived from public employment, for there is a substantial discrepancy between total reported income and consumption expenditures. For the three ministries polled (livestock, planning, and health) each household's expenditures exceeded total household incomes by about Sh 20,000 a month on average. If some part of this discrepancy is accounted for by illicit receipts, then, of course, separation from the civil service could have a substantial impact on the economic welfare of affected families unless alternative employment could be obtained. But as noted above, it appears that most of the civil servants currently report substantial amounts of earned income well in excess of their civil service wage and incentive receipts. Only a third of the interviewed employees reported no additional earned income. This suggests that many, if not most, civil servants do have alternative employments on which they could fall back on a full-time basis were they to be separated from government employment.

The concern for the aggravation of unemployment conditions is also misplaced. Relative to the country's total labor force, the annual reduction in central government employment over the reform period would appear to be very small. For example, a reduction of 12,000 during the first year would represent 0.4 percent of the estimated size of the nation's labor force. If all such reductions were to be effected in the Mogadishu region, they would probably not exceed 2.7 percent of the city's labor force, estimated at 450,000 people. Thus, even if all of those released were to be rendered unemployed, this would not increase the rate of unemployment by more than these percentages.

However, it is not reasonable to assume that all those released would be rendered unemployed. Indeed, one of the reasons for the high rate of absenteeism within the government is that workers hold other productive employments. Thus, it is likely that the majority of those released would simply devote a greater amount of time to their existing employment. The impact on the rate of open unemployment could then be expected to be negligible.

Financial implications

The financial implications of the proposed reform are substantial. The proposed wage structure in the last column of table 3.6 would require, in real terms, increases in January 1990 salaries by a factor of 11 at the bottom of the structure and by a factor of 18 at the top. These increases could not be effected at one time; they would have to be implemented over a period of several years. However, these adjustments do not impose unreasonable demands on government resources if comparisons are made with the past. For example, in 1974 the government's wage bill amounted to 3.4 percent of GDP. During the 1980s it declined to only 1.1 percent. For 1990 we estimate that total salary and supplement payments will amount to less than 1.0 percent of GDP. The reforms advocated here would increase the wage bill to 1.8 percent of estimated 1995

Table 3.8 Employment and salary projections for Somalia, 1995
(January 1990 shillings)

Occupation	Number of employees	Percentage of work force	Proposed average monthly salary	Annual wage bill (thousands)
Professional	3,500	14.0		
Education	1,500		75,000	1,350,000
Civil service	2,000		110,000	2,640,000
Technician, other nonprofessional	10,000	40.0		
Education	5,000		65,000	3,900,000
Civil service	5,000		75,000	4,500,000
Administrator, executive	1,400	5.5	125,000	2,100,000
Clerical	3,800	15.3	55,000	2,508,000
Service	2,000	8.0	41,000	984,000
Agricultural worker, machine operator, laborer	4,300	17.2	35,000	1,806,000
Total	25,000	100.0	65,960	19,788,000

Source: Author's estimates.

GDP. This modest increase in the proportion of GDP would nonetheless afford the 25,000 remaining central government employees salaries that come much closer to matching their opportunity costs.

The realization of reform of the salary structure might extend over a five-year period beginning in 1991. In order to estimate a wage bill for 1995 that would be consistent with the salary scale proposed in table 3.6, we estimate the distribution of employment by occupational grouping (table 3.8). In the same table, we estimate the average monthly salary and the annual wage bill corresponding to each group. The total wage bill of Sh 19,788 million represents a real increase of 281 percent over that provided in the ordinary budget for 1990. However, because the government currently pays salary supplements out of the development budget, part of the increase can be met by consolidating the salary supplements made through the development budget into the ordinary budget.[9] If supplements in 1990 are of the same order of relative magnitude as in 1987, then the projected wage bill for 1995 amounts to a real increase of only 180 percent over the consolidated wage bill for 1990. Spread over a period of five years, this increase should be feasible. Tables 3.9A and 3.9B summarize the annual increases that would be required to realize the proposed salary structure and the projected salary bills as a percentage of GDP.[10] (The data include those for the

Table 3.9A Salaries and employment, Somalia, 1990–95
(January 1990 shillings)

Year	Annual salary bill (thousands)	Percentage increase	Employment	Average monthly salary	Percentage increase
1990	5,192,260	n.a.	56,500	7,658	n.a
1991	6,230,712	30	44,500	11,668	52.4
1992	8,422,461	35	36,500	19,230	64.8
1993	11,355,472	35	31,500	30,041	56.2
1994	15,329,887	35	27,000	47,314	57.5
1995	19,788,000	30	25,000	65,960	39.1

n.a. Not applicable.

Table 3.9B Salary bill as share of GDP, Somalia, 1990–95
(January 1990 shillings)

Year	Annual salary bill (millions)	GDP (millions)	Share of GDP (percent)
1990	5,192.3	957,190	.54
1991	6,230.7	981,119	.64
1992	8,411.5	1,006,628	.84
1993	11,355.5	1,032,801	1.10
1994	15,329.9	1,059,654	1.45
1995	19,788.0	1,087,205	1.83

Source: GDP: World Bank estimates, base case; author's calculations.

Ministry of Education, accounting for the higher average salary for 1990 in comparison with that reported in table 3.2.)

Also to be considered as a cost of civil service reform will be the severance allowances that will be payable to those that are separated. Somali law requires a payment of one month's salary for each year of service. The annual cost of these allowances is estimated on the following basis. The average length of government service is assumed to be six years based on the finding of the 1985 public sector census that fully 45 percent of employees had been employed six years or less. We also assume the largest proportion of redundancy exists among employees in the lower grades, primarily C and D. If so, the average monthly salary of the separated workers will be less than the average civil service wage. We have arbitrarily selected an average salary for those released from service that probably overstates the true average, and since the average years of service we have chosen is also likely to be overstated, the cost estimates can be treated as maximum likely costs of severance allowances.[11]

As can be seen in table 3.10, separation allowances will loom as a significant cost relative to the total wage bill for the first two years of the reform period. It would not be unreasonable to seek the assistance of foreign donors for the purpose of defraying this cost. The dollar amount represents only a small charge relative to the total assistance provided Somalia. Even if it were to prove necessary to "sweeten the pie" in order to induce workers to accept separation, the dollar cost would be small. For example, if the separation allowance were to be matched by an equal expenditure to provide employees with a set of options, such as retraining, capital to start a business, relocation, and so on, the dollar cost would still be modest. In the first year, it would amount to only US$1.44 million.

The table also demonstrates that the cost per employee of eliminating redundancy mounts from year to year as salaries rise. Thus, it will be in the interest of the parties financing the separations to effect the largest

Table 3.10 Separation allowances, Somalia, 1991–95

(January 1990 shillings)

Year	Number of separations	Average monthly salary	Total cost (millions) Shillings	U.S. dollars[a]	Percentage of wage bill
1991	12,000	10,000	720	.720	11.6
1992	8,000	15,000	720	.720	8.5
1993	5,000	24,000	720	.720	6.3
1994	4,500	36,000	986	.986	6.4
1995	2,000	51,000	612	.612	3.1

a. Shillings have been converted to U.S. dollars at the approximate official exchange rate of 1,000 shillings to $1 prevailing in January 1990.
Source: Author's calculations.

number possible in the first and second year of the reform. An additional reason for striving for larger reductions at the early stages of the reform is that it might prove difficult to maintain the momentum of the process since the urgency of continuing retrenchment may decline with time. A final persuasive argument in favor of large early reductions is that employee resistance to separation can be expected to mount as the real salaries paid in the civil service rise.

Fortunately, it should be possible to achieve the goals set forth. In the first year, the removal from the rolls of all those who have not appeared for work for an extended period should be relatively painless. The Ministry of Education has achieved a very substantial reduction in its roster of employees in this fashion. Moonlighters that appear only briefly at their government office can be offered the choice of working full-time or retiring from government service. At least some can be expected to choose their outside employment, particularly if the sweetened severance allowance were to amount to the equivalent of a year's salary. Finally, the employment rolls may be expected to shrink as normal attrition occurs.

Conclusion

At the beginning of this chapter we advised the reader that we were embarking on a voyage through largely uncharted waters. We had been asked to estimate the extent of redundancy in the civil service and to propose reforms in employment and compensation practices in a context of extreme scarcity of reliable information that was essential to the task. We therefore had to resort to stratagems designed to establish numerical values that might prove more trustworthy than the incomplete data available from official sources. Obviously such a course runs the risk of estimating numerical values of employment and redundancy that depart substantially from a set of "true" values. How much confidence can be placed in a program of action that rests not on measures derived from employment censuses but on estimates reached indirectly using other bodies of information?

We hope to have demonstrated that it is possible to arrive at plausible estimates of employment from payroll data and, by resorting to a simplified concept of a production function, to estimate the extent of redundancy in the civil service. Because any estimation process is subject to error, we took care to bias our estimates in the direction of understating the degree of redundancy. We are confident that the immediate goal of a reduced labor force of 25,000 civil servants is one that can be achieved without compromising the quantity or quality of government services. Furthermore, we pointed out that the reform process, spread out as it is over a five-year interval, allows for adjustments to be made as the recommended institutional and administrative reforms are implemented and a more precise determination of appropriate staffing levels is reached.

Similarly, our proposals for adjusting pay scales sought to define their appropriateness by reference to the opportunity cost of labor, that is, the compensation available in nongovernmental employment alternatives. Again, the empirical basis for defining "prevailing market wages" proved elusive. A substantial private sector employing the range of skills found in the civil service is still lacking in Somalia. Furthermore, the rapid inflation of the years immediately preceding the study resulted in distorted interfirm comparisons of wages. Thus, although the proposed structure provides a reasonable target, it should be viewed as subject to modification as market information improves in quantity and quality.

Finally, we were able to address at least some of the concerns of public officials regarding the impact the release of public employees would have on open unemployment and on the living standards of those released. By pointing out the meager contribution that government salaries were making to total household expenditures and the alternative sources of employment and earnings currently realized by public employees and their families, it was possible to place these issues in perspective and at least allay the expressed concerns.

In short, by drawing on diverse sources of information it has been possible to establish a reasonably robust picture of the existing state of the civil service and a clearly defined set of objectives to be achieved by a reform program. In view of the enormity of the current deficiencies of the government sector, the implementation of our recommendations should prove extremely beneficial even if our estimated measures suffer from some degree of error.

Notes

1. "The Characteristics of Public Sector Employment and Key Issues of Manpower Development," Manpower Survey, vol. 1, Government of Somalia, Ministry of Labour and Sports, Department of Statistics and Manpower Planning, June 1985.

2. "The Manpower Implications of Current Development Strategies," Manpower Survey Project, vol. 1, Government of Somalia, Ministry of Labour and Sports, August 1972, pp. 42–48.

3. Somali government expenditure and employment figures are drawn from an internal World Bank report.

4. Information on class size and student-teacher ratios is drawn from an internal World Bank report from 1989.

5. Although the procedure applied above provides a rough approximation of the extent of overstaffing in the aggregate, it provides no guide to the deter-

mination of overstaffing in particular ministries and agencies. One would normally expect the extent of redundancy to vary across agencies. Thus, the true extent of redundancy requires a systematic determination of the staffing requirements of each unit of the government, which in turn requires effective job descriptions that specify the set of duties associated with each post that must be performed by each occupant.

6. Somali Civil Service Study, Government of Somalia, Ministry of Labour and Social Affairs, September 1984, pp. 5-5 and 5-7.

7. A. C. Edwards, "Teacher Compensation in Less Developed Countries." Paper prepared for the conference on Cost and Effectiveness of Teachers, World Bank, Washington, D.C., April 20–May 1, 1987, pp. 4–6.

8. According to World Bank sources, 1977 GDP in current shillings was Sh 6,338.2 million. Given a population of 4.406 million, a per capita GDP of Sh 1,439 is yielded. The lowest civil service grade, D14, had a basic salary of Sh 220 a month or Sh 2,640 a year. The ratio of 2,640 to 1,439 is 1.834. The per capita GDP values for 1989–90 are also taken from World Bank estimates.

9. In 1987, salary supplements paid out of the domestically financed development budget amounted to roughly 36 percent of the wage bill in the ordinary budget.

10. It should be emphasized that all the calculations undertaken here are in terms of January 1990 shillings. This implies that the real increases projected will be realized only if periodic adjustments are made in salary scales to compensate for increases in the price level.

11. In addition, "ghost workers" who have not appeared on the job for at least six months should be ineligible for allowances.

4

Public expenditure and civil service reform in Tanzania

Mike Stevens

In its first two decades as an independent nation, Tanzania fired the imagination of the development community.[1] Julius Nyerere, the country's first leader, won many admirers with his writings on African Socialism, blending socialism, self-reliance, and traditional African community values.[2] The Arusha Declaration of 1967 translated this philosophy into a blueprint for social and economic development. Although the subsequent nationalization of foreign-owned businesses and the creation of an extensive public enterprise sector now seem serious policy errors, the moves were consistent with the prevailing development paradigm of an interventionist government, a distrust of multinational corporations, and a desire to end exploitation. The launching of the *ujamaa* movement then followed, a program of village-based social and economic organization aimed at radically transforming the rural areas. Although it was one of the poorest countries on the continent, Tanzania became the leader in Africa in pioneering new programs of education and health. These stressed providing basic services to the mass of the population in ways that minimized costs, now the accepted approach. And there were many other areas (such as adult education) where Tanzania was an innovator. In addition, the government launched an ambitious program of industrialization, manufacturing locally in public enterprises goods that previously had been imported.

The programs through which the government sought to implement its philosophy of self-reliance and social equity excited donors. Tanzania became one of the highest per capita aid recipients in Sub-Saharan Africa, and a "concentration" country for many donor agencies. Aid relationships were cemented by the personal rapport between President Nyerere and the heads of aid agencies or donor governments.

All of these developments enlarged government responsibilities in the economy. With them came a rapid expansion of public sector employment and a rise in public expenditures. The government's strategy was that, while donors would finance the capital costs of programs, their operating costs would be covered by the growth of tax revenues, the profits of newly created public enterprises, and the savings of Tanzanian citizens. In this way, high aid inflows and the principle of self-reliance were reconciled.

Tanzania's brave new world of self-reliant socialism, supported by friendly foreign governments, began to tarnish in the decade that followed Arusha. Although signs of fiscal strain could be detected from the beginning of the 1970s, initially buoyant external conditions masked the growing gap between public resources and commitments. But by the middle of the decade, these strains had become more evident, and by the end of the decade a vicious circle of external shocks and inappropriate policy responses compounded by structural rigidities set in.[3] By the end of the decade the economy was stagnant. Prices had been distorted by poor macroeconomic policies and bureaucratic controls. Producer incentives were destroyed by large, inefficient agriculture marketing parastatals, and the public sector generally was in serious disarray, greatly overcommitted in relation to the resources, human and financial, at its disposal. In the face of such distortions there was little prospect that external aid would be used effectively. Consequently, many donors, including the World Bank, reduced their aid programs. Public finances were further strained by two additional events, which occurred toward the end of the decade. The first was the collapse of the East African Community. This obliged the government to absorb displaced community officials, and to recreate services that hitherto had been provided on a shared basis. The second was a costly war with Uganda that had been started by President Idi Amin's invasion of Tanzania's lake provinces. GDP growth, which had averaged more than 5 percent a year from 1970 to 1978, fell to around zero between 1978 and 1985.[4]

The turning point came midway through the decade. After a prolonged period of economic stagnation—punctuated by partial attempts at economic reform, which failed to gain the support of the international community—the Government of Tanzania launched its Economic Recovery Program in June 1986. The Economic Recovery Program was a comprehensive program of exchange rate, fiscal, monetary, and trade reforms and sector-specific measures aimed at arresting the decline of the Tanzanian economy and recreating the conditions for sustainable growth over the medium term. Agreement was reached with the major international donors, including the IMF and the World Bank Group, paving the way for significant external support from aid donors for Tanzania's reform program. Although external conditions have remained difficult, the policies being carried out today under the Economic and Social Action Program are a direct continuation of the Economic Recovery Program. While progress in some areas, such as public enterprise reform, has been slower than expected, Tanzania's reform program continues to be supported by the international aid organizations and by bilateral donors. Over the past six years, economic growth has been within an annual range of 4 to 5 percent, according to official national accounts data, a figure that would most likely be higher were it not for the difficulties of measuring activity in the informal sector, where growth has been the most dynamic, and the most visible.

This chapter is concerned with a single aspect of a multifaceted economic reform program, the reform of public service pay and employment. The latter has been one of the most difficult parts of the Economic Recovery Program for the government to tackle. Despite attempts made early in the program to impose a freeze on new hirings and to eliminate "ghost workers," a comprehensive public service reform program has taken time to emerge in Tanzania. Compared with some other countries in Sub-Saharan Africa, such as Ghana, which set civil service retrenchment and pay decompression targets and began to implement them relatively soon after the start of its structural adjustment program, Tanzania initially lagged behind.[5] On the other hand, some of the work that has been done analyzing the public service wage bill in relation to the budget as a whole remains distinctive. Specifically, this chapter describes the work that was done on public service wage and employment issues in the context of a public expenditure review carried out by government officials and World Bank staff in 1987–88. The story is therefore about how pay and employment in the civil service was investigated and analyzed prior to the design of specific reform measures. This work has since been continued by the Tanzanian government and now underpins current civil service reform efforts.

To understand the problems facing the public service in Tanzania by the mid-1980s, it is necessary to go back two decades. The story's starting point is the divergent path taken by government employment relative to revenues in Tanzania in the years preceding the Economic Recovery Program, and what this did to civil service pay, working conditions, and the productivity and morale of Tanzanian public employees of all categories.

Size and structure of the public service

When Tanzania became independent in 1961, it inherited a colonial pattern civil service. This was centered on a relatively small administrative elite, supported by executive and clerical workers. Publicly provided social services were available to only a small fraction of the population. A separate local government structure existed but was likewise limited in size. Civil service pay scales reflected wide differentials between the predominantly expatriate administrative class, the heavily Asian technical classes, and the African lower-level staff.[6] During the 1960s, in common with many other newly independent African countries, a program of civil service reforms was carried out. Targets for the Africanization of the civil service were set, and the training of local officials was greatly expanded. New pay scales more in keeping with local requirements were introduced. Schemes of services were devised for the different cadres of civil servants to provide a framework for training and career development. Teachers, health workers, and local government staff were integrated into a common pay structure with central government administrative staff. In addition, many of the responsibilities of the Public Service Commission were transferred to the government so that appointments, training, and promotions in the public service could be better integrated with other government policies. These reforms, which were inspired by contemporary management thinking in the advanced industrial countries, were part of a wave of public sector management reforms, subsequently adopted elsewhere in eastern and southern Africa.

At the same time, the public service in Tanzania began a period of rapid growth. This was consistent with a strategy of development that required the public sector, guided by Tanzania's ruling party, to play the leading role in the life of the nation.[7] In particular, the expansion in public service numbers was driven by the need to staff a growing primary education and health care network. Furthermore, there was a belief that the government had a responsibility to provide employment for school leavers through public sector job creation. The capital costs of these programs were readily financed by donors, but the staff and operating costs remained largely a domestic responsibility. To ensure equity between the public and private sectors, a national incomes policy was introduced. This was based on government pay scales setting the norm for both parastatal and private sectors. Again, the concept of a national incomes policy was in keeping with the spirit of the time, and was widely applied in the countries in the region. Government felt that the shortage of skilled indigenous workers, caused by colonial neglect of training, should not create a wage spiral.

Public employment growth in Tanzania in the decade and a half prior to the Economic Recovery Program was dramatic (figure 4.1). In the first decade of independence the civil service had more than doubled in size. In 1970 total formal sector employment was estimated at 376,000, of which 135,000 were employed directly by the government (central, provincial, and local) and 85,000 by the parastatal sector. By 1984 the total had risen to 633,000, with government and parastatal employment amounting to 302,000 and 186,000, respectively.

Over the period, therefore, government employment had risen from a little more than one-third of formal sector employment to nearly one-half. While total formal sector employment grew at 3.8 percent, government employment grew at 5.9 percent, and private sector employment contracted by more than a third. Especially rapid government payroll expansion took place in the decade immediately prior to the Economic Recovery Program, when government employment grew by 8.2 percent a year compared with only 3.3 percent for formal employment as a whole. By contrast, for the latter part of this period the economy was static, and the share of government revenues in GDP was declining. Thus, from about 1977 onward the trajectory of government employment became sharply detached from its domestic revenue base. By the middle

Figure 4.1 Public service expansion and stagnating output, Tanzania, 1970–84

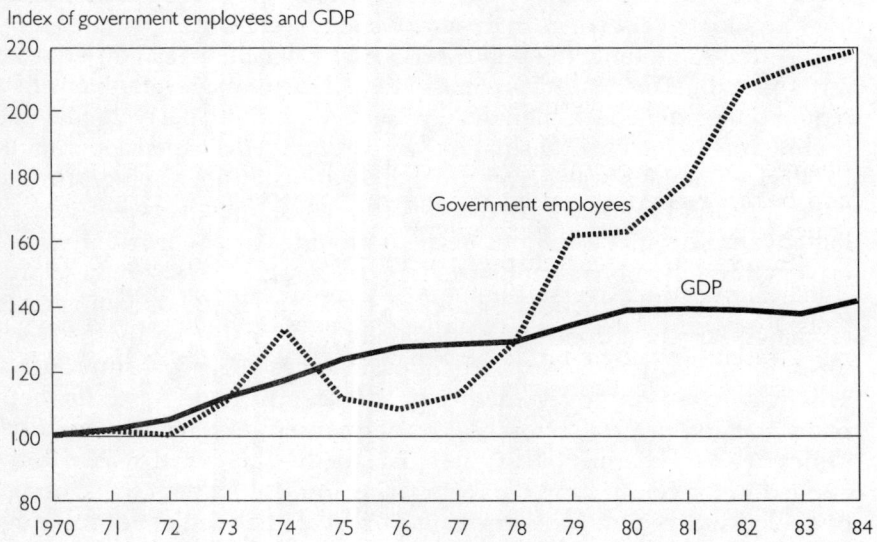

Index of government employees and GDP

Source: World Bank data.

of the 1980s public sector employment in Tanzania constituted more than three-quarters of formal sector employment.

Major changes also occurred in the balance between the central, regional, and local tiers of government. During the 1960s and early 1970s Tanzania had a local government structure based on elected district and urban councils, much like other Anglophone countries in Africa. In 1972 a program of government structural reform was announced. The official reason was to implement more effectively the social and economic strategy of the Arusha Declaration. Critics of the government said it was because elected councils challenged the one-party state. District and urban councils were abolished, and both their services and services hitherto provided by central government departments were made the responsibility of regional administrations. Regions became the primary units for coordinating economic development, and staff from headquarters ministries were seconded to them. In place of elected councils, popular participation was channeled through a hierarchy of village and district development committees. Regions, however, remained entirely dependent on central government for policy direction, staffing, and funding.

This pattern was reversed by the 1983 Local Government Act, which reinstated district councils. The move was in part an acknowledgment that central government had become overextended, and that the financial burden of education, health care, district roads, and water supplies should be shared with local communities. With the reintroduction of local authorities, the regional tier dwindled sharply as staff were reduced. Some were reabsorbed into central government ministries. Mostly, staff were transferred to the reinstated councils. With primary schools and health facilities returned to local authority budgets, about two-thirds of total government employees are now at the local level, but on pay scales linked to those of central government staff. Local authorities receive block grants from the central government to pay teachers' and health workers' salaries, but are supposed to raise their own revenues to cover the rest of their outgoings.

Successive changes in the structure of government led to institutional duplication, overstaffing, and a general erosion of payroll controls. Recognition that the size of the civil service might be excessive is not a recent development. In response to the strains the wage bill was imposing on budgets, the government carried out staff retrenchments on two occasions, in 1976 and 1985. But these proved to be little more than temporary blips in the inexorable upward surge in public sector employment. With such a small private sector, in practice constrained from expanding in many areas by government policy, there was little alternative in the formal sector to public employment. A view also prevailed among policymakers that adverse economic circumstances were temporary and somehow would reverse themselves. Furthermore, Tanzania, as an active member of the Non-Aligned Movement and promoter of the New International Economic Order, may have been the victim of its own rhetoric. This placed the onus on industrialized countries to compensate poor countries for adverse conditions, rather than on the latter to make internal adjustments. Many of the staff that were added each year to government payrolls were teachers and health workers, the consequence of ambitious targets for universal primary education and health care coverage, set a decade earlier.

Implications for pay and productivity

The implications of divergent financial and public employment trends, however, could not be avoided. Initially, both minimum and average wages were maintained in real terms. After 1975 both categories fell, the average wage more sharply. By 1986 the purchasing power of the minimum wage in public employment had fallen to less than a third of its 1969 value, and the average wage to less than a fifth. The erosion was especially marked for higher-level staff. A top public sector salary was worth nearly thirty times the minimum wage in 1969. By the mid-1980s it had fallen to less than six times the lowest scale and in the process had declined to a mere 6 percent of its former purchasing power value.[8]

In the first decade of Tanzania's independence the reduction in salary differentials was in part by design as the government sought to make public pay scales inherited from the colonial period more egalitarian. After 1975 economic circumstances rather than deliberate policy seems to have driven the process. Public sector salaries and wages were increased only in the light of available funds, with the largest increases awarded to those closest to the poverty line. Periodic salaries commissions made more realistic pay recommendations, but the resources were not there to implement them, and the government continued to make only partial compensation for inflation, and in ways that further compressed the pay structure.

A look at average public sector wages from 1969 to 1986 reveals dramatically the decline in the purchasing power of salaries from the mid-1970s onward (figure 4.2). Although some compensating adjustments to tax bands were made, the after-tax position of middle- and higher-level public employees deteriorated even more. By the late 1980s the ratio between the after-tax monetary incomes of top salary earners and incomes at the lower end of public wage scales fell to around 4:1. In relative terms, the after-tax purchasing power of managerial, professional, and senior technical cadre salaries in the civil service was about one-twentieth of its value a decade and a half earlier.

Not surprisingly, a decline in real pay levels and a narrowing of salary differentials of such a magnitude proved to be highly detrimental to civil service productivity. Work incentives, the recruitment and retention of technical and professional staff, and managerial responsibility all suffered. By the middle of the 1980s it had become clear to donors and government policymakers alike that the performance of the public service had become a drag on economic recovery. It also threw into question whether the resources donors were now prepared to provide to rehabilitate the Tanzanian economy would be used effectively. Increasingly, donors sought ways of protecting the projects and programs they were funding from the adverse effects of eroding civil service pay.

Public enterprise pay followed the same downward path as government sector pay. This was consistent with Tanzania's national incomes policy, which imposed wage conformity within the public sector. Government salaries commissions in Tanzania have traditionally made recommendations covering both government and public enterprise scales. In practice, however, the financially better-off parastatals were able to protect their staff by providing more generous cash allowances, benefits-in-kind, and other compensation arrangements. As a result, loss of central government technical staff to the parastatal sector accelerated. A perverse result of the constraints placed on parastatal pay by official

Figure 4.2 Decline of real public pay, Tanzania, 1969–86

Index of average public sector wages (1969 = 100)

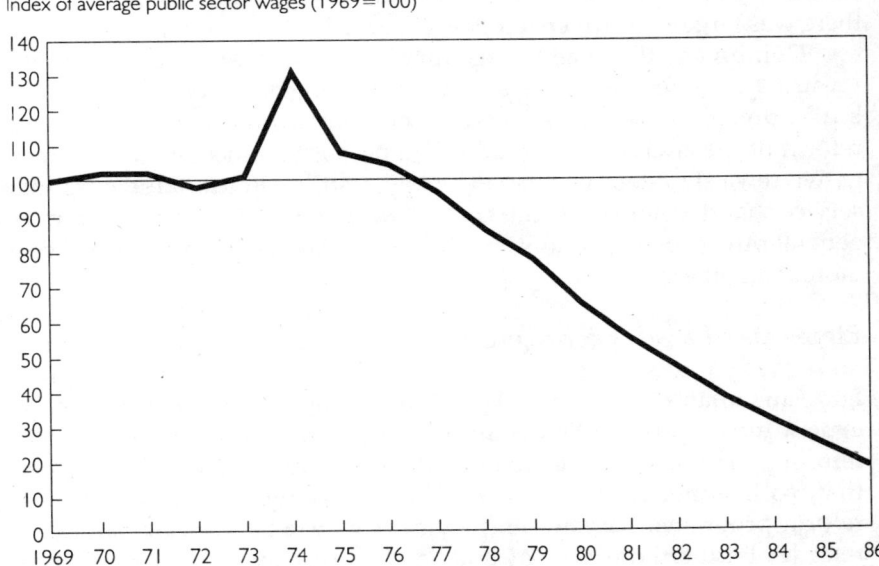

Source: World Bank data.

policy was a diversion of public enterprise investment into housing and transport, to insulate staff from the effects of government pay policy.[9]

The most direct effect of the erosion of pay was a reduction of work effort. Absenteeism became commonplace. Many middle-level staff sought alternative sources of income, and reduced the hours in their day spent on government business. Those with marketable skills undertook consultancy work for aid agencies, fortuitously catching a rising tide of local consultant use by the donor community.[10] Donors assisted by paying special allowances to staff attending training seminars or by supplementing the salaries of staff working on the projects they were funding. Both contravened government regulations, but were tacitly accepted as a way of rewarding staff. But even though this helped the staff directly concerned and preserved implementation capacity at the project level, it accelerated the breakdown of a unified public service. Government medical staff began to seek payment from patients directly (a sort of privatized cost recovery). Senior officials sitting on public enterprise boards relied heavily on directors' fees and other parastatal-provided benefits.[11] And the government itself introduced a number of special allowances to compensate staff for its inability to raise basic pay scales. Benefits in kind, the most prominent of which has been access to government pool housing at highly subsidized rentals, to some extent offset the decline in real pay. Finally, corruption, from which the Tanzania public service had hitherto been largely free, began to appear. In most instances it was on a petty scale, but in some areas, such as the customs department, there was large-scale diversion of revenues.[12]

Combined, these compensatory devices became an alternative reward system for the public service. They staved off complete collapse, but in doing so may have stood in the way of a more thoroughgoing reform of the civil service. In addition, because the benefits of the alternative reward system were so unevenly distributed, certain parts of the service that did not come into contact with either the private sector, the general public, or the donors, such as accountants and auditors, suffered more than others.

Elements of a reform program

For Tanzanian officials and World Bank staff engaged in the public expenditure review, identifying the main elements in a civil service reform program was a relatively straightforward exercise. It was clear that, as in other countries in Africa embarking on country strategy reform programs, pay and employment would be a major part of the reforms. Furthermore, the pay and employment component would need to have four elements.

- A significant increase in real pay.
- A pay structure with increased differentials between grades, and higher rewards for groups in greater labor market demand.
- Control of new hirings, elimination of "ghost workers,"[13] reductions in overstaffing, and streamlining of functions.
- Affordable and fair compensation arrangements for those retrenched from the public service.

In addition, it was realized that the "negative," staff-cutting aspects of civil service reform would also have to be balanced by "positive" features such as recreating a sense of purpose for the civil service, making training more effective, improving management, boosting morale, and involving staff in the reform process. However, these latter concerns lay beyond the scope of the public expenditure review exercise of the moment. Rather, the immediate objective was to analyze what had happened to pay and employment in the public service, and to gain a better understanding of the dynamics of the wage bill in the context of public expenditures overall.

Increasing real pay

On the issue of pay the question was not whether civil service pay needed to be increased, but the scale and affordability of the required increases. There was an understandable reluctance on the part of the government to embark, as other countries had done, on a reduction of numbers in the hope that the wage bill savings generated by retrenchment would create sufficient room for the necessary pay improvements to take place. Thus, the Tanzanian–World Bank team sought to approach the problem differently. It recommended that at the outset a view should be taken on the likely magnitude of increases that would be needed if a motivating wage structure for the public service were to be put in place—even if the latter in practice could be achieved only gradually—and to work back from there. Only when a view had been taken of the order of magnitude of pay increases needed to restore productivity would it be possible to analyze the tradeoffs between pay and numbers and the time path for achieving a new balance. Returning to the average real pay levels of the early 1970s implied at least a fivefold increase over current levels.[14] This was judged an unrealistic target since external circumstances had changed and a lesser target might suffice. Here, the analysis was done on aggregate terms, without attempting to differentiate between different groups of public employees. Clearly, the necessary pay adjustments for an accountant or engineer were likely to be greater than for a primary school teacher. But determining new pay relativities went beyond the scope of the public expenditure review exercise.

Reviewing incentives and differentials

Every public sector pay award in Tanzania since Independence had narrowed differentials. The gap between top and bottom scales in the early 1960s (greater than 40:1) was clearly excessive. Consequently, the civil service reforms that were carried out in the late 1960s had revised salary scales so that they were more in line with Tanzania's circumstances. However, the process of eroding differentials had continued throughout the 1970s and by the beginning of the 1980s had gone far beyond what might have been considered necessary for social equity. Thus, the recommendation was made that the experience of the past two decades be reviewed and a judgment made on the stage at which pay differentials seemed appropriate in the context of the country's level of development, labor market conditions, social and political considerations, and the need to reward skills and responsibility. The public expenditure review exercise also produced recommendations that nonwage benefits should be critically reexamined, on the grounds that they had become costly in budgetary terms, were unfairly distributed (particularly housing benefits), and imposed a rigidity on personnel management that ran contrary to what was required for efficient and flexible public service management.[15]

Controlling employment and retrenchment

On each of the two previous occasions that the government had attempted to reduce numbers, retrenchments had proved temporary. Public service employment had quickly resumed its upward path. The difficulty in getting reliable statistics about the government's own payroll, and the fact that recruitment freezes had been nominally in force for much of the period, were symptomatic of a larger problem of controlling staffing levels. The first requirement was to restore control over the establishment of new positions and to ensure that staffing decisions were made in the light of the budgetary resources available to a department. In practical terms this pointed to (1) an effective freeze on new hirings; (2) a civil service census to determine actual staffing levels and to remove ghost workers from the payroll; and (3) selective retrenchment of existing employees. The first would stabilize numbers, the second would eliminate fake payroll entries, and the third would address more fundamentally the imbalance between numbers and the ability of the government to meet the payroll and supporting expenditure consequences. The latter would be done in two ways: first, by identifying and eliminating overstaffing, and second, by reducing functions. Thus, the range of activities carried out by the government would need to be scaled back to a set of basic functions that it could perform effectively and that were needed to support a dynamic and balanced economy.

Assessment of pay and employment tradeoffs

Once the broad direction of civil service reform had been determined, the next stage was to examine the tradeoff between restoring pay and reducing total public service numbers. This was done by analyzing, in succession, four dimensions of the tradeoff. The first dimension was the impact of economic growth on the government's finances. Would the government sector grow into balance as the economy responded to the policies of the Economic Recovery Program and yielded more revenues for the government budget? If there was a prospect of this happening, painful staff reductions would not be needed. The second dimension was the scale of staff reductions that might be necessary. If government revenues were unlikely to grow fast enough to finance the required pay increase, reductions in staffing would be necessary. This was explored by looking at alternative retrenchment scenarios, comparing shallow and deep cuts in numbers and their respective potentials for wage bill savings, which in turn could be used to restore pay. The third dimension was the structure of the government pay scales. How much would it cost to decompress pay differentials, using different assumptions about the type and degree of decompression desired? As displayed in figure 4.3 for 1988–89 and projected for 1993–94, the final dimension was the relationship between the wage bill and the other main blocks of expen-

Figure 4.3 Government budget expenditure restructuring, Tanzania, 1988–89 and 1993–94 (projected)

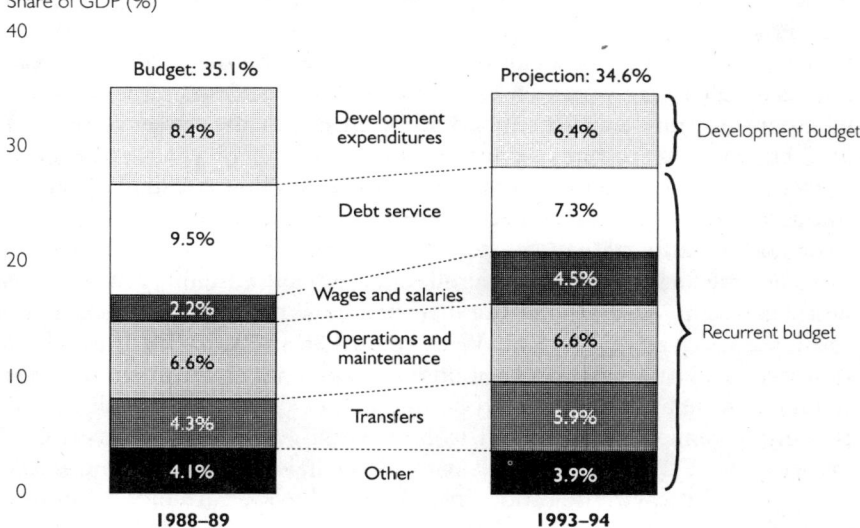

Share of GDP (%)

Source: World Bank data.

diture in the Tanzanian government budget, namely, investment spending (reflected in the development budget), debt servicing, transfers to subordinate levels of government and to budget-dependent agencies, grants, and what was termed in the language of the Tanzanian budget "other charges," that is, nonwage operations and maintenance expenditures. Since investment expenditures were largely financed by nonfungible donor aid, debt service was mandated, and the category of grants consisted mainly of transfers to local authorities for teachers and health workers salaries, it was decided to concentrate the analysis on the relationship between the central government wage bill and its budgetary complement, nonwage operations and maintenance expenditures. Thus, the question was whether by changing the ratio between "personal emoluments" and "other charges," civil service pay levels could be improved on a faster timetable without loss of efficiency.

To enable these four dimensions to be explored, it was necessary to have extensive background information on the wage bill and on the overall composition of the government's budget. In particular, the following sets of data were indicated: the government salary scales and the number of employees held against each grade, projections of GDP growth and government revenues, and the central government wage bill in the context of the other main blocks of budgetary expenditure.

Obtaining government pay scales and the number of staff held against each scale in central government proved to be a straightforward task. Data on the existing government salary scales and the number of staff on the central government payroll at each level were available from the Ministry of Labour and Manpower Development (table 4.1). This provided the basic information needed to estimate the cost of pay decompression and pay increase strategies. It also provided the shape of the government's employment pyramid. One issue that cropped up at this stage was whether and how adjustment should be made for the presence of ghost workers on the government payroll. At the time the government had conducted a civil service census, and it was known that substantial payroll fraud had been found. However, there were difficulties processing census data, and the information was not yet available. Therefore, it was decided to accept the fact that official payroll data probably contained many ghost workers and to assume that these would be eliminated in the course of implementing retrenchment. With regard to the growth of available resources, a simplifying assumption was made that government revenues would grow at a rate that would permit a real increase in expenditure of 5 percent a year. This was held to be consistent with a long-run GDP growth rate of 4.5 percent a year, with some allowance for revenue elasticity. The GDP growth projection, in turn, was the one currently being used by both the World Bank and the International Monetary Fund in the macroeconomic projections underpinning the structural adjustment program. Using the information on central government pay scales and establishments together with the projections of revenue growth, it was possible to answer some of the questions posed above.

Revenue growth alone

Combining existing budgetary data with the projections of GDP growth that had been made when the Economic Recovery Program was first designed, a number of public service pay restoration simulations were performed. The conclusions that emerged were as follows:

- Although budget revenues could be expected to recover quite strongly in response to economic growth and improved collection efficiency, they would not be sufficient to enable the Tanzanian pub-

Table 4.1 Central government employment by scale, Tanzania, 1987–88

Scale	Monthly pay (midpoint)	Wage compression ratio	Employees	Monthly wage bill (TSh millions)[a]	Share of total wage bill (%)
OS1	1,390	1.00	15,405	256.0	8.0
OS2	1,480	1.06	11,780	209.2	6.5
OS3	1,575	1.13	4,027	76.1	2.4
OS4	1,755	1.26	4,459	93.9	2.9
OS5	1,985	1.43	6,366	151.6	4.7
NTA	1,850	1.33	15,243	338.4	10.5
MU	1,680	1.21	1,373	27.7	0.9
MS1/NTB1	2,150	1.55	9,126	235.5	7.3
MS2/NTB1	2,810	2.02	19,825	668.5	20.8
MS3	3,610	2.60	8,081	350.1	10.9
MS4	4,820	3.47	5,497	317.9	9.9
MS5	5,790	4.17	2,926	203.3	6.3
MS6	6,230	4.48	2,260	169.0	5.3
MS8	6,540	4.70	632	49.6	1.5
MS10	6,700	4.82	245	19.7	0.6
MS11	6,740	4.85	119	9.6	0.3
MS12	6,930	4.99	159	13.2	0.4
MS13	6,970	5.01	73	6.1	0.2
MS14	7,100	5.11	112	9.5	0.3
MS15	7,229	5.19	55	4.8	0.2
MS16	7,255	5.22	12	1.0	0.1
MS17–19	7,980	5.74	7	0.7	..
Total			107,782	3,211.4	

.. Negligible.
Note: The graduate entry point is MS3. A senior economist with experience and postgraduate qualifications would be grades MS6–8, a commissioner MS12, and a principal secretary MS14–15.
a. TSh is Tanzanian shillings.
Source: Government of Tanzania, Ministry of Labour and Manpower Development.

lic sector to escape from its pay and employment trap within a realistic time frame. More precisely, it was calculated that if the incremental revenues were applied proportionally to the wage bill and other major expenditure categories (such as nonwage supporting expenditures or operations and maintenance), it would take more than thirty-five years to restore public service pay to the real level enjoyed by civil servants in the mid-1970s. During all this time, the size of the public service would have to remain frozen, with any fresh hirings offset by retirements, dismissals, and resignations.

- If, instead of allocating additional revenues evenly to all categories of expenditure, the wage bill were to receive a proportionally greater share, it was estimated it would still take twenty-five years of steady GDP growth and a freeze on total numbers before pay levels could be restored.

For obvious reasons restoration of civil service pay by economic growth alone was rejected as unworkable. There was little in Tanzania's past to suggest that staff numbers could be frozen indefinitely. Population growth would impose new demands on the government, particularly in the social spheres. And leaving the existing structure of public employment unchanged implied accepting massive overstaffing and inappropriate functions in many areas. Furthermore, for much of the period, real pay would have remained below desirable levels, perpetuating a demoralized civil service and the inefficient practices that had grown with it. In short, when public employment has grown two to three times as fast as revenues for a decade or longer, government wage bills cannot be expected to grow back into balance by revenue growth alone.

Retrenchment

The next step was to look at the contribution retrenchment could make to the wage bill, thereby releasing resources for improved pay. Retrenchment also would reduce the pressure on nonwage operations and maintenance expenditures in two ways. First, a reduction in numbers, other things being equal, increases the value of supporting expenditures per employee. Operations and maintenance allocations could either be maintained at their existing aggregate budgeted levels, or transferred to personal emoluments, thereby providing more resources for pay adjustment. Second, to the extent that these allocations were being used as pay substitutes, an improvement in pay would make it more likely that operations and maintenance allocations would be used as the budget intended. The critical factor, the Bank's budget simulations showed, was the scale of retrenchment, as the following findings illustrate:

- A 10 percent retrenchment (assumed evenly distributed across the grades) with no change in the ratio between personal emoluments and other charges released only enough resources for an 11 percent rise in real wages.

- A 20 percent retrenchment accompanied by an upward shift in the ratio of personal emoluments to other charges, corresponding to maintaining the latter constant in unit terms, enabled pay to be increased by 88 percent.
- Finally, a 30 percent retrenchment, also accompanied by a shift in the ratio of personal emoluments to other charges, created sufficient room for a 168 percent wage increase.

These simulations pointed to a difficult but inevitable conclusion. In countries where public sector employment has been on a divergent path from revenues for an extended period, it is only with deep cuts in public service numbers that sufficient savings occur to restore pay in a meaningful way.

A couple of simplifying assumptions were used to help the analysis. First, it was decided to ignore retrenchment costs. These consist of the cash compensation and pension costs of laying off staff, together with any additional social safety net costs or special training programs that might be provided for redundant staff. The simplifying assumption was that these costs would be met by a special fund set up by the donors. It was realized that matters would be more complicated in practice. Pension costs, which are contractually determined, would be a direct charge on the government budget. However, they would be quite low because of the eroded value of base pay. Social safety net costs, on the other hand, might well attract substantial donor assistance. However, since they address the social costs of the entire adjustment program, they are not specific to the country strategy reform program, although redundant public servants could be expected to be beneficiaries. The other simplifying assumption concerned operations and maintenance expenditures. Although the retrenchment scenarios assumed that unit operations and maintenance savings arising from the reduction in numbers might be transferred to the wage bill, in practice in many areas (for example, infrastructure maintenance, medical supplies, classroom materials) allocations were recognized as being already seriously deficient. A more comprehensive exercise, carried out on a sector-by-sector basis, utilizing expenditure norms derived from standard cost analysis and other techniques, would be needed to take account of this. Obviously, to the extent that operations and maintenance allocations are in an overall sense deficient, retrenchment would have to be even deeper.

Decompressing differentials

The final set of simulations analyzed the cost of decompressing salary scales. Various alternative decompression scenarios were analyzed, using data on the distribution of central government staff across the twenty-six different scales of the government salary structure. These ranged from general, proportionate decompression from a ratio of less than 6:1 to a set of target compression ratios, to selective decompression strategies concentrated on the middle-level, technical, and senior management scales. Overall, these showed that in contrast to general wage increases, salary decompression could be achieved relatively cheaply in wage bill terms, ranging from an additional 10 percent of the wage bill for selective decompression, to an additional 25 percent for general decompression, based on a target range of 12:1.

The conclusion these analyses pointed toward was that for Tanzania to escape from the pay and employment trap two decades of overly rapid public service expansion had created, a combination of measures would be needed. At the heart of the reforms there would need to be quite sharp reductions in numbers, more than probably could be achieved by reducing overstaffing and eliminating ghost workers alone. At the same time, account would have to be taken of the fact that many other parts of the budget were undergoing change as part of the structural adjustment process.

The task could have been made simpler by holding the wage bill to a constant share of GDP, but this was rejected as unrealistic. In the first place, there was some evidence that the central government wage bill share might have become too small, at just a fraction of total recurrent spending (it was about one-tenth in 1987–88). Second, the other major blocks of expenditure were themselves changing over time, partly due to their internal financial dynamics and partly for financial reasons.

To make the task manageable and to ensure consistency, a budget model was created, replicating the structure and classification system of the Tanzanian budget.[16] The model was projected forward five years, and incorporated a number of arbitrary assumptions about limiting or increasing the shares of certain categories of budgetary expenditures. Underlying the resulting budget scenarios was the assumption that the overall budget deficit, at the time 8.9 percent of GDP, would be progressively reduced, to 6.8 percent of GDP by 1993–94. This was consistent with agreements reached by the Government of Tanzania with the IMF. Among the assumptions made were:

- In the absence of detailed government debt projections, it was assumed that external debt servicing would continue at current levels. The rise in the shilling cost caused by further anticipated devaluation would be offset by the progressive substitution of existing debt by borrowing on more concessional terms. Internal debt servicing was estimated to fall as declining inflation reduced the average cost of borrowing.

- Transfers to local governments and budget-dependent agencies (such as universities) would have to rise as they implemented the same retrenchment decompression–pay increase package as the central government.
- Development expenditure was assumed to fall, reflecting the view that there were higher economic returns from rehabilitating and properly budgeting for existing services than from new investments.
- Parastatal restructuring, which in the short run would impose costs on the budget (mainly because of government-guaranteed debts), would be largely completed by 1993–94.
- Operations and maintenance allocations would stay constant as a share of GDP, but would rise by 50 percent in per capita terms, in response to the need to raise allocations per employee. In addition, a special increase in the budget allocation for government infrastructure was provided for.
- Finally, a number of shifts in the sectoral composition of both recurrent and development budgets were provided for, in response to changes in sectoral priorities. Government spending overall on industry would be sharply reduced, recurrent spending on agriculture and the social sectors would be increased, and both recurrent and capital spending on infrastructure (mostly for rehabilitation) would be increased.

A number of different pay and employment policy packages were then tested in the model to provide policymakers an idea of the depth of reforms that would be needed to bring the budget back into balance, given overall macroeconomic constraints, statutory expenditure requirements, sector policy considerations, and the need to raise pay to motivating levels and strengthen supporting expenditures. The tests described above had already shown that shallow retrenchment was unlikely to release sufficient resources to materially improve public service productivity. Eventually, a package of pay and employment reforms was adopted. This was based on a 30 percent reduction in staffing levels, a tripling of monetary pay accompanied by a reduction in nonwage benefits, and the decompression of salary scales to a 12:1 ratio.

Conclusion

The foregoing might suggest that pay and employment reform—cutting numbers and raising pay—is all that policymakers should be concerned about when designing civil service reform programs. This is far from the case. Civil service reform, of course, involves much more than reducing aggregate numbers and restoring former pay levels. Civil service management systems, the reinstatement of manpower controls, training, career development, accountability, bureaucratic values, inculcation of a spirit of service, staff morale, and the broad governance background to public sector management—all are issues that must be addressed. On top of all of this, the process of reform—"change management"—has to be carefully planned and managed so as to retain the confidence of staff and harness their energies. In addition, it may require a redrawing of the lines between the public and private sectors, and the withdrawal from or contracting out to the private sector of many functions hitherto performed by the state.

But for countries like Tanzania—and this includes most countries in Sub-Saharan Africa that have embarked on programs of reform to raise public sector productivity—reform programs will be on sound foundations only if they are first examined within the overall budgetary resources envelope. Indeed, it could be argued that failure to have done this lies behind the tendency for civil service reform programs to "stall" once they have completed the first rounds of employment reduction, with as yet little restoration of real pay.

The requirements for the type of budgetary analysis carried out in Tanzania are, it must be admitted, demanding. The exercise requires the collection of substantial amounts of data, not only on public services pay and employment, but also for the budget as a whole. Budget models cannot be constructed without a sound knowledge of the structure of administration, and of the multiple linkages between the different components. And skill and judgment are needed for interpretation.

Fortunately, in Tanzania the data needed for this type of analysis existed. Thus, it was possible both to track expenditures on the wage bill and other components over an extended period, and to chart the growth of public employment, the wage bill, and other budgetary magnitudes over time.

Since the work described in this chapter was completed, further progress in designing a comprehensive program of civil service reform has been made. The budget model described here has been taken over by a local task force and developed further. A more comprehensive civil service reform program has subsequently been developed and is now being implemented, with the support of the donor community.

Notes

1. Tanganika became an independent country in 1961, and joined with Zanzibar in 1964 to form the United Republic of Tanzania.

2. See *Ujamaa: The Basis of African Socialism*, published as a Tanzania African National Union pamphlet in 1962.

3. P. Collier, D. Buchan, and J. Ganning, *Economic Consequences of the Coffee Boom in East Africa: A Comparative Analysis of Kenya and Tanzania* (Washington, D.C.: World Bank, 1987).

4. National income statistics in Tanzania during this period should be treated cautiously because of the increasingly distorted price structure, bureaucratic controls, and the diversion of activity to the "grey" economy. For the first half of the 1980s official statistics probably underestimate the fall in production. For the second half of the decade they most likely understate the recovery.

5. Louis de Merode, "Civil Service Pay and Employment Reform in Africa: Selected Implementation Experiences," World Bank, Africa Technical Department, Washington, D.C., 1991.

6. In the years leading up to Tanzanian independence a few Africans had been admitted into the administrative class, but this was limited by the small number holding university degrees and by strict entry requirements.

7. Mainland Tanzania became a one-party state through the Interim Constitution of 1965, when the Tanzania African National Union (TANU) became the sole legal party. In 1977 TANU merged with Zanzibar's Afro-Shirazi Party to form the Revolutionary Party, Chama Cha Mapindusi (CCM).

8. T. R. Valentine, *Wage Adjustments, Tax Rates, Accelerated Inflation in Tanzania* (Dar-es-Salaam: Economic Research Bureau, 1983).

9. A visitor to Dar-es-Salaam in the middle of the 1980s could not help noticing that, although little productive investment was taking place, the construction sector was hard at work building staff housing estates for public enterprise workers.

10. Various fictions were used to avoid blatantly breaking civil service rules. Staff would take "leave of absence" to undertake work for a donor that, in more normal times, would have been done as part of their routine duties. Others, in their spare time, would informally associate themselves with university-based consultants, providing government data that the consultants would have had difficulty obtaining on their own.

11. This was a practice that cannot have made officials enthusiastic about pressing ahead rapidly with public enterprise divestiture. It also put ministries at risk of "capture" by profitable but protected parastatals.

12. An informal canvas of private sector companies by the author in 1988 elicited the general view that, with the exception of the docks, corruption was still on a minor scale, and regarded by most firms as a cost of doing business.

13. A "ghost worker" is a fictitious name on the payroll whose salary is collected by someone else.

14. Calculating pay restoration factors was complicated by the price liberalization concurrently taking place under the Economic Recovery Program, and the fact that in earlier years civil servants enjoyed preferential access to some price-controlled goods.

15. When access to housing at heavily subsidized rents becomes the most desirable part of a civil servant's remuneration package, transfers are opposed and it becomes impossible to rotate staff between headquarters and field units.

16. This ruled out using consolidated data from the Tanzanian Bureau of Statistics, which were classified according to national accounts conventions and were not as up to date as budget estimates and expenditure outturn data.

5

Recognizing labor market constraints: government-donor competition for manpower in Mozambique

Peter R. Fallon and Luiz A. Pereira da Silva

Adjustment policies for government pay and employment have usually focused on the shorter-term issue of reducing fiscal deficits. Although adequate macroeconomic management is a necessary condition for stabilization, attention to the microeconomic consequences of restrictive public sector wage policies is also necessary. In Mozambique the central features of the civil service pay and employment structure pose real obstacles to economic recovery. Dominant among these features is the ease with which international agencies—in contrast with the government—are able to set wages for skilled manpower. Recently, donor-driven competition for skilled personnel has led to an escalation of wages paid to locally recruited staff.

The Mozambican labor force is both uneducated and unskilled, even by Sub-Saharan African standards—a fact strongly reflected in the lack of sufficiently skilled and experienced manpower in public administration. Better-qualified civil servants are seriously underpaid relative to comparable workers in other sectors of the economy, further straining the ability of the civil service to discharge its functions effectively. Pay differentials range from about 400 percent to as high as 1,000 percent for the same occupational category (table 5.1). A cleaner's salary (in the international agencies sector), for example, is roughly equal to that of a national director (in the civil service sector). The government faces severe problems of turnover and low morale among its skilled employees as a result of these imbalances. Although these problems originated in the difficult internal and external constraints imposed on the country since its independence, improvement could be achieved through decisive policy action. This will be particularly important in the next few years, as the government will need to increase its administrative capacity considerably if it is to implement future resettlement, rehabilitation, and reconstruction programs.

This chapter surveys the salient problems faced by the public administration system in Mozambique. The first section describes the fiscal and macroeconomic background that contributed to the present situation. The second section analyzes the main features of civil service pay and employment. And the third section assesses the impact of increased donor and private sector activity on both the market for skilled manpower and the performance of the civil service. Finally, some policy conclusions are drawn.

Fiscal and macroeconomic background

Five centuries of colonial rule did little to develop social and physical infrastructure in Mozambique. Later, Independence and the subsequent flight of human capital (to Portugal and South Africa) left the country with an acute shortage of skilled manpower. Against a background of international hostility and armed opposition to the FRELIMO (Frente de libertaçâo de Moçambique) government, authorities adopted inappropriate economic policies to address the urgent development needs of the country. The effects of the war, including disruption in production, collapse of the rural marketing system, and widespread destruction of infrastructure, soon compounded the classical distortions of centrally planned economies—erosion of market structures, repressed inflation and shortages, overvaluation of the exchange rate, and lack of economic incentives. By 1986, real GDP had fallen to about two-thirds of its 1980 level, exports had been reduced to less than one-third of their 1980 value and accounted

Table 5.1 Pay structure across sectors, Mozambique, end of 1990
(average monthly salary in thousands of meticals and in U.S. dollars)

Employment category	Civil service		Parastatal		Private		International organization	
	MZM	US$	MZM	US$	MZM	US$	MZM	US$
Senior administrative staff	438	243	308	171	n.a.	n.a.	n.a.	n.a.
Professional staff	488	271	137	76	2,000	1,111	2,440	1,355
Lower-level technician	86	48	75	42	75	42	880	489
Clerical staff	58	32	42	23	69	32	586	325
Driver	45	25	87	48	87	48	567	315
Unskilled manual worker	35	20	26	14	26	14	396	220

n.a. Not applicable.
Note: MZM is Mozambican meticals.
Source: Authors' calculations.

for only about 15 percent of imports, and the financing of external imbalances had led to the accumulation of arrears in external debt.

In early 1987 the government initiated an Economic and Social Rehabilitation Program to tackle the economy's structural problems and distortions. The central objective was to shift toward a more market-based economy with fewer administrative controls, and with more reliance on international and domestic market mechanisms to provide signals to economic agents. The program has stressed the importance of stabilization, with implementation of reforms leading to price liberalization (including unification of the exchange rate markets), fiscal adjustment, tight monetary policy, and improvement in the efficiency of public administration.

Fiscal constraints have also been crucial in limiting the wage and salary bill of the civil service. Such constraints have taken two forms: constraint on the overall level of recurrent expenditure and constraints on the composition of such expenditures. The overall fiscal constraint grew out of the macroeconomic position faced by the economy. Prior to 1987, fiscal austerity was forced on the government by a difficult external position. In 1987, at the start of the Economic and Social Rehabilitation Program, the economy suffered from widespread shortages and considerable depression in its domestic production. Even though increased external capital assistance had enabled higher domestic investment, and increased availability of imports had alleviated shortages and enabled a partial recovery in domestic production, this had to be viewed in the light of Mozambique's substantial external current account deficit and its high debt service ratio. One early effect of "opening up" the economy through the 1987 reform program was to increase the current account deficit (including grants) from 9.9 percent in 1986 to 25.1 percent in 1987. Although this jump in the deficit was financed through increased concessional loans, debt service as a proportion of exports of goods and nonfactor services was 227.6 percent. To improve its external position, it was necessary for Mozambique to restrict domestic absorption while maximizing, within existing constraints, growth in GDP. To achieve this and the further objective of controlling domestic inflation, both credit limits and fiscal targets were set. While the program has recognized the importance of key items of recurrent expenditure, the fiscal deficit (including grants) has fallen as a percentage of GDP, from 11.8 percent in 1987 to 7.1 percent in 1989.

The need to keep the fiscal deficit under control would in itself have put pressure on the government's ability to pay wages and salaries, but further constraints can be traced to a deteriorating internal security situation and distortions arising from the prevailing administrative allocation mechanisms. Worsening internal security in the 1980s necessitated increases in defense expenditures (these grew by more than 50 percent in real terms from 1980 through 1987), and as scarcities appeared on official markets the unofficial economy flourished, with a consequent shrinkage of the tax base. In addition, the destruction of some public enterprises, combined with the mounting financial losses of others, gave rise to substantial growth in subsidies to parastatals. By 1986 such subsidies exceeded defense expenditures. Growing interest payments on public debt have further worsened fiscal difficulties in recent years. Since public investment in Mozambique is heavily supported by concessional external finance, and is consequently donor-driven, the authorities reacted to the deteriorating fiscal situation by applying stringent expenditure controls on fungible items within the recurrent budget, namely, goods and services and the civil service wage bill.

As a result, wages and salaries fell as a proportion of recurrent expenditure, from 36.1 percent in 1980 to 16.6 percent in 1987. In real terms, this represents an average annual decrease in expenditure on wages and salaries of 10 percent a year. The crowding out of wages and salaries and other recurrent items caused by increases in defense expenditures, subsidies to public enterprises, and interest payments may be crudely inferred from the fact that the aggregate share of these items in recurrent expenditure rose from 33.2 percent to 61.6 percent over the same period—an average annual increase in real terms of 9.0 percent. These crowding-out effects have also been to the detriment of the government's ability to provide education, with, in turn, an adverse effect on the supply of skilled manpower.

Since 1987 the Economic and Social Rehabilitation Program has imposed continued fiscal restraint, but the degree of crowding out in the government budget has been lessened by a substantial reduction in subsidies to enterprises. At the same time, the real value of government expenditure on wages and salaries has risen at an average annual rate of 9.2 percent from 1987 through 1989, although the wage bill's share of government expenditure remains very low in relative terms when compared with that of other Sub-Saharan African countries.

Civil service pay and employment

Mozambique employs an estimated 105,000 civil servants (out of a total labor force of some 6.2 million).[1] Parastatals and the military forces are believed to employ a further 122,000 and 72,000 people, respectively. About 88 percent of civil servants are in local government—an extremely high proportion. Employment in the civil service is relatively small when compared with that of other Sub-Saharan African countries (table 5.2). Mozambique has about seven civil servants for every thousand inhabitants, a proportion similar to that found in Malawi and Mali and lower than the ratios in other countries considered. Although the number of military personnel per thousand population is relatively high in Mozambique, this is not true of employment in the public sector as a whole (civil servants, military personnel, and employees of parastatals). There are about twenty public sector employees per thousand population in Mozambique, compared with an estimated 14.5 in Mali, 20.0 in Nigeria, 23.1 in Liberia, and 42.0 in Zambia. Considering the relatively small size of the civil service, redundancy does not appear to be as great a problem in Mozambique as elsewhere.

What is striking in Mozambique, even in comparison with other Sub-Saharan African cases, is the low level of education (general and technical) of most public employees, posing an enormous obstacle to the development of a modern public administration. The economic and administrative problems of the educational system have rendered it incapable of supplying the public sector with enough people with even a reasonably good elementary or junior high education. Less than 20 percent of higher-level civil servants have university degrees. And 16 percent have no formal schooling at all. The problem is pervasive: among chiefs of departments in the central government, only 61 out of 247 were college-educated; among provincial directors, the corresponding num-

Table 5.2 Public employment, selected Sub-Saharan African countries, various years

| | | | Civil service | | |
Country[a]	Year	Population (mid-year, millions)	Total civil service	Central government	Local government
Angola	1988	9,481	250,137	—	—
Ghana	1983	11,750	200,000	—	—
Liberia	1983	2,040	33,600	—	—
Malawi	1983	6,820	50,368	—	—
Mali	1980–83	7,050	50,066	49,116	950
Mozambique[b]	1989–90	15,696	105,000	12,911	92,089
Nigeria	1983	93,120	1,101,778	279,665	822,113
Senegal	1980	5,710	88,390	—	—
Sudan	1983	20,530	335,759	—	—
Zambia	1983	6,250	131,646	—	—

— Not available.

a. Coverage may vary across countries (see Lindauer and others, "Government Wage Policy in Africa").

b. Based on Ministry of State Administration of Mozambique, census of the civil service (preliminary results). Parastatal employees are estimated. Data come from an industry survey covering 707 enterprises, of which 428 are public or under state intervention.

Source: World Bank, World Development Report (various years); D. Lindauer, O.A. Meesook, and P. Suebsaeng, "Government Wage Policy in Africa," World Bank Research Observer, vol. 3, no. 1 (January 1988); "The Military Balance 1990–1991," International Institute for Strategic Studies (London, 1990); "World Military Expenditures and Arms Transfers, 1988," U.S. Arms Control and Disarmament Agency; authors' estimates.

bers were 21 out of 133; among chiefs of provincial departments, only 5 in 199; and of the 199 district directors, none was college-educated. Four central institutions had the following high percentages of employees with only basic or elementary schooling: the Ministry of Labor, 56.6 percent; the Ministry of Finance, 86.4 percent; the National Planning Commission, 55.0 percent; and the Bank of Mozambique, 61.0 percent. Within the education sector itself, qualifications are very low. Out of a total of over 30,700 elementary and junior high teachers giving classes in 1990, more than 18,500 had completed only elementary school.

The government is obviously constrained by a general, nation-wide scarcity of skilled workers. In 1990 only about 3,000 to 4,000 employees (including about 2,000 expatriates) in the country held a university degree. This number represents only 0.05 percent of the labor force. The 1,000–1,500 Mozambican public employees holding a university degree thus represent a substantial proportion of the country's skilled manpower.

Pay levels in the civil service

Although it is true that the average wage paid to civil servants in Mozambique is greater relative to per capita GNP than in a number of

Military personnel	Parastatal employees	Total public employment	Public sector as a percentage of formal employment (1981)	Civil servants per 1,000 population	Military personnel per 1,000 population
147,500	376,363	774,000	75	26	16
8,000	—	—	—	17	1
5,000	10,000	48,600	21	16	2
6,000	—	—	—	7	1
8,000	45,401	103,467	66	7	1
72,000	122,048	299,048	—	7	5
144,000	621,741	1,867,519	65	12	2
18,000	—	106,390	45	15	3
86,000	—	—	—	16	4
16,000	136,420	284,066	75	21	3

other Sub-Saharan African countries (table 5.3), this statistic is misleading as an indicator of the appropriateness of existing wage and salary levels in public administration. Although wages at lower levels may not be inappropriate in light of the excess supply of unskilled labor and possible overstaffing at lower grades, wages at middle and higher grades are grossly inadequate considering the prevailing labor market conditions.

Reviewing pay levels in the Mozambican civil service as of November 1990 and making comparisons is unusually difficult. First, salaries are often paid in a mixture of local and foreign currency. This is particularly true at professional and administrative levels. Employees and consultants in both the private sector and the international agencies receive most of their remuneration in foreign exchange. This system resulted from certain distortions that prevailed prior to the 1987 reform program and that have proved difficult to remove.

Over the years the overvaluation of the exchange rate had provided a rationale for the operation of parallel market activities. And in response to the limited availability of goods on local markets, a number of legal procedures to circumvent local market scarcity had been put in place. The basic principle was to allow a dual market of transactions in the economy through the selling of imported goods in duty-free shops (*lojas francas*) to be accessed exclusively by holders of foreign exchange.

Table 5.3 Civil service pay levels, selected Sub-Saharan African countries, various years

Country	Year	GDP in current US$ millions	GNP per capita in current US$	Central government expenditures as a percentage of GDP
Angola	1988	7,400	600	—
Ghana	1983	4,057	310	6
Liberia	1983	1,067	480	23
Malawi	1983	1,221	210	16
Mali	1980–83	1,079	160	27
Mozambique	1989–90	1,296	80	—
Nigeria	1983	89,770	770	11
Senegal	1980	2,465	440	19
Sudan	1983	7,339	400	13
Zambia	1983	3,343	580	26

— Not available.
Source: World Bank, *World Development Report* (various years); D. Lindauer, O.A. Meesook, and P. Suebsaeng, "Government Wage Policy in Africa," *World Bank Research Observer*, vol. 3, no. 1 (January 1988); "The Military Balance 1990–1991," International Institute for Strategic Studies (London, 1990); "World Military Expenditures and Arms Transfers, 1988," U.S. Arms Control and Disarmament Agency; authors' estimates.

Initially, employers with access to foreign exchange, such as donor agencies and nongovernmental organizations—realizing that basic commodities were unavailable through metical-denominated transactions—issued employees foreign exchange–denominated vouchers to be exchanged for food items (known as the food basket) at the lojas francas. Over time, the practice evolved into one in which foreign exchange is paid directly.

Payments in foreign exchange became a common incentive in compensation schemes and were extended to higher-level employees and consultants throughout wide sections of the economy. Although the dollarization of some incomes permitted the payment of adequate levels of remuneration to foreign *cooperantes* [2] and expatriates, the practice of paying wages in foreign exchange fed parallel market activities in spite of substantial improvements in the domestic supply situation. Among employees of the major local donors, even those at the lowest levels, such as guards and janitors, received the bulk of their salaries in foreign exchange.

In the public sector, a "technical subsidy" (*subsídio técnico*) was introduced in January 1989 as a short-term measure aimed at raising the salaries of higher-level staff.[3] Officially, the technical subsidy applies only to the highest-level categories of the civil service—in the managerial career, to directors and heads of ministerial departments, and in the technical career, to specialists and higher-level technicians.

Government expenditure and net lending		Government wages and salaries			Government average monthly wage as a percentage of per capita GNP
As a percentage of GDP	In current US$ millions	As a percentage of government expenditure and net lending	In current US$ millions	Government average monthly wage in current US$	
29.8	2,204	29	642	214	36
8.2	333	25	82	34	11
34.3	366	37	136	337	70
28.8	352	19	68	112	53
31.5	340	24	80	134	83
47.5	616	9	58	46	57
21.2	19,031	8	1,446	109	14
26.8	661	34	226	213	48
20.3	1,490	—	—	—	—
33.4	1,117	29	323	204	35

The technical subsidy is equivalent to a dollar allowance deposited every month in a convertible currency–denominated bank account. A ceiling for cash withdrawals of US$300 a month was established by the Ministry of Finance. The amount of the annual technical subsidy depends on the grade of the employee. The rates are $2,000 a year for a specialist, $1,500 for category A higher-level technicians and for national directors, and $1,000 for other applicable categories. At the end of 1990 an average monthly technical subsidy of $125 represented about 225,000 Mozambican meticals (MZM) a month at the parallel exchange rate. This calculation is based on a conservative estimate of the parallel exchange rate of MZM 1,800 per U.S. dollar, and compares with the official rate as of November 1990 of MZM 930 per U.S. dollar. This was roughly equal to the base salary of a national director (the highest position in the civil service). About 2,600 higher-level staff were receiving a technical subsidy at the end of 1990.[4]

Analysis of government pay is also complicated by the wide variation across the civil service in the proportion of total remuneration attributable to fringe benefits. Two kinds of fringe benefits were identified. For lower-level civil servants, the government offers a subsidized food basket through entitlement (*cartões*) or food stamps. The amount of goods that can be purchased through such entitlement varies according

Table 5.4 Civil service pay structure, Mozambique, end of 1990
(MZM thousands unless otherwise specified)

Employment category	Average base salary	Average base salary including technical subsidy	Fringe benefits	Total compensation
Managerial career				
National director	213	438	120	558
Department director	163	313	100	413
Division chief	131	131	0	131
Technical career				
Specialist	188	488	20	508
Higher-level technician	123	348	20	368
Lower-level technician	86	86	0	86
Secretarial career				
Clerk	58	58	0	58
Support staff				
Driver	45	45	0	45
Unskilled manual worker	35	35	0	35

Note: Base salary is an average that takes into account, when applicable, the existence of three steps within a grade. Specialist denotes holders of a doctoral-level university degree. Higher-level technicians usually have master- or bachelor-level university degrees.
Source: Government of Mozambique; and authors' estimates.

to the number of dependents in the household. For example, for a household of five persons, the end-1990 metical value of the *cartão* is estimated at MZM 9,000 a month at market prices. This compares with a minimum wage for unskilled workers in the public sector of about MZM 26,000 a month. For higher-level staff, the government provides, in some cases, housing benefits not exceeding about MZM 50,000 a month and gasoline and car allowances (only for the highest-level managers) worth about MZM 100,000.

The noticeable dispersion among the salaries paid to various categories of public sector workers also complicates matters. These disparities occur for at least two reasons: differences in the speed of implementation of the 1985–87 reforms governing the reclassification of employees, although for some careers (for example, technical and managerial) the unification of salary scales is almost complete; and differences between salaries in central and local governments.

The payment of fringe benefits and the technical subsidy keeps the civil service pay structure decompressed (see table 5.4 for a more detailed breakdown of civil service pay). The bulk of the remuneration received by civil servants at the highest levels of the managerial and technical cadres is in the form of fringe benefits and technical subsidies. Such payments are, however, nonexistent at lower levels.

Total compensation in U.S. dollars			Compression ratios		
Official exchange rate	Parallel exchange rate	Fringe benefits as a percentage of base salary	Including fringe benefits	Excluding fringe benefits	Excluding technical subsidies
600	333	27	16	12	6
445	247	32	12	9	5
141	79	0	4	4	4
547	304	4	14	14	5
396	220	6	10	10	4
93	51	0	2	2	2
63	35	0	2	2	2
49	27	0	1	1	1
38	21	0	1	1	1

After the launching of the Economic and Social Rehabilitation Program in 1987, a number of modifications were progressively introduced in the salary scales. These changes were aimed at restoring the incentives for skilled labor in the civil service (through decompression), correcting nominal wages for the purchasing power losses experienced during 1975–85, and addressing the large number of pay categories. In addition, steps were taken to separate the civil service salary scale from those of other sectors.

The behavior of the real wages of civil servants is difficult to analyze in the Mozambican context because of the large number of occupational categories. Table 5.5 illustrates a tentative exercise in which average salaries, expressed in nominal units of domestic currency and in real U.S. dollars, are compared for some broad categories. Two significant patterns emerge: as expected, a substantial decline in the real wage is seen between 1975 and the 1980s; after 1987, the real wage rates of most workers continue to decline, while those of the top managerial grade show some improvement. However, these improvements still prove inadequate to attract and retain qualified higher-level civil servants.

Comparisons with other sectors of the economy

We compared civil service pay with that in parastatals, the private sector, and international organizations or donors (see table 5.1). To ensure consistency in treatment across sectors, the technical subsidy is consolidated into the average base salary of civil servants, while in other sectors, average wage rates are calculated. Payments in foreign exchange are converted into local currency at the parallel exchange rate. We exclude fringe benefits from the comparisons as these are difficult to assess outside the civil service.

Table 5.5 Nominal wage developments, Mozambique, selected years, 1975–90

(base monthly salary)

Employment category	1975		1980		1985	
	US$	Escudos	US$	MZM	US$	MZM
Senior administrative	2,090	26,700	141	3,500	81	3,500
Professional staff	1,878	24,000	483	12,000	278	12,000
Lower-level technical	768	9,800	125	3,100	72	3,100
Clerical staff	552	7,050	85	2,100	49	2,100
Driver	396	5,050	—	—	—	—
Unskilled manual worker	274	3,500	63	1,563	36	1,563

— Not available.

Note: US$ salaries are in constant (1985) U.S. dollars at the official exchange rate, excluding fringe benefits and excluding the technical subsidy in 1990.

Source: Various ministerial decrees; and authors' estimates.

With few exceptions, parastatal salaries are lower than those paid to civil servants, and it is hardly surprising that parastatals report problems of absenteeism and turnover similar to those found in the civil service. It is much more difficult to measure salaries paid to Mozambicans in the private sector. At both the managerial and professional levels, most of the firms interviewed employed expatriates. Such individuals, while nominally receiving administratively set compensation levels, in fact receive the overwhelming bulk of their remuneration in the form of offshore payments. Although few Mozambicans are employed at senior levels in the private sector, evidence for one observable professional group (engineers) indicates an average total remuneration level of about MZM 2 million a month—more than four times the comparable rate in the civil service. At lower occupational levels, private sector remuneration rates only exceed those paid by parastatals if the parallel rather than the official exchange rate is used to convert foreign exchange payments into meticals. Foreign exchange payments to employees are absent in parastatals, but increasingly commonplace in private sector firms with foreign exchange earnings. The amounts paid by such firms seem to vary between 10 percent and 40 percent of salaries, depending on grades and scale points.

Donors' pay structures are organized according to standard salary scales, usually with about ten steps for each category of worker. Although the average compression ratio is not significantly different from that of the civil service (about 14:1), the base salary for a senior administrative staff member is about five times that of a national director in the civil service. For most donors, payment is made in a mix of meticals and foreign currency (usually U.S. dollars). The proportion paid in foreign currency is generally high and varies across donors (from 66 percent to as high as 100 percent). In addition, staff are granted a number of fringe benefits such as family allowances, education allowances, medical assistance, and sometimes free transport (senior staff only).

1987		October 1988		April 1989		January 1990	
US$	MZM	US$	MZM	US$	MZM	US$	MZM
123	37,500	166	96,132	138	117,762	192	213,500
123	37,500	166	96,312	138	117,982	123	136,859
86	26,250	97	56,206	80	68,852	72	80,000
45	13,875	68	39,905	57	48,884	51	56,000
—	—	29	16,875	24	20,672	27	30,000
17	5,250	27	15,750	23	19,294	23	25,100

There is strong evidence that salary payments in the civil service for middle- and higher-level staff are low compared with other sectors of the economy (international agencies and the private sector). Senior administrative staff earn a little less than one-fifth what they could earn from comparable employment elsewhere, such as local consultancies. The situation is similar for professional staff, although the rates of pay for this group are considerably dispersed outside the public sector. Clerical staff in the civil service receive pay that is considerably less than that paid by donors. The compression may not be appropriate, however, since the white-collar employees of international agencies need considerable proficiency in foreign languages. Certainly, the pay rates of clerical staff in the private sector are much closer to civil service levels. Possession of language skills may also partly explain the huge dispersion in the pay of drivers outside the public sector. Manual workers, whether skilled or unskilled, face much lower intersectoral differences in pay levels. The main finding, though, is that civil service pay levels are much too low for occupations requiring a substantial degree of education.

Although inadequate pay has not led to substantial turnover from the civil service as a whole, there has been a net loss of some of the most highly qualified personnel. Senior posts have sometimes been filled by promoting relatively inexperienced staff. Moonlighting and absenteeism are common among middle- and higher-level personnel. Among the highest grades in particular, these problems are compounded by donor-funded payments of travel expenses and allowances that unnecessarily take staff away from their duties.

Another difficulty arising from the practice outside the public sector of paying portions of wages and salaries in foreign exchange is income tax evasion. From available evidence, remunerations paid in foreign exchange either go totally untaxed, or are made in meticals equivalent to the income tax owed expressed in foreign exchange converted at the official exchange rate. As metical prices are often related to dollar or rand prices converted at the parallel exchange rate, the effective tax rate is reduced substantially below the nominal rate. Undercollection of personal income tax has important implications for public sector wage and employment policy, as it both widens the gap between civil service wages and net-of-tax wages in other sectors and reduces the government's ability to finance much-needed increases in its wage bill.

The impact of donors and the private sector

Increased donor involvement, coupled with a recent upsurge in private sector activity, has created considerable upward pressure on the demand for highly skilled manpower in Mozambique. Since the government has so far been unable to raise wages sufficiently, there has been a drain of skilled manpower from the civil service. However, because donors rely on key government officials to assist in the implementation of their projects, they increasingly have sought ways either to cross-subsidize their salaries or to hire their services on a part-time basis.

Excess demand for skilled manpower

To appreciate the problem of donor-driven demand for professionals, it is important to reemphasize the desperate state of the market for skilled manpower in Mozambique. Of a total estimated labor force of 6.2 million, there are fewer than 2,500 Mozambicans with university-level qualifications. Of these, only twenty have doctorates. The paucity of skilled manpower can be traced to the colonial legacy bequeathed to the country in 1975. At that time the literacy rate among the local population was only 7 percent, and the overwhelming majority of domestically produced university graduates were Portuguese nationals. At Independence, most skilled administrative, professional, and technical workers left the country, stripping Mozambique of the bulk of its human resources.

The small stock of indigenous high-level manpower has spurred the demand for skilled workers from abroad. Such workers are almost always funded directly out of donor-funded projects or technical assistance. Although estimates vary, it is thought that about 3,000–5,000 expatriate technical assistants are working in Mozambique. The number is likely to decrease, however, with the anticipated decrease in technical assistance from Russia and Eastern Europe and subsequent departure of their personnel, thus worsening the shortage of skilled labor. The relatively low production of new university graduates will only add to the problem.

The total number of cooperantes has to be considered in the context of, first, the 1,500 local, higher-level technicians and managers who constitute the top-level categories of the civil service and, second, the roughly 150 local university graduates turned out annually. Were the government to absorb all university graduates, regardless of their specific qualifications, then at the present outturn of university graduates it would take almost two decades to replace all the present foreign technical assistance specialists. Even though this observation should be tempered by the fact that much of both the demand and supply of expatriate workers is generated by donor activities, it is undeniable that such workers also play an important role in public administration.

The demand for highly skilled labor has increased sharply with the growing number of development projects in the country. From 1985 to

1989, concessional external capital assistance (grants and multilateral loans) rose from US$0.38 billion to $0.66 billion. Since the number of expatriate workers has increased only modestly, this has meant a tremendous increase in the demand for highly skilled Mozambicans. More recently, the demand for such workers has risen still further because of the emergence of the private sector. Moreover, while the government was heavily constrained in its ability to raise the pay of its employees, donor agencies and other employers have had less difficulty setting competitive wage rates for skilled labor. As a result, skilled wage rates rose substantially in nongovernmental sectors, with an associated shift of some highly qualified personnel away from government employment.

Indicators of the demand pressure on skilled labor arising from the flow of external assistance into Mozambique show that, during 1985–90, the growth rate of cooperantes—the majority of highly skilled workers in Mozambique—was substantially lower than the growth rate of both unrequited official transfers and government investment expenditure (two indicators that can be related to the demand for skilled labor; table 5.6). It is thus likely that the demand for administrative, financial, and other professional skills arising from increased inflows of foreign assistance has grown more quickly than the supply. It is thus hardly surprising that pay levels for highly skilled workers have also grown rapidly.

In the market for qualified manpower, donors engage in both direct recruitment from government service and the purchase, on a part-time basis, of the services of existing civil servants. Often, staff are recruited

Table 5.6 Tentative indicators of the demand for skilled labor, Mozambique, 1985–90

Indicator/index	1985	1986	1987	1988 (estimated)	1989 (estimated)	1990 (estimated)
Cooperantes	3,500	3,000	3,409	3,873	4,401	5,000
(1985=100)	100	86	97	111	126	143
Unrequited official transfers, excluding technical assistance (current US$ millions)	139	213	304	377	388	427
(1985=100)	100	153	219	271	279	307
Government investment expenditure (current US$ millions)	155	230	235	264	287	349
(1985=100)	100	148	151	170	185	225
Ratio of cooperantes to unrequited official transfers	25	14	11	10	11	12

Source: For number of cooperantes, United Nations Development Programme study and World Bank staff estimates; for unrequited transfers, Government of Mozambique balance of payments figures; for government investment expenditure, Government of Mozambique, Ministry of Finance.

locally from the civil service, the parastatals and, to some extent, the local staff of other donor agencies. This draws heavily on the limited pool of qualified local personnel. Examples exist of senior civil servants being attracted away from their posts with salaries as high as US$4,000 a month, and of projects "poaching" staff from each other. Within project implementation units, there are also considerable nonsalary benefits accruing to locally recruited staff. Ready access to training and study tours abroad with associated benefits are common features. Project vehicles are normally provided, as well as other ancillary benefits.

Donor compensation practices

Within bilateral and multilateral agencies, a considerable dispersion exists across basic salaries. This is reflected in the substantial differences observed between maximum and minimum salaries within each occupational group. To quote examples from individual scales (using the official exchange rate), in one agency the salary scale of an office assistant or gardener starts at US$3,136 annually, and reaches $4,072 over ten increments. By contrast, in another agency the scale for the same group begins at $2,036 annually, and reaches $2,756 over five increments. There is thus about a 50 percent difference in the starting points and about 33 percent in the end points between the two donors' salary scales for this grade. However, if one compares salaries paid to the higher grades within the same two agencies, the situation is reversed. The agency with the lowest pay for gardeners pays between $24,000 and $28,500 annually (over ten steps) at the higher grades. The other agency pays only between $17,261 and $22,436 at the upper levels. Here, the difference in salaries is less pronounced and is merely on the order of 20 to 25 percent. Taking into account salary supplements does not alter these differences significantly. Nonsalary benefits are difficult to quantify. However, there are no contrasting features between agencies that could plausibly change the rankings of the net real value of their salary packages.

These discrepancies are not surprising for higher-level staff in view of the widespread shortage of qualified employees in this segment of the labor market, but such disparities are more difficult to justify at lower occupational levels. Although donors doubtless are guided by efficiency wage motives in setting wages above those in other sectors, there seems to be no such explanation for the plethora of pay rates that currently prevails.

The situation creates considerable difficulty for the Mozambican government as well as for the donor agencies themselves. As the government's administrative capacity weakens, it becomes increasingly difficult to implement existing projects. Donors have thus sought ways and means to persuade key civil servants to remain in their posts. One approach that has been adopted, that of topping up the salaries of individual civil servants, has arisen in cases where donor-funded projects are implemented by government departments or agencies. The practice of topping up civil service salaries appears prevalent in Mozambique, although donors are reluctant to admit its existence in their own activities. However, five agencies acknowledged paying cash salary supplements at one time or another. At least two of the five were active in topping up the salaries of government officials as of December 1990. In one case the supplement varied between US$145 and $490 a month, while in the other a supervising engineer was topped up at $2,500 a month. Topping-up does, of course, take forms other than cash payment. Some donors have provided housing, others vehicles. A more common incentive is provided through access to overseas training and study tours and through daily subsistence and travel allowances.

Some donors also contribute to the Incentive Fund in the Ministry of Finance. The fund has been in place since 1987, and in January 1990 it had US$4 million available. Administered at the sole discretion of the minister, the fund is used to top up the salaries of specific public officials and to pay technical subsidies. Between $1,000 and $2,500 is given to each beneficiary annually, in addition to a round-trip air ticket to Western Europe or North America. Such tickets are transferable, and may therefore be resold. Overall, the Incentive Fund lacks openness in its implementation, with the criteria used to select recipients and determine amounts paid unclear. Furthermore, the fund is restrictive in its application and creates acrimony that could lead to demoralization within the civil service.

It could be argued that, as a result of donor-funded fringe benefits, effective remuneration in specific cases among the highest ranks of the civil service is catching up with that of competing sectors. However, this is not true for higher-level staff as a whole, since many, if not most, higher-level staff benefit little from government-funded or donor-funded fringe benefits. It is reasonable to assume that some individuals in development-related ministries will fare well under this system. But this will not be the case in ministries that are not directly involved in donor activities. The picture that emerges is an untidy one, with information mainly anecdotal and incomplete.

Donor-driven competition for skilled personnel is creating immense problems for the government. The preoccupation of many donors with ensuring that their local administrations have a full complement of qualified staff and with securing, at all costs, the manpower required to implement their projects is depriving the government of the capacity to effectively manage its administration. The government's response through the Incentive Fund is not a serious answer to the problem; rather, it is, at best, an ad hoc measure to ease the government's predicament in the very short term.

Policy conclusions

A rigid and limited supply of skilled labor is not an uncommon feature of labor markets in Sub-Saharan African countries. And in Mozambique, considering the deficiencies in the education sector (especially at the university level), the shortage of skilled manpower is likely to last for some time. The cooperante scheme has played an important role in relaxing this supply constraint over the past ten years. However, the future supply of cooperantes is threatened by the decreased supply of Soviet and East European workers. Thus, government policy on external cooperation and the foreign supply of managerial skills will be crucial in the near future. In the long run, the only measure that will relieve the pressure on the government's administrative capacity is to increase the supply of skilled manpower. In the past, Mozambique has maintained an unusual degree of openness in its labor market for skilled manpower. And although it is understandable that heavy reliance on skilled expatriates has serious drawbacks and is often justifiably resented, it seems desirable that this approach be maintained to meet the needs of the growing private sector and future rehabilitation programs.

In the short to medium term, there are three general policy directions that could be followed to improve civil service wages. First, the wages of experienced and highly skilled civil servants could be raised to the extent allowed by existing budget constraints. Second, motivation and discipline could be improved if a substantial number of annual salary increments or steps were established within the salary scale for each higher- and middle-level grade. Finally, there may be scope for increased revenue generation through the collection of income tax. To finance future increases in the wage bill, in principle, payments in foreign currency should be subject to income tax collected in a way that matches the value of the original payment. This would of itself narrow the gap in net earnings between the civil service and other sectors. Weaknesses of the tax collection system, as well as some donors' unwillingness to report taxable payments made to local staff, often mean that legally taxable wage and consultancy payments in foreign exchange are not fully reported to the tax office. Where such payments can be identified, income tax should be levied so that the metical value corresponds to the real purchasing power of the payment made.

It must be recognized, however, that the impact of these measures is likely to be limited because of the severity of the problem. The government's ability to grant wage increases is limited by existing fiscal constraints, and, as argued earlier, the potential savings from feasible staffing reductions are likely to be relatively small. The problem is that the government is competing with employers who are much less constrained. And it is far from clear that the outcome of this competition is optimal, given the interdependence of government and donor interests.

Donors are aware of the pay differentials between their local staff and public sector employees. Moreover, many donors have expressed concern about the distortions these disparities cause. The donor community has even tried to improve its knowledge of pay differentials by disseminating questionnaires among the various donors and organizing internal discussions on the subject. However, apart from these commendable initiatives, few commonly agreed policy rules have been applied to the recruitment of local staff. On the contrary, noncooperative behavior has been observed among donors, particularly when the staffing of a project coordination unit is at stake.

The advantages to be gained from a donor agreement on remuneration levels are significant. There is wide variation in pay practices among donor agencies and nongovernmental organizations, particularly with respect to local consultants, and fees paid are often extremely high. This reflects to some degree a competitive bidding process for scarce, highly skilled labor. At the middle and lower skill levels, it is clear that donors pay far more than the supply price of such labor and that substantial rents are being earned by the recipients of such payments. A cooperative agreement seems to be the only short-term workable solution to reduce significantly the huge intersectoral pay differentials. More moderate and less dispersed pay levels for Mozambicans in the donor sector would confer the joint advantages of freeing up donor resources for other activities and reducing job dissatisfaction among civil service employees.

Indeed, the donor community has not sufficiently internalized the adverse externality that can occur when a highly skilled individual is attracted away from public administration. While the donor employing that individual will gain the marginal product associated with the addition of his services, the same donor, as well as other donor agencies, will find it marginally harder to implement activities because the administrative capacity of the government will have been reduced. Negative externalities may also be felt in parastatals and the private sector. Thus, as donor activities increase over time, and growing numbers of experienced public officials are drawn away from the civil service, donors will find it more difficult to successfully conduct their affairs. An ideal solution would be for donors to agree to limit their recruitment of skilled Mozambicans so as to eliminate this negative externality. Limiting donor pay levels is not an appropriate solution since it could place donors at a competitive disadvantage in relation to the emerging private sector. This, in turn, would lead to excess donor demand for highly skilled labor and thus increase the chances of a breakdown in the arrangement. Although it is difficult to imagine recruitment practices being fully specified and agreed, it would be useful if the government and the donors could agree at least on a general code governing recruitment and the use of government officials for part-time consultancy work.

Mozambique is an extreme example of a classic public pay and employment profile in Africa and in many other parts of the world— that of a small, poor country, with a weak human resource endowment and few skilled nationals, attempting to carry out a rapidly expanding development agenda, fueled by massive inflows of (mainly project-dedicated) foreign aid. What is clear from this and other cases is that the determination of appropriate government pay levels depends largely on demand factors that can be multiple and complex. These factors can include, among other things, external demand from donors or from overseas opportunities, and domestic demand driven by the expansion of government employment and by the needs of the public and private enterprise sectors. The experience in Mozambique also illustrates the much discussed "enclave" problem—the inherent tension between staffing donor-funded projects for essential development activities as against building the government's long-term institutional capacity through provision of adequate incentives to civil servants. Decisive policy approaches to these troubling issues will need to be taken if the effectiveness of development assistance is to be improved throughout the world.

Notes

1. This figure is based on preliminary results from a census of the civil service conducted during 1989/90 by the Ministry of State Administration. The actual number of civil servants in Mozambique is still to be determined: this is understandable in a country that has been facing a civil war since its Independence. The number of 105,000 civil servants is based on two parallel estimates: the preliminary results of a 1990 census of the civil service carried out by the Ministry of State Administration and a reconciliation of this census with the payroll carried out by the Ministry of Finance. Since November 1990 the government has been taking a number of important steps aimed at (1) determining the total number of civil servants within the 1990 structure of grades and salary scales; (2) elaborating a new, unified, and decompressed salary scale in conjunction with new, unified grades across the whole civil service; and (3) integrating progressively the civil servants into the new grades and the new salary scale. In parallel with this three-stage process, the Ministry of Finance has refined its sur-

vey of the civil service payroll. Initial results at the end of September 1991 suggest that about 90,000 civil servants (instead of 105,000) are on the government payroll. As of October 1991 the three-stage process had been completed for about 58,000 civil servants.

2. *Cooperantes* has two definitions in Mozambique: all resident expatriate workers other than diplomatic staff; and resident expatriates working for the government. Here, the wider definition is applied. Apart from those imported as part of technical assistance from Eastern Europe, most cooperantes are from Latin America.

3. The Department of Foreign Exchange of the Ministry of Finance reported that the cost of this special incentive amounted to US$1.9 million in 1989.

4. The technical subsidy was extended in 1990 to firms in the productive sector that have earnings in foreign exchange. In this case, the firm can spend up to 2.5 percent of its foreign exchange gains on this type of internal incentive. However, this is subject to the approval of the Department of Foreign Exchange of the Ministry of Finance and dependent on the availability of foreign exchange.

6

Preparing for civil service pay and employment reform: a primer

Mike Stevens

The term "civil service" is often used loosely. Sometimes it implies everyone on the government payroll. At other times it can mean a small administrative elite. The first requirement in designing a civil service reform program is to decide what parts of total public employment are to be covered by the program.

Deciding on the universe

The best advice is to start with a broad canvas and take stock of the public service as a whole, narrowing the focus as appropriate. A program that addresses only the administrative inner core is likely to be easier to design and implement, as well as being less costly. On the other hand, if common salary scales operate throughout the public sector, as they do in many countries, then changing the terms and conditions of the basic reference group will have a ripple effect throughout public employment, unless the nexus is explicitly broken.

Assessing the public employment structure

Mapping public employment is an essential first step in designing a civil service reform program. To do this it is necessary to know the structure of government. A typical structure for public sector employment (shown in schematic form in figure 6.1) will include, first, on the central government payroll an inner core of administrators. In some countries this is a broadly based category comprising large numbers of immigration officials, statisticians and economists, accountants, architects, engineers, clerks, typists, and drivers, as well as managers and administrators. In other countries it comprises an elite group of administrators, small in number and powerful—a true inner core.

Next there may be large numbers of employees in separate services that are nevertheless paid out of government budget funds, on pay scales linked to the central administration. Typical examples are teachers, health workers, and the police. Collectively or individually, these groups may outnumber the administrative core group. Directly dependent on the central government budget, but in a special class of its own, is the military. Customarily, the armed forces are not included in civil

Figure 6.1   Public sector employment

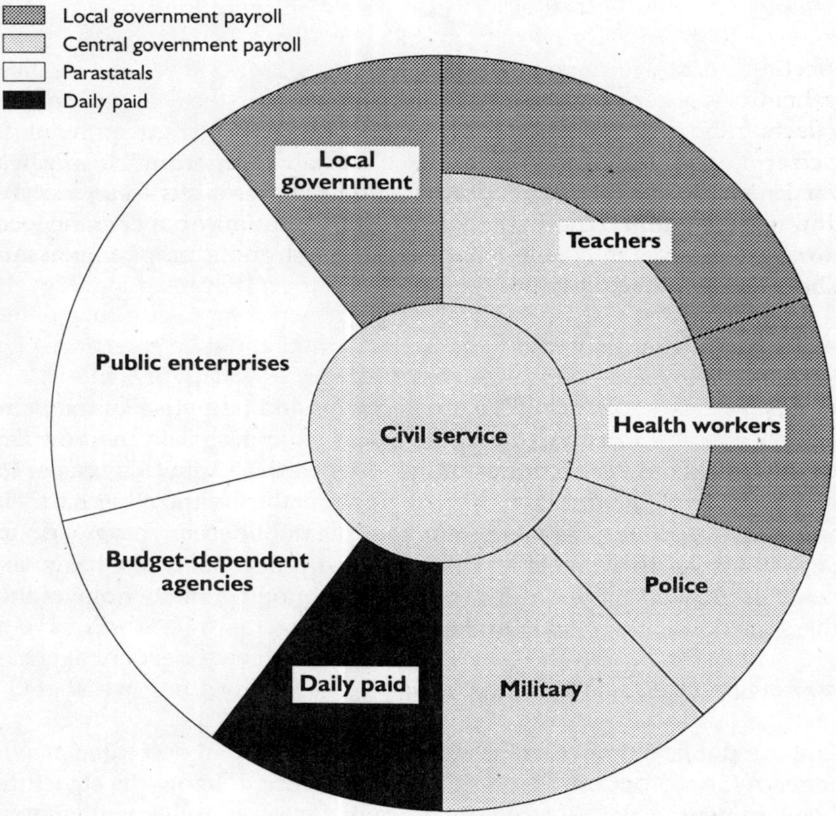

Note: The proportions indicated are illustrative and are not meant to correspond with the public employment shares of any particular nation.

service reform programs, but ripple effects from changes in civil service pay may affect the central budget and, thus, the military.

Also a charge on the central budget is "daily paid" staff. Strictly speaking, these employees are not part of the permanent establishment and may therefore lie outside the purview of a civil service reform program. But government salary reviews typically include recommendations for daily as well as permanent staff, and the budgetary implications have to be taken into account. Furthermore, in many countries staff hired on a daily paid basis have become absorbed into the permanent establishment, with the line between the two categories no longer distinct. Indeed, part of the reform program may be to redraw the line more sharply.

Another question is whether to include local government workers. In many countries local government pay and conditions have been brought into line with those of central government, and it is hard to imagine that central government conditions can be changed without affecting local government employees. In some cases cadres like teachers or health workers are split between central and local governments, reflecting the different responsibilities of the two tiers of government. In such circumstances, a civil service reform program covering both central and local government employees may be too ambitious to undertake. However, the impact a central civil service reform may have on the local government wage bill needs to be kept in mind, and it may be necessary to plan for a subsequent reform program for the local government level.

Finally, there is the parastatal sector, which comprises public enterprises and budget-dependent agencies. Normally, public enterprises are not included in civil service reform programs, especially if the thrust of policy is to make them more commercially autonomous. This in turn implies severing the link with civil service pay scales if in the past this has been the basis of remuneration. Budget-dependent agencies are another matter. Although it may in the long run be desirable to give them greater independence in pay matters, their staff often are employed on civil service–equivalent terms and traditionally have seen their pay and conditions linked to that of the civil service proper. Whether or not that link should continue will be something the reform program will have to resolve, but certainly at the outset the staff of budget-dependent agencies are part of the universe to be considered before deciding whether the reforms should have broad coverage or a narrower focus.

Obtaining employment numbers

It is difficult to decide what parts of public employment to include in the civil service reform program without a clear picture of the numbers of people involved. Obtaining these figures is often a problem. Consolidated information may not be readily available (itself a symptom of something wrong with civil service management). When different sources of information are compared, they may not agree, necessitating painstaking work to arrive at a consistent set of data. Some of the differences may be definitional (for example, approved positions compared with staff in post); others may be due to different collection methods (for example, an employment survey compared with payroll data). Furthermore, the presence of "ghost workers"[1] may prevent drawing a true picture of civil service numbers; this phenomenon, common to many countries, points to the need for a civil service census.

To provide a complete picture of civil service numbers, data ideally should be presented as follows:

- *Historically*, to show the growth in public employment over time, when and where expansion has occurred, and whether past efforts at retrenchment or freezing recruitment have had any effect. In many countries it is illuminating to compare the growth in civil service numbers with underlying government revenue growth and the general performance of the economy. Often this will show that over an extended period the growth in public employment exceeded the growth in government resources. Indeed, for many countries this has been the primary cause of present-day civil service problems.
- *Departmentally*, to show which parts of the government are the big employers, and thus where the reform effort needs to be concentrated. If departmental data are available on a historical basis, it should be possible to link expansion in numbers with the introduction of new policies and programs (for example, the adoption of higher transition rates from primary to secondary education as a goal of social policy).
- *By service*, again to show where the main areas of employment are. Typically, this will mean separate data series for local governments, teachers, health workers, police, and so on. In many countries the first two categories account for the bulk of staff in public employment. Obtaining aggregate numbers for each service is essential if a decision has to be made to restrict the civil service reform program to less than the full public service.
- *By professional cadre*, if the main service groupings are broken down this way. This information is necessary if the cost of selective pay increases targeted at particular categories of public employees (for example, accountants, engineers, doctors) is to be estimated.
- *By salary grade*, to show the shape of the employment pyramid and to enable calculation of the cost of differential salary adjustment strategies, such as the decompression of pay scales.

Building up information on public service numbers is likely to take time and typically requires going to several different sources and comparing the results. The following are some of the main sources of data on civil service numbers:

- *Budget documents* provide a great deal of information on the structure of governments for those prepared to invest time in understanding them. In some countries the budget documents will show the number of approved positions alongside the proposed departmental financial appropriations. Alternatively, the budget documents may show departmental manpower in a summary table. This is particularly likely in countries that have expanded the range of budget documents to include informational material as well as proposed appropriations.
- *The public service ministry* is another primary source of data on civil service employment, and if responsibility is divided, the *public service commission* is a good source as well. Normally, one would expect the public service ministry to keep records on total manpower in post by department, going back several years. There may also be some sort of establishment register listing by department the authorized positions department managers may recruit against. Actual numbers may exceed approved levels in countries where establishment (or complement) control has broken down. But where it is still effective, staff in post are typically 90 to 95 percent of authorized positions.
- In large countries where personnel management has been delegated to line agencies and departments, the central ministry may not have a full record of staff numbers, in which case there is no alternative but to seek the information from the *personnel departments of the major agencies*. However, even where authority to recruit has been delegated, staff summaries should still be reported to the civil service ministry.
- Daily paid staff present a special problem, since they are, strictly speaking, not part of the civil service proper and are paid through different channels than regular civil servants. The public service ministry often will not have records of daily paid staff, so it may be necessary to go directly to the *principal employing ministry* (typically, the public works ministry). Alternatively, if returns on daily paid staff are made to the finance ministry, as part of budgetary expenditure reporting, then this ministry may be a source of data. The number of daily paid staff may fluctuate through the year, typically due to seasonal factors (if there is a distinct construction season, for example) or budgetary resources (if funds tighten during the financial year, in which case daily paid staff are likely to be the first laid

off). Thus, an average rather than an exact number for daily paid staff is a more realistic objective.

- If teachers and local government workers are part of a separate service, then the appropriate body for administering that service (for example, the *education ministry* for teachers, the *local government ministry* for local government workers) will need to be approached. Furthermore, in some countries there may be a separate *local government service commission*. A similar approach may be used for the police.
- Military personnel numbers raise a different set of issues. If it is deemed necessary to obtain rough numbers of the size of the armed forces, and government sources are not forthcoming, the *international publications* of such organizations as the U.S. Arms Control and Disarmament Agency, the International Institute for Strategic Studies, and the Stockholm International Peace Research Institute provide comparable figures of force strength by country.
- An obvious port of call for someone seeking data on civil service numbers is the *government statistics bureau*. Statistics bureau staff may already have obtained and consolidated figures from the public service ministry figures. In addition, the statistics bureau may have generated its own data in the course of employment and other labor market surveys. The statistics bureau will also be a source of information on public and private sector wage rates and earnings.
- It would be a mistake to neglect the *planning ministry* or agency (when this exists) as a source of information. Planning ministries often contain manpower planning units that collect data and analyze employment in both the public and private sectors. The classification of these data may be different from civil service groupings, but the staff may have access to raw civil service data not obtainable elsewhere. Because manpower planning has traditionally been carried out on a "needs" basis, projections of civil service employment made by manpower planners may be much higher than the budget allows.
- Finally, the *finance ministry* should be consulted for payroll data. In most countries civil servants are paid centrally through a computer payroll system (in some countries there may be separate systems for different groupings, such as teachers). A payroll is potentially a rich source of information about staff numbers, by department and by grade. However, it may be technically difficult to extract the data; furthermore, since ghost workers are in the last analysis a form of payroll fraud, the numbers may be biased upward. Nonetheless, payrolls directly drive the budget and can be the most up-to-date source of civil service employment data available.

Building up information on public service numbers is thus likely to be a time-consuming process that may result in conflicting data series and the need to exercise judgment. The compensation is that in the process of obtaining the numbers, a great deal will be learned about the structure of the public service and how it operates.

Studying compensation

The next requirement is information on pay scales. Obtaining the scales is likely to be an easier task than finding out about civil service numbers. In many countries government pay scales are published in budget documents, and even where they are not, they should be readily obtainable from the finance ministry, the public service ministry, or the public service commission. They will have been reviewed by civil service salary commissions, whose reports, if published or otherwise obtainable, will provide the existing scales. Finally, the government statistics office may have the information.

By themselves, government pay scales reveal no more than the number of salary grades and projections of the level and spread of staffing. A key is needed to interpret them. Obviously, the top civil servant in a ministry is likely to be on or close to the highest scale, while drivers, office messengers, and cleaners are going to be at the bottom (if they are not daily paid staff). To fill in the middle it is necessary to know, for example, such things as the secondary school and graduate entry points, and where in the scales different occupational groups, such as teachers, engineers, and accountants, fit. This information should be available from the civil service ministry. In some countries there may be separate sets of scales, based on different civil service divisions or classes.

Some simple exercises in analyzing pay scales can then be undertaken. Compression ratios can be measured (from the midpoint of the highest scale to the midpoint of the lowest scale), and their evolution over time can be investigated (this is likely to be more revealing than intercountry comparisons, which vary greatly even between civil services that operate effectively). The cost of alternative decompression scenarios (if pay differentials have been eroded) can be tested, provided data on the shape of the public employment pyramid are available.

Pay comparisons can also be made between the public and private sectors if private sector compensation by occupation can be obtained. In addition, information should be obtained on income tax rates, which may in turn need reform if the income bands on which they are based are tied to government scales that are no longer realistic. In some countries (such as Sri Lanka) civil servants are not subject to income tax, and salary scales are supposed to reflect this. And in some cases where civil servants' incomes are taxed, allowances may be exempted, likely diluting the impact of taxation.

The hidden reward structure

Whereas in industrial countries the monthly paychecks of civil servants constitute the bulk of their remuneration, in developing countries a range of fringe benefits usually has to be taken into account. In part this is a colonial inheritance. Allowances that were deemed necessary for expatriate administrators were carried over largely unchanged into post-independence civil services. As monetary pay in many countries has deteriorated, allowances and other benefits in kind have taken on a special value, and attempts to reduce them have been strongly resisted. Unreformed income tax regimes with outdated tax bands reinforce this tendency. Furthermore, in some countries, faced with the unaffordability of a general wage increase, governments have deliberately resorted to special allowances, which may not be scheduled or widely known, as a means to remunerate key staff.

The more the purchasing power of monetary pay has declined, the greater the need to analyze other channels of remuneration. In practical terms this presents the analyst of civil service pay and employment with a formidable problem. Although it might be possible to obtain a list of the officially sanctioned allowances, the manner of their distribution is often difficult to find out. Aggregate expenditure on allowances can be determined from the budget, if they are separately coded (as is usually the case). However, in countries where civil service pay has been seriously eroded, the amounts paid as salary supplements may greatly exceed the amounts ostensibly allocated to allowances (supplements may, for example, be funded through a central contingencies vote or by transfer from other categories of expenditure), and this will require considerable detective work. Special attention needs to be paid to housing benefits, which are, in effect, largely off-budget. Housing can easily become the most important component in a civil servant's total remuneration if monetary pay scales have collapsed; however, the government housing stock is usually limited and distribution of these benefits is seldom transparent or uniform across the civil service.

The objective of these investigations is to achieve a comprehensive picture of the reward system under which different groups of civil servants operate. To some extent the picture can be drawn by studying the allowances and benefits available. Ultimately, it will have to be completed from interviews, and even then, unless confidence is established, the picture will be incomplete. However, it is prudent to assume that where official scales are badly eroded, substitute systems have come into being, far less transparent than the salary scales and probably unequally distributed.

Severance pay and pensions

If retrenchment is likely to be part of the reform program, the costs to the government budget need to be estimated, whether they are incurred through voluntary departure schemes or through forced redundancies. In the short term the costs may well exceed the wage bill savings. This means ascertaining separation costs on termination and pension costs.

Separation terms will be provided either by legislation or in the contractual terms and conditions of government employment. In some countries the financial obligations on the government may be quite low; in others the costs can be very large. Where they are low, governments may decide to augment severance pay for political or social reasons. Where they are high, the rate at which the civil service can be downsized may be constrained by budgetary factors. In most countries separation terms have evolved in personnel management policies in response to individual cases of dismissal or retirement—and not with the inhibiting implications of large-scale retrenchment in mind.

Pension costs also need to be taken into account. First, it may be necessary to raise pensions for straightforward equity reasons. In many countries governments have failed to adjust pensions in line with inflation, with the result that they have fallen behind even more than have salaries (there is seldom a compensating system of allowances for pensioners). Second, any method of retrenchment that includes voluntary or other early forms of retirement is likely to raise the government's immediate pension liability. If staff leave well before their retirement age, the immediate cost to the government could be in the form of a lump sum payment out of contributions to the civil service pension fund, if the scheme is funded, or directly from the budget, if it is not.

Estimating severance and pension costs is a matter of establishing the legal obligations of the government as employer, and any other payments the government may consider necessary, and multiplying these by the numbers likely to leave the civil service through reduction in overstaffing and rationalization of functions. In many countries these calculations will show that the financial savings from a program of retrenchment are unlikely to be harvested immediately. Indeed, it may be several years before the wage bill savings outweigh retrenchment costs. Unless concessionary external aid is available, the financial costs of retrenchment are likely to exercise a brake on the speed at which a civil service can be downsized.

Underpinnings of compensation policies

Preparing for a civil service reform program also entails finding out how governments have set pay and conditions for the civil service in the past. In the 1960s and 1970s national incomes policies were in vogue. They had validity in countries where modern sector skills were in short supply and public and private sector competition for scarce manpower was considered undesirable. By the 1980s incomes policies had collapsed in most countries, and there is no longer a belief in their efficacy. But vestiges often remain, notably the alignment, at least notionally, of parastatal pay with central government pay. There may also be policies tying local government pay to central government scales, as well as similar policies for teachers. Another line of inquiry is whether minimum wage legislation is in effect, how minimum wage levels are set, and the extent to which this binds the government at the lower end of its scales.

It is necessary to know about past government pay policy, not because it should continue unchanged into the future, but because making explicit the changes that are needed (which may require amending legislation) should feature in the resulting civil service reform program.

The budgetary context

Civil service reform programs that are designed without reference to the overall fiscal context of the government are unlikely to succeed. The history of public administration in developing countries is replete with examples of carefully worked out reform proposals shipwrecked on the rocks of budget realities. Part of the preparatory work for a reform program, therefore, is establishing clearly the budgetary resource envelope that the reforms must take place within. This means taking the government budget and breaking it into the main building blocks: capital (or development expenditure), debt servicing and other mandated or statutory expenditure, the government wage bill, nonwage operations and maintenance, and transfers. It also means assessing the revenue side of the budget, since in some countries revenue-raising capacity is itself artificially depressed due to collection weaknesses that in turn are related to civil service deficiencies. Reforms to customs and tax administrations may be needed before pay levels can be effectively addressed.

Because each of these budgetary blocks has its own dynamics, and in turn may be influenced by government policy, it is useful to try to project them forward in some form of medium-term expenditure plan. If, for example, a high share of the budget has been absorbed by transfers to loss-making parastatals or by consumer subsidies, reforms in these areas will affect resources available for civil service pay. Alternatively, if operations and maintenance allocations are significantly less than what is required to support efficient government services, then this must be addressed in parallel with the resources envelope for the wage bill. Indeed, in many countries, even where civil service pay is badly deficient, there may be little point in proposing salary reforms unless there is a matching increase in supporting operations and maintenance allocations. Thus, these two expenditure blocks have to be considered together. In many cases it will simply not be possible to restore both pay and supporting expenditures to realistic levels without a drastic reduction in the numbers on the public payroll, or without a radical change in the way government services are paid for and delivered.

In weighing the balance between the wage bill and nonwage operations and maintenance it is useful if studies of the optimum level of operations and maintenance provision (such as "standard cost" analysis) can be carried out alongside or before the design of the civil service reform program. It is also necessary to have a feel for how much of what presently passes for operations and maintenance is in fact a substitute for monetary pay—for example, allowances paid as direct augmentation of salaries as against compensation for travel and accommodation costs incurred on legitimate field trips.[2]

Judging the scale of reforms

Once the basic information on staff numbers, the wage bill, and severance costs has been gathered, a preliminary look may be taken at the scale of the reforms needed to rectify imbalances in civil service pay and numbers. Although pay and employment reform is by no means the totality of civil service reform, unless these two elements can be brought into better balance in many countries, no amount of reform effort in other areas is likely to be effective.

Civil service reform in recent years has been based on three large goals:
- Reduction in numbers by eliminating payroll fraud and reducing overstaffing, utilizing a census to expose ghost workers, conducting functional reviews to identify areas of excess staffing, and implementing voluntary departure schemes.
- Utilization of the financial savings from retrenchment to decompress salary scales, to incorporate allowances into monetary pay, and to raise the real level of remuneration over time.
- Improvements in civil service management, particularly establishment control, record-keeping, and training.

Looking back at some of the longer-running civil service reform programs, it may be asked whether the model just outlined is viable in all cases. In many countries—especially in those where over a decade or more public service numbers have grown two or three times faster than the underlying growth in revenues, and where, under the pressure of prolonged fiscal crisis, civil service pay has collapsed—the reform model described above may not be adequate. Gradual reductions in staff numbers to generate the savings needed to decompress salary scales and improve the employment terms and conditions of civil servants may simply be too little too late.

A conceptual framework for looking at the pay, employment, and performance equation might group countries into three categories. Countries in category I would be those where pay scales remain sufficient to motivate staff, but have slipped relative to private sector comparators and may have become too compressed. Under these conditions, it is difficult to recruit and retain personnel with key skills or to reward staff that take on additional responsibilities. Conventional programs that freeze or slow down recruitment and decompress salary scales, perhaps combined with management changes, are likely to be the main elements of a reform package for category I countries.

Category II countries would be those where salary scales are more seriously out of line, but still represent a living, if not motivating or competitive, wage. There also may be significant overstaffing. In such countries the conventional civil service reform model—combining pay reforms with reductions in overstaffing—may be sufficient to rectify the imbalances if combined with management improvements and shifts in the composition of the budget. Particularly important are reinstitution of effective staff complement controls, a better linking of staffing decisions with the budget, and achievement of a better balance between the main blocks of expenditure, such as the wage bill, nonwage operations and maintenance, capital spending, and transfers.

The final group of countries, category III, would be those where real monetary pay has completely collapsed and alternative reward systems have taken over. Conventional civil service reform programs are difficult to apply in such circumstances, since the imbalance in numbers is likely to extend beyond overstaffing. Functional reviews, the conventional technique for identifying overstaffing, do not normally question the underlying merit of departments. For countries in category III, a much more radical review of the scale and scope of the functions the state has taken upon itself is indicated. Since such countries typically are often high aid recipients, the role of donors in supporting key programs and the forms in which their aid is provided are likely to be an intrinsic part of such a review.

Thus far, most civil service reform programs have been predicated on the assumption that the reforming countries are in either category I or category II. However, many of the countries that are now embarking on civil service reform programs appear to be contenders for category III. There is thus an urgent need to devise sustainable reform approaches for this group of countries, a challenge that both governments and donor agencies will need to take up in the coming years.

Notes

1. A "ghost worker" is a fictitious name on the payroll whose salary is collected by someone else.

2. Although no empirical work has been done to determine the optimal ratio of personnel emoluments to other running costs, and standards would obviously vary by sector and country, a personnel expenditure–operating cost ratio of 60:40 or better would seem to be a reasonable target.

PART II

ATTEMPTS AT REFORM

7

Experience with civil service pay and employment reform: an overview

Barbara Nunberg

Recent efforts to overhaul developing country economies have placed in stark relief the need for adequate public sector administrative capacity, especially within the core civil service. Increasingly, the ability of civil services to carry out the critical—much less the routine—functions of government is severely constrained. Furthermore, the size and cost of many civil services are excessive. These deficiencies have become key targets of structural adjustment programs supported by international donors such as the World Bank. This growing concern with containing the size and improving the performance of the civil service signifies a redimensioning and redefining of the state, reflecting a fundamental shift in the direction of economic development policy. The new wisdom is to "manage less—but better."

This chapter surveys recent World Bank experience in support of developing country civil service reform and begins to assess the progress made. Civil service reform as practiced in World Bank operations has focused on two separate but related dimensions. One deals with the shorter-term, emergency steps to reform public pay and employment policies. These reforms usually center on measures to contain the cost and size of the civil service, mostly in the context of structural adjustment lending. The other reform dimension deals with longer-range civil service strengthening efforts, some of which may support various of the nearer-term cost containment measures, but most of which are directed toward ongoing, sustained management improvements. Many of these longer-term reforms have been included in technical assistance projects—either those that stand alone as "development management" operations or those that constitute direct institutional support for specific actions taken in structural adjustment loans. Although references are made to the second reform dimension, it is the former work on pay and employment reform that is the main subject of the analysis that follows.

This narrow lens is consistent with the other material in this volume; it is in no way intended to convey the belief that cost containment is the more important objective in reforming civil services, or that it is on its own sufficient to make governments function more effectively. But the focus does reflect the view that pay and employment reforms are a necessary condition to civil service improvements in many countries. Finally, the topic was thus construed because of the Bank's extensive experience on pay and employment reform. It is time to take a systematic look back to see how well such programs have fared.

The section that follows briefly lays out the analytic assumptions underlying most civil service reform programs.[1] The discussion then turns to the operational experience, examining first the cost containment and then the remuneration rationalization aspects of reform. The impact of these efforts is then assessed. The final section draws conclusions and suggests directions for future work.

The need for reforms

Recent analytic work on public pay and employment issues provides the following broad outline of the civil service problem: Governments in many developing countries are unable to manage and finance their civil services. These civil services are frequently too large, too expensive, and insufficiently productive; and civil servants, especially those in managerial positions, get few incentives and are poorly motivated. Civil services are too large in the broad sense that in many states the public sector is overextended, that is, it possesses too many agencies and organizations, charged with too broad a span of responsibilities; and in the narrower sense that too many of these agencies employ numbers of people excessive to requirements (in the sense of people and skills needed to fulfill officially assigned economic and administrative tasks). They are too expensive in the sense that public sector wage bills constitute too high a percentage of total government revenues and account for too high a percentage of GDP. The agents within civil services tend to be poorly motivated in that remuneration scales for upper and middle managers are low, often extremely low, in comparison with those of roughly equivalent posts in the private and frequently the parastatal sector; and wages are often severely compressed, with the highest paid earning low multiples of the wages of the lowest paid. Many civil servants are insufficiently productive in the sense that they do not fulfill the tasks assigned to them (they are ineffective), or they carry out their assignments partially, with great delays, at high cost (they are inefficient).

World Bank programs have tried to tackle this civil service syndrome by focusing on four principal problems: excessive government wage bills, surplus civil service employment, salary erosion, and wage compression. Guided by this analytic construct, the World Bank began to lend money to developing countries to correct this syndrome through civil service reform. We turn now to an examination of the operational experience to date, keeping in mind the caveat that experience has been poorly documented and that data are not always reliable and are often partial. Thus, a full assessment is beyond the reach of this analysis, but tentative lessons from the accumulating body of evidence can still be drawn.

The operational record

In the period between 1981 and 1991, civil service reform was a prominent feature of ninety World Bank lending operations.[2] Of these, sixty were structural adjustment loans (SALs) and thirty were technical assistance loans (TALs), mainly in support of SALs. (Table 7.1 lists World Bank operations with civil service reform components.[3])

Africa, where the magnitude and intensity of the issue is clearly greatest, leads as the region with the most civil service reform operations, numbering fifty-five. But other regions are catching up: Latin America and the Caribbean have been the locus of twenty such operations. Asia and the Middle East and North Africa lag with nine and six operations, respectively. Data do not yet reflect activities among countries of recent membership from Eastern Europe and Central Asia. (Figure 7.1 shows the regional distribution of Bank operations with civil service reform components by lending instrument.)

Activities are relatively new in this field. Prior to 1981 the World Bank was only tangentially involved with civil service reform, and that involvement, limited to the occasional report on public administration issues or support for training government staff through the strengthening of public service institutes, was mainly on the project, not the policy level. By the beginning of the past decade, however, structural adjustment lending, with its emphasis on demand management and improving the performance of adjusting governments, drove the World Bank deeper into civil service reform.

The recognition of the heavy fiscal burden posed by large government wage bills was the main reason for increasingly including civil service reform in Bank adjustment operations. In the early 1980s, for exam-

Table 7.1 World Bank operations with civil service reform components, 1981–91

Region/country	Loan/credit type	Loan/credit number	Amount (US$ millions)	Approval date
Africa				
Angola	Economic Management Capacity	Cr 2274	23.0	06/91
Benin	Structural Adjustment I	Cr 2023	45.0	06/89
	Structural Adjustment II	Cr 2283	55.0	06/91
Burkina Faso	Structural Adjustment	Cr 2281	80.0	06/91
Cameroon	Economic Management	Ln 3110	9.0	07/89
	Structural Adjustment	Ln 2866	70.0	07/89
Central African Republic	Technical Assistance I	Cr 1150	4.0	05/81
	Technical Assistance II	Cr 1581	8.0	04/85
	Structural Adjustment I	Cr 1732	14.0	09/86
	Structural Adjustment II	Cr 1916	40.0	06/88
	Structural Adjustment III	Cr 2162	45.0	06/90
	Economic Management	Cr 1971	13.2	12/88
Comoros	Macro-Economic Reform	Cr 2270	8.0	06/91
Congo	Structural Adjustment	Ln 2866	70.0	06/87
Gabon	Structural Adjustment	Ln 2933	50.0	04/88
	Technical Assistance	Ln 3114	5.0	08/89
Gambia, The	Structural Adjustment I	Cr 1730	5.0	08/86
	Structural Adjustment II	Cr 2032	23.0	06/89
Ghana	Structural Adjustment I	Cr 1777	34.0	04/87
	Structural Adjustment Institutional Support	Cr 1778	10.8	04/87
	Structural Adjustment II	Cr 2005	120.0	04/89
	Economic Management Support	Cr 2224	15.0	03/91
	Private Investment	Cr 2236	120.0	05/91
Guinea	Technical Assistance	Cr 1559	9.5	03/85
	Structural Adjustment I	Cr 1659	25.0	02/86
	Structural Adjustment II	Cr 1926	65.0	06/88
	Economic Management Support II	Cr 1963	14.5	11/88
Guinea-Bissau	Structural Adjustment I	Cr 1798	10.0	05/87
	Technical Assistance II	Cr 1935	9.7	06/88
	Structural Adjustment II	Cr 2019	23.4	05/89
Malawi	Structural Adjustment III	Cr 1644	30.0	12/85
	Institutional Development	Cr 2036	11.3	06/89
Mali	Technical Assistance	Cr 1307	10.4	12/82
	Structural Adjustment	Cr 2188	70.0	12/90
Mauritania	Structural Adjustment	Cr 1812	15.0	06/87
	Development Management	Cr 1865	10.0	12/87
Mozambique	Rehabilitation III	Cr 2021	90.0	05/89
Niger	Structural Adjustment	Cr 1660	20.0	02/86
Rwanda	Structural Adjustment	Cr 2271	90.0	06/91
São Tomé and Principe	Structural Adjustment I	Cr 1825	4.0	06/87
	Structural Adjustment II	Cr 2165	9.8	06/90

Region/country	Loan/credit type	Loan/credit number	Amount (US$ millions)	Approval date
Senegal	Structural Adjustment II	Cr 1656	20.0	02/86
	Structural Adjustment III	Cr 1802	50.5	05/87
	Structural Adjustment IV	Cr 2090	80.0	02/90
	Development Management	Cr 1910	17.0	05/88
Sudan	Public Enterprise & Economic Management	Cr 1789	9.0	05/87
Togo	Structural Adjustment II	Cr 1599	27.8	05/85
	Technical Assistance III	Cr 1600	6.2	05/85
	Structural Adjustment IV	Cr 2194	55.0	11/90
Uganda	Technical Assistance II	Cr 1434	14.2	12/83
	Economic Recovery I	Cr 1844	65.0	09/87
	Economic Recovery II	Cr 2087	125.0	02/90
Zaire	Structural Adjustment	Cr 1831	55.0	06/87
	Economic Management & Institutional Development	Cr 1832	12.0	06/87
Zambia	Economic Recovery Program	Cr 2214	210.0	03/91
Asia				
Bangladesh	Public Administration	Cr 1349	12.0	04/83
	Import XIII	Cr 1655	200.0	02/86
Laos	Structural Adjustment	Cr 2037	40.0	06/89
Nepal	Structural Adjustment	Cr 1769	50.0	03/87
Papua New Guinea	Structural Adjustment	Ln 3218	50.0	06/90
	Public Sector Training	Ln 3290	20.8	01/91
Sri Lanka	Economic Restructuring	Cr 2128	90.0	05/90
Thailand	Structural Adjustment I	Ln 2097	304.5	03/82
	Structural Adjustment II	Ln 2256	175.5	03/83
Middle East and North Africa				
Tunisia	Structural Adjustment	Ln 2962	150.0	06/88
Turkey	Structural Adjustment II	Ln 1987	300.0	05/81
	Structural Adjustment III	Ln 2158	304.5	05/82
	Structural Adjustment IV	Ln 2321	300.8	06/83
	Structural Adjustment V	Ln 2441	376.0	06/84
Yemen	Institutional Development & Public Administration	Cr 2015	10.8	05/89
Latin America and the Caribbean				
Argentina	Public Sector Reform Technical Assistance	Ln 3362	23.0	06/91
	Public Sector Reform	Ln 3394	325.0	07/91
Bolivia	Economic Management Strengthening	Cr 1977	9.7	12/88
	Public Finance Management II	Cr 2279	11.3	06/91

(Table continues on the following page.)

Table 7.1 continued

Region/country	Loan/credit type	Loan/credit number		Amount (US$ millions)	Approval date
Costa Rica	Structural Adjustment I	Ln	2518	80.0	04/85
	Technical Assistance	Ln	2519	3.5	04/85
	Structural Adjustment II	Ln	3005	100.0	12/88
Dominica	Structural Adjustment	Cr	1817	3.0	06/87
Guyana	Structural Adjustment I	Ln	1948	14.0	02/81
	Structural Adjustment II	Cr	2168	78.0	06/90
Haiti	Economic Recovery	Cr	1766	40.0	03/87
	Technical Assistance	Cr	1786	3.0	04/87
Honduras	Structural Adjustment	Cr	2208	20.0	01/91
Jamaica	Structural Adjustment II	Ln	2315	60.2	06/83
	Public Administration Reform	Ln	2423	4.5	05/84
	Structural Adjustment III	Ln	2478	55.0	11/84
	Financial and Program Management	Ln	3386	11.5	06/91
Peru	Public Sector Management	Ln	2204	10.2	09/82
Uruguay	Structural Adjustment I	Ln	2836	80.0	06/87
	Structural Adjustment II	Ln	3081	140.0	06/89

Note: Includes operations through July 31, 1991. Operations in which training is the only civil service reform component have been excluded.
Source: World Bank.

ple, following rapid expansion of government employment, the civil service wage bills of many African countries rose to more than half of total government revenues. Such increases were tolerable as long as total revenues increased. But with the prolonged economic crisis and the attendant stagnation of growth in government revenues, the difficult-to-reduce wage bill began to "crowd out" other critical current expenditures, such as maintenance and depreciation and essential supplies and equipment. This led to the increasingly common situation of teachers without books, doctors lacking medicine, postal workers with no stamps to sell, and so on.

The second rationale for increased attention to civil service reform concerned low effectiveness and efficiency levels in government administrations, often reflected in the breakdown of basic public functions: the degradation of state-maintained physical infrastructure, high transaction costs and pervasive delays in doing business with government, and the prevalence of corruption among public officials. The ultimate goal of administrative reform was to improve government efficiency and effectiveness, but it was recognized that achieving this objective would be a complicated, problematic, longer-term effort. In light of this long-term goal, then, cost containment and reductions might arguably be more appropriate down the road, preceded by a systematic assessment of

**Figure 7.1 World Bank civil service operations, 1981–91
(through July 31, 1991), by region and lending instrument**

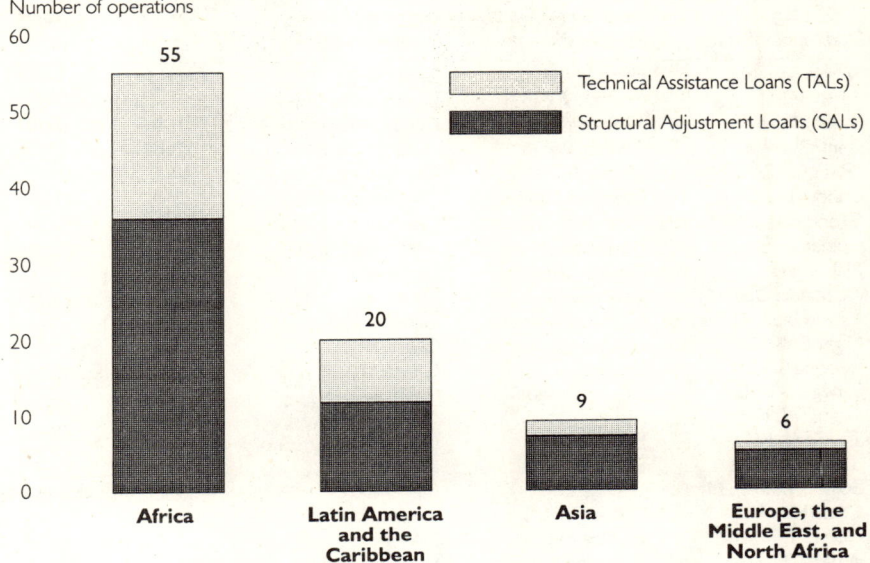

Number of operations

Technical Assistance Loans (TALs)
Structural Adjustment Loans (SALs)

Note: SALs include Economic Recovery Credits and Public Sector Reform Loans. TALs include Economic and Development Management, Institutional Development, Public Administration, and Public Sector Management. *Source:* World Bank.

what the organizations of the state need to do, what physical and human resources they need to do it, and how they should go about doing it. But the magnitude and intensity of fiscal problems have proved overwhelming, and cost containment steps have been given highest priority. Cost containment measures can thus be said to be to efficiency-effectiveness promotion what stabilization has been to the restoration of growth in adjusting economies—in other words, issues of demand management take precedence over and are easier to effect than the restarting of growth.

Cost containment

World Bank operations dealing with government pay and employment issues have supported a range of reform approaches. Many of these have been implemented on a trial-and-error basis, and we are only beginning to learn which are working and which are not. (The key measures taken by countries to reform pay and employment policies are summarized in table 7.2.) One way to analyze these actions is to rank them on a continuum of political difficulty ranging from the easiest to

Table 7.2 Components of civil service reform programs, 1981–91

Studies, diagnostics	Civil service surveys, head counts, functional reviews	Data collection, mechanization of personnel management functions	Wage and salary structure reform (decompression, grading, freezes and cuts)
Angola Eco. Mgt. Cap.	Benin SAL II	Benin SAL II	Benin SAL I
Benin SAL II	Central African	Burkina Faso SAL	Burkina Faso SAL
Burkina Faso SAL	Republic SAL I	Central African	Cameroon SAL
Central African	Central African	Republic SAL I	Central African
Republic SAL	Republic TAL I	Central African	Republic SAL
Gabon TAL	Comoros Macro-	Republic TAL II	Congo SAL
Ghana Eco. Mgt. Sup.	Eco. Ref.	Central African	Gabon SAL
Guinea TAL	Congo SAL	Republic SAL III	Gambia SAL
Mali SAL	Gambia SAL	Comoros Macro-	Ghana SAL I
Mauritania Dev. Mgt.	Ghana SA Inst. Sup.	Eco. Ref.	Ghana SA Inst. Sup.
Mozambique Rehab. III	Ghana Priv. Invest.	Gabon TAL	Ghana SAL II
Niger SAL	Ghana Eco. Mgt. Sup.	Ghana SAL I	Ghana Eco. Mgt. Sup.
Rwanda SAL	Guinea SAL	Ghana SA Inst. Sup.	Ghana Priv. Invest.
Senegal SAL III	Guinea-Bissau SAL	Ghana SAL II	Guinea SAL
Togo TAL III	Mauritania SAL	Ghana Priv. Invest.	Mali SAL
Togo SAL IV	Rwanda SAL	Ghana Eco. Mgt. Sup.	Mauritania SAL
Bolivia Eco. Mgt.	Senegal SAL III	Mali TAL	Mauritania Dev. Mgt.
Bolivia Pub. Fin. Mgt. II	Uganda ERP I	Mali SAL	Mozambique Rehab. III
Costa Rica TAL	Uganda TAL II	Mauritania SAL	Niger SAL
Haiti ERP	Zambia ERP	Mauritania Dev. Mgt.	São Tomé & Principe
Jamaica PA	Argentina PS Reform	Senegal SAL II	SAL I
Jamaica SAL III	Bolivia Eco. Mgt.	Senegal Dev. Mgt.	São Tomé & Principe
Peru PSM	Guyana SAL II	Senegal SAL IV	SAL II
Bangladesh IPC	Jamaica SAL II	Togo SAL IV	Senegal SAL II
Bangladesh PA		Uganda ERP II	Senegal SAL IV
Thailand SAL I		Argentina PS Reform	Togo TAL III
Thailand SAL II		Argentina PS Ref. TAL	Togo SAL IV
Yemen ID PA		Jamaica Fin. Mgt.	Uganda ERP I
		Bangladesh PA	Uganda ERP II
		Yemen ID PA	Zaire SAL
			Zambia ERP
			Argentina PS Reform
			Bolivia Eco. Mgt.
			Costa Rica TAL
			Dominica SAL
			Haiti ERP
			Haiti TAL
			Jamaica PA
			Jamaica SAL III
			Jamaica Fin. Mgt.
			Peru PSM
			Uruguay SAL I
			Uruguay SAL II
			Bangladesh IPC
			Bangladesh PA
			Papua New Guinea SAL
			Sri Lanka Eco. Restr.
			Thailand SAL I
			Thailand SAL II
			Tunisia SAL

Staff reductions, employment freezes, enforcement of early retirement age	Voluntary departure, redeployment, re-training, compensation, severance	Creation or strengthening of personnel management institutions	Training (public administration schools, twinning, overseas fellowships, etc.)
Benin SAL I	Benin SAL I	Benin SAL II	Angola Eco. Mgt.
Benin SAL II	Cameroon SAL	Central African	Cap. Bldg.
Cameroon SAL	Central African	Republic SAL I	Benin TA Pln. & Eco. Mgt.
Central African Republic	Republic SAL I	Central African	Gabon TAL
SAL I	Central African	Republic TAL II	Ghana SA Inst. Sup.
Central African Republic	Republic TAL II	Central African	Ghana Eco. Mgt. Sup.
SAL III	Central African	Republic SAL III	Guinea TA Eco. Mgt.
Comoros Macro-	Republic SAL III	Comoros Macro-	Guinea Eco. Mgt. II
Eco. Ref.	Comoros Macro-	Eco. Ref.	Madagascar Acct. & Mgt.
Congo SAL	Eco. Ref.	Gambia SAL	Malawi ID
Gabon SAL	Congo SAL	Ghana SAL I	Mali Eco. Mgt. & Train.
Gambia SAL	Gambia SAL	Ghana SA Inst. Sup.	Mauritania Dev. Mgt.
Ghana SAL	Ghana SAL I	Ghana SAL II	Mauritania TAL II
Ghana SA Inst. Sup.	Ghana SA Inst. Sup.	Ghana Eco. Mgt. Sup.	Mozambique Eco.
Ghana Eco. Mgt. Sup.	Ghana SAL II	Guinea SAL	& Fin. Mgt.
Ghana Priv. Invest.	Ghana Eco. Mgt. Sup.	Mali TAL	Niger Eco. & Fin. Mgt.
Guinea SAL	Guinea SAL	Mauritania Dev. Mgt.	Niger Ed.
Guinea Bissau SAL	Guinea Bissau SAL	São Tomé & Principe	Rwanda TA Pub. Fin.
Mauritania SAL	Mali SAL	SAL II	Mgt.
Niger SAL	Mauritania Dev. Mgt.	Senegal Dev. Mgt.	Senegal Dev. Mgt.
São Tomé & Principe	Senegal SAL II	Senegal SAL IV	Trinidad & Tobago TAL
SAL I	Senegal SAL IV	Togo TAL III	Uganda TAL II
Senegal SAL II	Argentina PS Reform	Uganda TAL II	Zambia TAL II
Senegal SAL IV	Costa Rica SAL	Uganda ERP II	Argentina PSM
Uganda ERP I	Guyana SAL	Argentina PS Ref. TA	Argentina PS Ref. TA
Uganda ERP II	Haiti TAL	Jamaica PA	Bolivia Pub. Fin. Mgt. II
Zambia ERP	Laos SAL	Jamaica SAL III	Brazil PSM
Argentina PS Reform		Jamaica Fin. Mgt.	Haiti Ed. & Train. IV
Costa Rica SAL		Peru PSM	Jamaica Fin. & Prog. Mgt.
Guyana SAL		Bangladesh PA	Peru PSM
Haiti ERP		Papua New Guinea	Bangladesh PA
Haiti TAL		SAL	Papua New Guinea
Honduras SAL		Papua New Guinea	PS Train.
Uruguay SAL II		Pub. Sect. Train.	Algeria TAL
Nepal SAL		Sri Lanka Eco. Restr.	Jordan Manpower Dev.
Papua New Guinea SAL		Turkey SAL V	Morocco PA
Sri Lanka Eco. Restr.		Yemen ID PA	Yemen ID PA
Turkey SAL II			
Turkey SAL III			

Note: Includes program information through July 31, 1991. SAL is Structural Adjustment Loan; TAL is Technical Assistance Loan; ERP is Economic Recovery Program; PA is Public Administration; PSM is Public Sector Management; IPC is Import Program Credit; ID is Institutional Development.
Source: World Bank.

the most difficult. Viewed this way the main steps a country can take to contain costs through pay and employment reforms are the following:

- Removal of "ghost" or nonexistent names and workers from the government payroll.
- Elimination of officially sanctioned posts that are not currently filled.
- Retrenchment of temporary or seasonal workers.
- Enforcement of retirement age.
- Freezing of recruitment.
- Elimination of guaranteed entry to the civil service from the educational or training system.
- Suspension of automatic advancement.
- "Voluntary," incentives-induced retirement of surplus workers.
- Containment of wages (restraints or freezes).
- Dismissal of serving civil servants.

These measures have been undertaken in a number of countries through World Bank–supported programs, utilizing a variety of technical tools and political techniques. Although country-specific accounts of the implementation experience with these measures are found in the case studies that follow this chapter, the following discussion conveys a more general, comparative assessment of these approaches.

Removing ghosts and posts

The reduction of civil service cadres through the elimination of ghost workers[4]—the first and least politically sensitive approach to employment reform—appears to have been an effective technique in emergency cost containment programs, although comprehensive data on reductions accomplished through this method are not available. (Table 7.3 presents various measures taken by selected countries to reduce employment.) For Ghana and Uganda, for example, ghost elimination represented a useful instrument of employment reform.[5] Ghost removal was also cited as a significant feature of reforms in various other countries. After a staff audit in 1987 in Guinea, for example, approximately 1,091 ghost names were stricken from the civil service payroll. In Cameroon approximately 5,000 fictitious names were eliminated. In general, ghost reduction incurs low political costs because the only opposing constituency are the system abusers themselves, for whom a public admission of fraud would be necessary to stake a claim to continuing payment. Indeed, in none of the above cases did ghost removal generate a public outcry.

The first step in ghost removal is a civil service census to determine the number and type of government employees. In many countries, such a poll will be the first time in many years (or perhaps the first time ever)

Table 7.3 Employment reduction by mechanism, selected countries, 1981–90
(number of reductions)

Country	Ghost removal	Enforced/early retirement	Voluntary departure	Retrenchment (regular staff)	Retrenchment (temporary staff)	Other mechanisms	Total[a]
Cameroon	5,830[b]	5,000	0	0	0	0	10,830
Central African Republic	2,950[b]	0	1,200	350–400	0	0	4,500–4,550
Congo	0	0	0	0	0	2,848[c]	2,848
Gambia, The	0	0	0	919	2,871	0	3,790
Ghana	11,000[d]	4,235[e]	0	44,375[e]	0	0	48,610
Guinea	1,091[f]	10,236	1,744	0	0	25,793[g]	38,864
Guinea-Bissau	800[d]	945	1,960	921	0	0	3,826
Laos	0	0	16,890	0	0	0	16,890
Mali	0	0	600	0	0	0	600
Papua New Guinea	0	0	0	2,300	0	0	2,300
São Tomé and Príncipe	0	0	4	0	294[h]	0	298
Senegal	497	747[i]	1,283	0	0	0	2,527
Sri Lanka	0	30,000[j]	0	0	0	12,000[c]	12,000
Uganda	20,000[k]	0	0	0	0	0	20,000

a. Gross figures not adjusted for new recruitment and attrition.
b. Elimination of ghosts and double payments.
c. Attrition through hiring freeze.
d. Refers only to ghosts identified. Their removal has not been verified in technical analysis.
e. Includes staff in district assemblies and the education services.
f. Ghosts in Guinea Conakry. A second census in 1989–90 identified a large number of additional ghosts.
g. Of this figure, 10,810 officials were assigned to a "personnel bank" and placed on administrative leave, and 14,983 were removed from civil service rolls through liquidation and the transfer of employees of mining joint venture company rolls. Whether all of those placed on administrative leave have left the service or not remains unclear.
h. An undetermined but small portion of these may be regular staff.
i. An additional 2,123 officials have applied for voluntary departure or early retirement.
j. Officials who have opted for early retirement and are scheduled to leave the civil service by 1/31/91.
k. Estimate based on savings from ghost removal exercise divided by average civil service wages.
Source: World Bank.

an attempt has been made to get an accurate picture of public employment, establishing who is, and who is not, legitimately enrolled on the civil service rosters and payroll. Such a step is paramount for all subsequent reforms.

Civil service censuses and payroll sanitization have been features of a number of pay and employment reforms. Few reforming governments have ignored the issue, though some have proceeded without a cleanup exercise. Laos, for example, is reported to have shed an estimated 10 to 30 percent of government workers using a payroll listing as the sole form of personnel record. For most countries, though, prior data collection and cleanup are necessary. These serve several useful purposes, including regularizing payroll lists through the elimination of ghosts, quantifying the often large ranks of temporary staff, and providing information leading to the enforcement of the statutory retirement age.

The usefulness of a census is related to its level of comprehensiveness and sophistication. The most elemental census-taking exercise may be little more than a "head count" that simply establishes the number and the structure of government employment (that is, the number of employees at various professional levels or in different regional locations). Censuses of the head count variety have tended to be designed and carried out by governments themselves. The results of these counts have often been disappointing. Findings have been incomplete and inaccurate, mainly because counts have been based on existing civil service rolls rather than verification of physically present employees. Although not expensive to undertake, head counts of this sort can still be a waste of scarce resources, since they must usually be followed by more rigorous censuses carried out with technical assistance from outside consultants. On the other hand, even flawed head counts can serve useful purposes. In Ghana the initial civil service survey revealed the overall structure of employment, which at least suggested overstaffing at lower grades of the bureaucracy, providing a starting point for policy reform discussions.

Even censuses that are more sophisticated in their validation methodologies may have only limited applications. Successive censuses carried out by international consultants in Ghana used the payroll mechanism to count civil servants, requiring that legitimate payroll claims be made in person and that each bonafide employee receive a numbered chit to be presented thereafter to collect his or her pay. Although some impostors might have slipped through this process, the likelihood was that fraud was significantly reduced. The Ghanaian census exercise also stopped short of establishing durable links between the computerized payroll system in the Ministry of Finance, the personnel records in the Office of the Head of the Civil Service, and the annual budget. The censuses did, however, provide important, one-shot, baseline data to begin the employment reduction program, thus fulfilling an essential function.

At least two problems are associated with the Ghanaian approach. One is that, without the institutional capacity to utilize the data in a computerized monitoring system, the quality of census data is subject to rapid erosion. Results become outdated quickly as new recruits enter the civil service (openly or clandestinely) and as other employees leave. Personnel data that might provide an overall profile of the administration also change, so that information about aspects such as the age structure and promotion patterns is no longer valid. Moreover, it is important to be able to capitalize on the results of the census quickly because the patience of civil servants to endure successive surveys wears thin, as has been the case in Ghana after three such exercises in a period of a few years. But "doing it right" also imposes administrative and financial burdens. In Madagascar the census was more rigorous; enumerators were hired and civil servants had to be present at the place of census. The penalty for noncooperation was severe: suspension of paycheck. Thus, participation was high. The cost of this elaborate exercise was a nontrivial 5 percent of the wage bill. Furthermore, the organizational requirements for execution of the census—organizing review committees, engaging enumerators, establishing census centers at both central and district levels—were also considerable.

In general, recent experience with census design and implementation suggests that such mechanisms are important first steps to getting the reform process moving, that their design should be kept simple but strategic in the sense that they should be conceived as part of the establishment of an ongoing system of controls,[6] and that their successful conceptualization and implementation generally requires external technical assistance.

Two other measures with relatively low political costs can be implemented to reduce civil service employment. One is the elimination of officially sanctioned but currently unfilled posts in the civil service. Such posts may have had (usually nominal) budgetary funds slotted against them, and thus their abolition leads to savings. Their removal also lowers expectations about future employment by prospective civil service entrants, producing a forward-looking orientation toward permanently downsized government. The main constituency for retaining such posts is found among recent public service institute graduates and among those higher- and middle-level bureaucrats whose administrative power derives at least to some extent from the number of staff under their supervision. Although the elimination of unfilled posts is in theory an "easy" downsizing measure, longer-term costs can be incurred from the inability of government to fill essential vacancies when they arise. In the

Gambia, for example, the Ministry of Finance's zeal in adhering to its administrative reform policy of post elimination prevented the Public Management Office from filling staff inspector positions, ironically inhibiting the implementation of the very personnel measures civil service reforms were intended to carry out.

Laying off temporary or seasonal workers is another employment reduction measure that can be implemented with relative political ease. Such workers can be dismissed without elaborate legal obligations or severance and pension entitlements. Their expectations about employment security often tend to be low. They are likely to be unskilled, uneducated, and unorganized in labor unions or political movements or parties and therefore less capable of mounting opposition to layoffs. The bulk of early government employment cuts in the Gambia were applied to temporary workers. This category had been a nontrivial source of employment expansion in many government sectors; the hiring of such workers had been subject to few controls because they do not figure in the civil service establishment proper.

Enforcing retirement rules

Strict enforcement of retirement for overage civil servants has been a feature of a number of reform programs (including those in Benin, Cameroon, Costa Rica, Gabon, Ghana, Guinea, and Senegal). In Guinea, for example, all civil servants over 55, or all those who had completed thirty years of service, were to be placed in automatic and effective retirement. The result was a reduction of more than 7,000 employees. Even though such programs present an attractive option for employment reduction because they cause little political opposition, their impact has been minimal. This is due in part to the unreliability of most information about age—even when gathered by modern survey techniques through civil service censuses—and in part to the overall age profile of most civil services in most developing countries. This is especially the case in Africa, where the average age of civil servants is below 40. Thus, the removal of overage employees usually targets a small group, and often one that is quite valuable, considering the dearth of trained professionals.

Freezing civil service recruitment

Freezing or limiting civil service recruitment is an often applied mechanism for reducing government employment. It is marginally more difficult on political grounds than ghost elimination or enforcement of retirement age. The difficulty is due to the disruptions that might be caused by aspiring civil service candidates, such as occurred during student strikes in Côte d'Ivoire. Hiring freezes have been widely used, with varying results. Senegal instituted a hiring freeze in 1983 and created a high-level interministerial commission to supervise the process. The commission, the secretariat of which met weekly, reviewed all departures from the civil service, with a view to determining whether it was necessary to fill the particular vacancy; if so, with whom; and if not, whether the staff of the organization could then be reduced by one or whether the organization had some pressing personnel need in another area that justified a position. Between 1,000 and 1,500 reductions (amounting to less than 1 percent of currently serving civil servants) were reported to have been effected in the first two years of the commission's operation. Variations on this theme include allowing hiring only if it does not result in a net creation of civil service posts (Kenya has tried this); or limiting hiring to essential professional staff (in force in Malawi, Mali, and Nigeria).

Eliminating guaranteed entry rights

Automatic hiring has been discontinued in some African countries that had traditionally guaranteed government jobs to school graduates. This reform measure turns out to be somewhat complicated to implement, as the case of Senegal demonstrates. When the hiring freeze was instituted in Senegal, there were more than forty government schools and training centers. Prior to the freeze, entry to these centers equaled entry to the civil service. The freeze forced the Senegalese to curtail severely the admission to and the ongoing activities of these centers; the result to date has been the continued existence of most of these institutions, but with ever-declining numbers of students or trainees. Still, the Senegalese government, as most others have done when faced with this problem, maintained its employment commitment to those already in the training pipeline, meaning that it may be some years before an effect from this element of restructuring can be perceived. The Senegal case raises another issue: the parallel reform in the parapublic sector is resulting in reduced transfers to and, it is hoped, eventual reduction in the numbers of public enterprises. But many of the staff now employed in Senegalese public enterprises are "tenured" civil servants who chose or were assigned to service in the enterprise. If they are dismissed they have the legal right to a post in the civil service proper. Legal rights can be amended, of course, but only at the expense of time, effort, and some of the government's political base.

In general, the record of both hiring freezes and elimination of guaranteed employment appears mixed. Where these measures have signified a halt to automatic civil service recruitment from universities or public administration training institutions, they apply a significant brake on civil service expansion. But recruitment freezes may constrain government from achieving the necessary skills mix through renovation of its cadres with young entrants.

Suspending automatic advancement

One frequent cost containment measure in the interstice between employment and pay reforms is the suspension of automatic increases and step advancements. This is of particular relevance in the francophone African countries where advances in grade and pay tend to be based solely on years of service. In such instances, freezing recruitment or even making modest reductions in the total number of civil servants sometimes has a limited effect on wage bill growth. Senegal, for example, froze recruitment as early as 1983, and even succeeded over two years in reducing total numbers. Still, it found that automatic step and grade increases kept the wage bill on the increase. The fiscal result of what the Senegalese regarded as a heroic and politically dangerous effort was reduction in the annual average growth rate of the wage bill from 14 percent to 9 percent. In order to dampen this sort of wage drift in the civil service, Burundi and Côte d'Ivoire temporarily suspended automatic pay increases. Burkina Faso also restructured its pay system so that promotions are now offered on a selective rather than automatic basis.

Implementing early retirement and voluntary departure programs

Increasingly, countries find that implementing the "easier" options does not result in sufficient cost cutting. They thus begin to explore ways to actually cut numbers of serving employees. Even at this stage, governments are loath to take the most difficult political route—that of involuntary dismissal. A number of strategies have been tried with varying degrees of success. Usually, these options are offered as one among several in a mixed approach to staff reductions.

Early retirement is an option that has been proposed in several countries. This program targets civil servants who are within a few years of normal retirement age and either pays them a lump sum separation package with pension benefits that begin with normal retirement age or starts their pensions at the early departure date. Although systematic analysis has not yet been performed on these types of programs, their benefits (in terms of reduced numbers and wage bill decreases) would seem to be minimal and their costs significant. First, the net present value of the savings stream is likely to be low since the savings represent only three to four years of staff reductions instead of savings that would occur if younger workers were to be removed. Furthermore, early retirement programs target the most experienced employees—both at managerial and support levels. This poses a particularly acute cost for those civil services in which once-high standards of professional performance and training have broken down. Early retirement means that the collective experience of the older employees, who might be the sole keepers of the flame of an earlier, more efficient era, is lost to the newer generation.

Voluntary departure schemes have been a feature of several civil service reform programs. In general, such schemes are viewed as politically palatable because they are not coercive. These programs, not unlike early retirement schemes, can be problematic in that they often attract the best and brightest civil servants, the very ones whom government would most wish to retain. Carried out on a large scale, voluntary departure schemes are expensive. In Guinea voluntary departure with an associated premium was to be financed with an earmarked fund of 6.5 billion Guinean francs (GF). The benefits involved a three-option plan in which departees might choose to draw a salary with accompanying rice rations for sixty months, take 40 percent in cash and the remainder in regular salary payments, or take a share of the severance allowance as a down payment on a new private sector business venture. In its proposed voluntary departure scheme, Senegal would offer sixty months of salary to voluntarily departing civil servants. The government has requested financial support for this scheme from the World Bank.

Although voluntary departure programs are obviously politically easier than involuntary ones, they cannot solve large-scale redundancy problems at affordable cost for most countries, particularly when carried out without external financing (as is predominantly the case). On a smaller, more targeted level, however, voluntary schemes might be combined with retrenchment to reduce employment.

Containing wages

Restraining or freezing wages is another frequently used measure to contain costs. Ways of instituting a wage freeze or at least restraining wages are numerous: holding wages to existing levels in current terms; holding wages steady in constant terms; allowing increases equal to a portion of, but less than the rate of, inflation; or agreeing that the wage bill cannot surpass a particular ratio (for example, as a percentage of government expenditure). Although such measures may be politically distasteful, governments have clearly viewed them as the lesser of two evils when faced with the alternative option of employment cuts. Such choices were for a long time reinforced by external actors, especially the International Monetary Fund (IMF), whose conditionality was largely indifferent to alternative methods of wage bill reduction as long as personnel expenditures were decreasing. Wage restraint has resulted in the overall erosion of salaries and the particular decline of professional-level wages in the civil service in many countries. The result was the compressed wage structure so common to African civil services, often betraying regime preferences for financial penalties falling on higher- rather than lower-level employees, calculated to be the more important political constituency. Sometimes wage freezes are effected through wage ceilings for each grade level. Such freezes have often been obviated by structural grade drift whereby a general inflation of grade levels occurs, promoting staff arbitrarily in order to raise salaries.

Retrenching civil servants

Retrenchment—the direct and explicit dismissal of redundant civil servants—is the most difficult and politically contentious measure used to reduce employment. Governments have resisted these remedies, adopting them only as last-resort options. This reluctance is related to the nature of the state in many developing countries. An important purpose of government is construed as the distribution of political patronage and social welfare through the provision of public posts to loyal followers and otherwise deserving clients. Overt employment reduction thus strikes at this basic definition of the role of government. Moreover, the fear of most political regimes that retrenchment will incite destabilizing social upheaval and political opposition serves to stiffen resistance to overt employment reduction measures. The task of opponents to staff cuts has been made that much easier by concerns about the capacity of the (often fledgling) private sector to absorb retrenched workers. The degree to which these fears have foundation must be subjected to analysis of the empirical experience with these reforms so far. Considerably more analysis needs to be done, but it would appear that the potential for political destabilization from such reforms is much smaller and the extent of labor mobility much greater than most governments anticipated.

Governments' anxieties about swallowing the bitter retrenchment pill are reflected in difficulties and delays in country compliance with staff reduction conditionality in World Bank adjustment operations. Bank-country dialogue often results in tacit acceptance of fewer dismissals and lengthier time frames than originally negotiated. Frequently, second- and third-generation adjustment operations repeat, in somewhat stronger terms, employment reduction conditions contained in the first structural adjustment loan (for SAL 1, "enforce retirement age regulations"; for SAL 2, "strictly enforce retirement age regulations").

Despite the resistance of governments to undertake what they perceive to be politically risky measures, retrenchment has taken place in several countries. Although reliable employment figures are difficult to come by, just under 45,000 civil servants (roughly 12 percent of the total) were retrenched in Ghana since the inception of their program. In the Gambia, following a census and staff audit, approximately 3,350 government employees (including 2,600 temporary employees) were dismissed. And in the Central African Republic between 350 and 400 civil servants have been removed so far, with more reductions planned for subsequent years.[7] Perhaps the most impressive cases come from Latin America. The World Bank–financed Public Sector Reform Loan in Argentina provided support for the net reduction of 120,000 civil servants, about 20 percent of the starting base.[8] Independent of external financing, Chile appears to have cut 57 percent of central government employment, reducing civil service cadres from 305,000 to 130,000 between 1973 and 1990, independently of external support.[9]

Governments have frequently been able to carry out these retrenchments with the help of a variety of techniques designed to mitigate the political and social impact of employment cuts and to consolidate the technical basis for the reform program. Some of these techniques are elaborated below.

Public information campaigns were seen as a useful tool to defuse opposition and assuage employee concerns about their fate. In Guinea and the Central African Republic (and planned for Senegal) expatriate consultants assisted government in the design of public information campaigns to inform government employees, through radio broadcasts and newspaper articles, of detailed administrative and financial aspects of the staff reduction programs. This was reportedly useful in informing employees of their rights under the law and in giving them sufficiently advanced warning to arrange for alternative employment.

Competency exams constitute another technical support mechanism for retrenchment. In Guinea, competency tests for sitting civil servants provided technical criteria to determine which personnel would be classified as surplus. Those who passed the test were to be retained, and those who failed would be entitled to a severance package related to length of service. (They would not, however, be able to opt for the more lucrative package offered those electing voluntary departure.) Recruitment in subsequent years would be determined according to the new qualifications testing, and the promotion of employees retained would follow a logical procedure coupled with training. Although the exams were first geared to university-level standards in France for professional-level positions, the requirements were later relaxed to fit local capabilities. The objectivity and credibility of the program were validated by the presence of external consultants, and this apparently enhanced acceptance of the practice. Despite this acceptance of the principle of testing, the exercise has proved cumbersome to administer, causing conflict and delays in the overall civil service reform program in Guinea.

Personnel banks were coupled with competency testing in Guinea. A special personnel bank was created in which those government employees who passed exams, but were considered otherwise redundant, were placed in a special category. These people remain on the payroll for six months. If they do not find jobs, they are removed and dismissed. They also have the option of leaving of their own volition with a severance package somewhat less generous than that offered to voluntary departees. There are approximately 14,487 employees in this category as of this writing. (This figure may include some 3,400 public enterprise employees, however.) The administration of this personnel bank has proved exceedingly complicated, and there is no clear indication that any of those placed in the pool have actually left government. There is concern that this category of employees will continue to impose an onerous burden on the wage bill without contributing to civil service productivity. Moreover, the presence in government of an (officially) idle class of disgruntled employees may demoralize other government personnel. A similar mechanism has been utilized in Argentina where between 70,000 and 90,000 civil servants are being removed to a personnel bank with an average of six months' income maintenance until they are redeployed elsewhere in government or dismissed from public service with severance.

Severance packages have accompanied retrenchment programs in most countries. Although the absolute value of these separation packages is impossible to compare, the formulas themselves appear to be relatively generous (table 7.4). These formulas are mostly embellishments on the basic legal obligations of government to dismissed employees, worked out through negotiations among various interested parties. The size as well as the administration of the severance packages appear to be among the most important determinants of the level of acceptance of the overall employment reduction program by affected employees. In Ghana delays in the calculation and distribution of separation entitlement in the first year of the reform program stirred some disruptive opposition among affected civil servants. Protests were smoothed over in the second year when severance payments began to be awarded on time.

The importance of severance payments in facilitating the retrenchment process has stirred a debate about how such benefits should be financed. So far, severance has been paid for directly by governments in a few cases such as Argentina, utilizing counterpart funds made available by World Bank policy-based adjustment loans for public sector management reform. To the extent that severance constitutes a recurrent cost, the World Bank has, on principle, refrained from supporting them. The growing importance attached to the downsizing of central government (and in parallel, state enterprises) and the centrality of severance packages to the success of these exercises have caused some to advocate a revision of this policy, however. Proponents of a policy shift argue that donor financing of onetime severance payments represents a crucial investment in sound government that will pay off in the long term. As of this writing, the policy remains unchanged.

Functional reviews have provided an important technical rationale for employment cuts in some countries. These are essentially an organizational audit of the functions of component agencies of government, and the number and type of staff presently carrying them out, in an attempt to determine the optimal staffing arrangements for basic government tasks. These reviews are conducted on a sample or selected priority list of central government ministries and often consist of a variety of activities, including:

- Job inspections, which review the structure and staffing of agencies in government to assess what work needs to be done to fulfill the organization's objectives; whether the organizational structure is appropriate for its activities; whether the staffing numbers, grades, and levels of responsibility are appropriate to the needs of the

Table 7.4 Severance formulas, selected countries

Country	Formula
Argentina	Varies, but on the average provides 75 percent of basic salary for six months, followed by severance payment averaging US$3,000 (depending on years of service), which is paid in six installments
Central African Republic	Forty months' salary and the employee's accumulated pension fund contribution
Gambia, The	1.2 months' salary per year of service[a]
Ghana	Four months' basic salary, plus two months' basic salary per year of service
Guinea	Flat amount equal to about five years' basic salary for the average worker, with 30 percent paid up front and the balance paid in twenty monthly installments[b]
Guinea-Bissau	One year's salary paid in monthly installments
Laos	One year's salary

a. Nonpermanent staff received only one month's salary.
b. Voluntary departure program formula.
Source: World Bank.

work; and whether some degree of consistency is maintained across agencies.

- Organization and method studies, which evaluate the efficiency of a particular service to identify main performance weaknesses and to find and remove bottlenecks and institute simplifying procedures, thus affording staff savings and promoting efficiency.
- Budgetary analysis, which examines financial data to pinpoint areas where manpower is being inefficiently employed in order to identify potential targets for budgetary savings, often analyzing by exception: for example, focusing on agencies where the proportion of personnel emoluments to total expenditure is particularly high, or where trends in personnel emoluments have deviated significantly from observed trends in other program expenditure.
- Ratio analysis, which applies staffing norms tailored to the precise functions and objectives of the organization or sector concerned, for example, medical officer–bed ratios, teacher–nonteaching staff ratios, agricultural extension officer–population ratios, and cost of tax revenues collected per tax collector. These ratios are then reviewed against government targets to assist in highlighting regional disparities and, in particular, in flagging areas of apparent staff shortages or surpluses relative to the average. Ratio analysis is indicative, pointing to the need for more specific policy reviews and, ultimately, more detailed plans for recruitment, training, and staff development. In the immediate, it helps identify functions that are obsolete, overlapping, or otherwise redundant.

Functional reviews are difficult to administer (they are usually carried out through technical assistance), and they are time-consuming. Indeed, in the two cases where they figured most prominently in the reform program (the Gambia and Ghana) many of the employment cuts actually took place before the functional reviews had been started. Nonetheless, carrying out these exercises even well into the implementation of a retrenchment program provides an assurance that there is at least an intention to pursue staff reductions in a rational, technical, and just manner. This assurance appears to have helped quiet opposition to the retrenchment programs.

Retraining, redeployment, and credit programs are offered by some countries, including training for jobs in the informal sector, public works programs, and credit schemes at favorable interest rates for small business or agriculture. On a technical basis, these programs have been less than fully successful; in some instances their justification may be questioned.

First, retraining for informal sector activities, which is where many redundant workers tend to go, may be largely irrelevant. In Ghana, for example, where this type of program was offered through the Program of Action to Mitigate the Social Costs of Adjustment and Development, the demand for such training was low. In most countries the existent institutions do not have the expertise to handle training for the informal sector or to accommodate the potentially large number of trainees in the event of massive public sector layoffs. An attempt was also made in Ghana to provide training through an apprenticeship program, but this proved difficult and costly to organize and ultimately reached only a limited target group. This program was undersubscribed as well. Credit for small business and agricultural activities, another aspect of the program, also generated little demand. In the Gambia the Institute of Business Advisory Services administered a similar program, which received roughly 700 applications (out of more than 2,000 workers laid off by the government) and provided credit or training services, or both, to only about 300 people.

Public works programs have been used on a limited basis to cushion the shock of retrenchment. In Bolivia a public works program was organized through the Emergency Social Fund to provide transitional employment for tin mine workers dismissed from COMIBOL, the state mining company. It appears that many miners did not take advantage of these programs. They chose instead to use the cash payment provided by generous separation packages (up to US$3,000 per worker)[10] to relocate and start enterprises in the informal sector, or to find construction employment elsewhere.

Small business credit programs have been created, for example in Guinea, where the government set up a special office, the Bureau d'Aide à la Reconversion des Agents de la Fonction Publique, to assist departing civil servants in applying for credit to finance private businesses. There is some concern that this credit program may have permanently damaged the country's credit system; indeed, there are now on the books large numbers of loans to departed civil servants with little hope of recoverability. The Gambia's small business credit scheme for redundant civil servants fared little better. Its loan recovery rate was 30 percent (as compared with 65 percent, for example, for a European Community–financed credit scheme with more stringent eligibility requirements).

This experience suggests that the technical rationale for these programs is weak. It would appear that many civil servants being retrenched neither need nor expect to be retrained or redeployed. Most go into the informal sector for which there are few adapted credit schemes. It would be administratively easier, and would probably have a more beneficial economic impact, to simply award cash severance payments to departing staff.

Another point is that redeployment programs require considerable institutional capacity to administer. In the Gambia the program only got off the ground one and a half years after retrenchment had begun. In Ghana the lag time was two and a half years. In Guinea the program began on the anticipated date, but proved very difficult to manage. Typically, there are a number of institutions whose activities must be coordinated, and the preparation requirements are considerable. Moreover, because existing training and credit institutions are inadequate, new mechanisms often are required, imposing substantial additional costs.

For some countries, the need for special mechanisms to rechannel labor into private markets may be less than anticipated. There is some preliminary evidence to suggest that labor absorption has been easier than expected—or than governments typically contend. In Africa, for example, urban workers appear to have moved with relative ease into agricultural activities (which, in many cases, partially occupied civil servants on a moonlighting basis even before retrenchment). In Bolivia the ability of the informal sector to absorb redundant public sector employees appears to have been considerable. The technical rationale for retraining and credit programs under these circumstances is thus somewhat fragile.

These programs do perhaps have an important symbolic value to the extent that dismissed workers place value on access to this kind of assistance, whether they avail themselves of it or not. Such programs thus serve an important function in defusing potential discontent among retrenched employees. In general, it may make more sense to concentrate on severance packages in designing employment reduction programs, as this is where most employee interest and demand are focused.

Rationalization of remuneration

Increasingly, pay and employment reform programs have also been addressing specific pay conditions for civil servants in an attempt to remove demotivating distortions in government remuneration structures. A number of reform programs have aimed at improving pay conditions, rationalizing the overall system of remuneration, and building an institutional capacity in government to formulate and implement sound salary policies on an ongoing basis. Such measures are more difficult to rank according to their political feasibility than employment reform actions because the winners and losers they create are less predictable, and the relative power of the affected interest groups varies from one country case to another.

Monetization of remuneration, for example, may be politically easy or difficult depending on the degree to which monetized salaries compensate for lost nonwage benefits, the nature of the existing system of distribution of nonwage benefits among different employee levels, and the extent to which potential losers and winners are influential or organized politically. Similarly, wage decompression tends to be applauded by higher-level staff and opposed by lower-echelon workers. In countries where the latter are unionized, organized, and form an important support base for the ruling regime, wage compression may be a more politically volatile issue than in countries where this group is weaker and less highly mobilized. Thus constrained, the following remuneration rationalization measures are not discussed in order of political difficulty.

Monetizing remuneration

Rationalizing remuneration by reducing the proportion of pay from nonwage benefits has been an important objective of civil service reform. In many countries these benefits constitute an unacceptably large percentage of total compensation, as real wages have been steadily eroded by inflation and expanding employment. Several governments have taken concrete steps to reduce allowances. Cameroon reduced housing allowances, for example, Guinea's rice rations were eliminated, and special performance premiums were abolished in Bolivia. The impact of these measures appears to be negligible. Nonwage benefits as a percentage of total compensation have increased on average by nearly 8 percent for those countries for which data were available (table 7.5).

One reason for the slow movement on this issue is the difficulty in getting systematic information and disentangling the enormously intricate webs of benefit structures. For many countries—in particular, those in francophone Africa—it may well be that reform will only result from

Table 7.5 Composition of civil service remuneration, selected countries, various years

Country	Year	Benefits as a percentage of total compensation	Salary as a percentage of total compensation
Bolivia	1982	70	30
Cameroon	1987	19	81
Central African Republic	1984	38	62
	1987	41	59
Gambia, The	1982	12	88
	1988	22	78
Senegal	1980–85	25	75
	1989	43	57

Source: World Bank; Coopers and Lybrand, "Efficacité de la Fonction Publique: Programme de Réduction" (Senegal); David Lindauer, Oey Meesook, and Parita Suebsaeng, "Government Wage Policy in Africa: Some Findings and Policy," *World Bank Research Observer,* vol 3, no. 1 (January 1988), pp. 1–25.

a simple declaration nullifying the entirety of the present convoluted benefit system, and replacing it with a salary-based reward system. Unfortunately, it is politically difficult to dispense with nonwage mechanisms without redressing the inadequacies of the salary structure that stimulated the emergence of nonwage distortions in the first place. Bolivia's recent attempts to legislate a more rational salary system have been circumvented, for example, by spontaneous nonwage bonus features to reward some employees outside of the strict wage system.

Equalizing pay discrepancies

Inequities in pay among various parts of government have also been the target of rationalization. Although civil servants are, in principle, paid according to a unified scale, some high-visibility ministries, such as the finance ministry, may offer pay and benefits that exceed those of less prestigious ones, such as ministries of agriculture or education. Civil servants have been hired under widely varying remuneration policies, with different rights and benefits, even in countries with unified civil service recruitment rules.

Closing the gap in pay and benefits among different parts of the public sector was the goal of some reform programs. In Jamaica, as in many other countries, parastatal bodies were able to attract qualified candidates away from the civil service because they offered substantially higher salaries. The World Bank's third structural adjustment loan instituted the conditionality that higher-level management posts in the civil service be remunerated at 85 percent of equivalent grades in statutory bodies through a three-phase pay hike. Although two raises for managers did occur, the opposition to differential wage increases from unionized civil servants at lower skill levels prevented the third increase from being enacted. As a result of this delay and the continuing wage erosion through inflation, qualified professionals and managers continue to be in short supply in central government.[11] In general, policies to promote civil service pay parity with parastatals have been pursued only on a limited basis, reflecting increasing questions about the feasibility and the wisdom of linking state enterprise pay to bureaucratic norms rather than profitability and productivity.[12]

Simplifying the salary structure

In some countries, salary grids and job classification systems have become overly complicated and elaborate, drawing fine distinctions among employees based on very small increments. Pay and grading studies have been carried out in a number of countries, resulting in recommendations to simplify these salary grids. The case of Dominica was extreme, but not extraordinary; the remuneration system, consisting of more than 100 pay scales, was converted to a structure of fourteen grades for middle and lower management; almost all jobs are now included in this new pay scale system. In Guinea the problem was less severe; consultants performed a job evaluation exercise and reduced nineteen grades to twelve.

Decompressing wages

For many countries, the erosion of average wages was the big problem to be addressed by pay reform. But particularly in Africa, a principal objective of pay reform is the decompression of the wage structure. This is essential in view of the difficulties in recruitment and retention of higher-level staff whose salaries have sunk to very low multiples of the lowest ranked workers. (Table 7.6 shows compression ratios, that is, the

Table 7.6 Wage compression ratios, selected countries, various years

Country	Earliest period	Latest period	Reference period
Argentina	4 : 1	—	pre-1990
Burundi	17 : 1	—	1984
Cameroon	22 : 1	—	1989
Central African Republic	9 : 1	9 : 1	1985–88
Gambia, The	8 : 1	6: 1	1985–88
Ghana	6 : 1	10 : 1	1984–92
Guinea	9 : 1	5 : 1	1985–89
Guinea-Bissau	5 : 1	4 : 1	1988–89
Laos	3 : 1	7 : 1	pre-1988–1988
Malawi	33 : 1	30 : 1	1975–83
Mali	16 : 1	—	1985
Mauritania	7 : 1	3 : 1	1975–85
Mozambique	2 : 1	9 : 1 [a]	1985–90
Niger	18 : 1	15 : 1	1975–85
Nigeria	18 : 1	9 : 1	1975–83
Senegal	8 : 1	6 : 1	1980–85
Sudan	13 : 1	9 : 1	1975–84
Togo	12 : 1	—	1985
Uganda	6 : 1	—	1983/84
Zaire	47 : 1	—	1985
Zambia	14 : 1	7 : 1	1975–84

— Not available.

Note: The compression ratio is the ratio of the salary of the top civil servant (for example, permanent secretary equivalent) to that of the lowest civil servant (for example, messenger).

a. Excludes technical subsidy paid in U.S. dollars, which would increase ratio to 17:1.

Source: World Bank; D. Robinson, "Civil Service Pay in Africa," ILO, Geneva, 1990; David Lindauer, Oey Meesook, and Parita Suebsaeng, "Government Wage Policy in Africa: Some Findings and Policy Issues," *World Bank Research Observer,* vol. 3, no. 1 (January 1988), pp. 1–25.

ratio of the salary of the highest- to the lowest-echelon civil servant, for selected countries.) Decompression of the salary structure was a goal in Ghana where in 1984 the compression ratio was approximately 2.5 to 1. It rapidly moved to 5.7 to 1 in that year, and by 1989 it had decompressed to 7.8 to 1. By 1991 it had reached 10 to 1, thus falling short of the government's stated objective of a 13-to-1 ratio, but clearly moving in the right direction. In Laos salaries decompressed from 3 to 1 to 7 to 1 under a program supported in its later stages by the IMF and the World Bank.

Providing salary supplements

Where reform of the salary structure has not been imminent, a number of countries have resorted to interim programs aimed at attracting qualified professionals into government. Salary supplements are the most common mechanism used to compensate for low civil service pay at upper echelons. Salary supplements appear to be widely utilized. In countries where international donor assistance provides an alternative employment market for skilled professionals, salary supplements may be provided by externally financed projects in several different ways. Civil servants may accept supplements to top up their civil service pay without taking leave from the government rolls. In Mozambique, for example, Bank and other donor projects have hired individuals working in ministries to staff special project units at higher salaries while still retaining their government jobs. The obvious potential for conflict of interest is enormous. Moreover, the demoralizing impact of such mechanisms on those government employees lacking access to topping-up benefits can be devastating.

Some civil servants may take leave or actually separate from the civil service. Although this is a "cleaner" arrangement in principle, the cost may well be the loss of the skilled individual from government service over the short and long runs. In such countries as Mozambique where human capital is so scarce, this brain drain could paralyze government functions. Moreover, on a large scale, such supplementation is affordable only with sustained external financing. The siphoning off and rewarding of the best and the brightest undercuts government motivation to improve conditions for the majority of individuals.

In some countries salary supplements consist of those payments provided to higher-level civil servants over and above their civil service grade salary. These payments are offered largely because it is feared that, without topped up salaries, the most capable personnel will be lured into internationally financed projects or better-paying parastatals, or (where this is an option) into the private sector. There is little doubt that salary supplements have a corrosive and distorting effect on civil service morale and management. Most important, they undermine the possibilities of meaningful structural reform in the longer term. The insidious aspect of this problem is that in many instances the offenders are the donors.

In a few instances, innovations have been proposed to deal with this problem. In Bolivia international donors contributed US$6 million to form a foundation to finance 500 key high-level government positions— all performance-evaluated—outside of the budget and outside of the IMF targets for the wage bill. While this was not seen as a long-term solution to the salary problem, it was viewed as a means of bringing some order to the chaotic pay supplement situation. In Ghana the World Bank assisted an innovative skills mobilization scheme to finance local consultancies for key government positions essential to the economic recovery program. Fees for these consultancies were to be at local private sector rates—well above civil service levels—and the positions were not to be filled by serving government employees. The idea was to attract skilled professionals from the private sector, and perhaps even repatriate skilled Ghanaians living overseas. After considerable debate over the terms of these contracts, the scheme was made operational, but appears to have had little impact. At time of writing, forty-one people had been identified as eligible for the scheme and registered on a consultants roster, but only three government slots were actually filled through this mechanism.

The impact of reforms

The above discussion has focused on aspects of implementation of government pay and employment reforms. Although a fair amount can be determined about how these programs are working from this implementational perspective, a sense of the real contribution of these reform programs can only be achieved by looking more closely at their outcomes and trying to assess the degree to which they have accomplished their stated objectives. (Note again that the usual warnings obtain about the limited extent and low quality of the data.)

Wage bill

The primary objective of most reforms was to reduce the aggregate wage bill. To what extent has this occurred in recent years? Is there any way to link changes (positive or negative) in the wage bill to government pay and employment reforms? (Table 7.7 shows nominal wage bill trends for selected countries.) For the fourteen countries with available

Table 7.7 Government wage trends, selected countries, 1980–88

Country	1980	1981	1982	1983	1984	1985	1986	1987	1988
Bolivia (thousands of Bolivianos)									
Wages and salaries	10,106.2	8,341.1	7,600.9	6,640.3	6,755.3	7,662.1	5,206.1	6,101.7	6,594.2
Materials and supplies	1,181.9	1,699.2	1,035.5	1,090.1	1,025.5	1,389.3	1,656.8	1,441.2	1,219.7
Total expenditures	19,079.0	13,893.4	11,791.0	11,091.3	11,148.7	12,657.0	10,862.9	13,247.9	11,450.6
W&S/total expenditures (%)	53.0	60.0	64.5	59.9	60.6	60.5	47.9	46.1	57.6
M&S/total expenditures (%)	6.2	12.2	8.8	9.8	9.2	11.0	15.3	10.9	10.7
Cameroon (billions of CFA francs)									
Wages and salaries	—	—	172.6	220.0	224.5	280.0	265.0	—	—
Goods and services	—	—	—	—	—	—	—	—	—
Current expenditures	—	—	392.8	440.5	455.5	533.5	479.8	—	—
Total expenditures	—	—	725.0	866.5	926.4	1,228.8	796.8	—	—
Total revenues	—	—	722.6	736.5	911.4	765.0	625.0	—	—
W&S/current expenditures (%)	—	—	43.9	49.9	49.3	52.5	55.2	—	—
G&S/current expenditures (%)	—	—	—	—	—	—	—	—	—
W&S/total expenditures (%)	—	—	23.8	25.4	24.2	22.8	33.3	—	—
G&S/total expenditures (%)	—	—	—	—	—	—	—	—	—
Central African Republic (billions of CFA francs)									
Wages and salaries	18.7	21.7	23.7	23.9	23.4	24.5	24.9	25.4	25.4
Goods and services	6.8	6.6	6.9	8.0	5.6	5.5	6.7	7.5	8.3
Current expenditures	—	—	36.4	38.6	37.0	38.3	40.2	42.3	43.6
Total expenditures	—	—	—	—	64.7	83.2	85.1	84.7	84.0
Total revenues	—	—	35.8	36.5	39.5	41.7	40.1	38.1	40.6
W&S/current expenditures (%)	—	—	65.1	61.9	63.2	63.9	61.9	60.2	58.2
G&S/current expenditures (%)	—	—	19.0	20.8	15.1	14.5	16.8	17.7	19.0
W&S/total expenditures (%)	—	—	—	—	36.3	29.4	29.2	30.1	30.2
G&S/total expenditures (%)	—	—	—	—	8.7	6.7	7.9	8.8	9.9

Costa Rica (millions of colones)

Wages and salaries	2,936.0	3,501.0	3,044.0	7,730.0	9,822.0	10,981.0	13,651.0	15,611.3	18,983.0
Goods and services	303.0	426.0	669.0	1,158.0	1,460.0	1,803.0	2,012.0	2,388.0	3,230.0
Current expenditures	6,352.0	8,663.0	15,072.0	20,953.0	26,586.0	30,144.0	36,859.0	43,629.0	53,906.0
Total expenditures	8,332.0	10,769.0	17,284.0	26,044.0	31,978.0	35,946.0	46,277.0	50,355.0	61,845.0
Total revenues	5,053.0	7,770.0	14,026.0	21,417.0	27,012.0	32,005.0	38,030.0	44,642.0	54,200.0
W&S/current expenditures (%)	46.2	40.4	33.5	36.9	36.9	36.4	37.0	35.8	35.2
G&S/current expenditures (%)	4.8	4.9	4.4	5.5	5.5	6.0	5.5	5.5	6.0
W&S/total expenditures (%)	35.2	32.5	29.2	29.7	30.7	30.6	29.5	31.0	30.8
G&S/total expenditures (%)	3.6	4.0	3.9	4.5	4.6	5.0	4.4	4.7	5.2

Gambia, The (thousands of dalasis)

Wages and salaries	—	—	—	52,775.0	63,929.0	66,190.0	62,271.0	73,090.0	78,387.0
Goods and services	—	—	—	24,978.0	22,280.0	26,017.0	40,846.0	58,603.0	60,121.0
Current expenditures	—	—	—	129,563.0	151,827.0	180,912.0	315,371.0	379,954.0	404,611.0
Total expenditures	—	—	—	—	—	—	—	—	—
Total revenues	95,780.0	76,520.0	87,050.0	103,100.0	122,970.0	146,040.0	213,190.0	294,620.0	—
W&S/current expenditures (%)	—	—	—	40.7	42.1	36.6	19.8	19.2	19.3
G&S/current expenditures (%)	—	—	—	19.3	14.7	14.4	13.0	15.4	14.9
W&S/total expenditures (%)	—	—	—	—	—	—	—	—	—
G&S/total expenditures (%)	—	—	—	—	—	—	—	—	—

Ghana (millions of cedis)

Wages and salaries	2,253.0	1,257.0	2,274.0	2,501.0	5,282.0	14,524.0	26,194.0	35,920.0	49,464.0
Goods and services	—	3,869.0	4,798.0	—	15,644.0	28,597.0	42,142.0	60,538.0	—
Current expenditures	4,179.0	6,330.0	8,603.0	13,401.0	23,326.0	38,642.0	60,834.0	80,583.0	111,006.0
Total expenditures	4,668.0	7,719.0	9,530.0	14,755.0	30,040.0	52,726.0	98,075.0	142,832.0	199,222.0
Total revenues	2,951.0	3,234.0	4,804.0	10,185.0	21,727.0	38,692.0	69,759.0	105,009.0	142,238.0
W&S/current expenditures (%)	53.9	19.9	26.4	18.7	22.6	37.6	43.1	44.6	44.6
G&S/current expenditures (%)	—	61.1	55.8	—	67.1	74.0	69.3	75.1	—
W&S/total expenditures (%)	48.3	16.3	23.9	17.0	17.6	27.6	26.7	25.2	24.8
G&S/total expenditures (%)	—	50.1	50.4	—	52.1	54.2	43.0	42.4	—

(Table continues on the following page.)

Table 7.7 continued

Country	1980	1981	1982	1983	1984	1985	1986	1987	1988
Guinea (billions of Guinean francs)									
Wages and salaries	3.4	3.8	4.2	4.5	—	—	18.2	21.3	36.8
Goods and services	—	—	—	—	—	—	45.8	51.8	37.3
Current expenditures	—	—	—	—	—	—	86.7	106.8	122.4
Total expenditures	—	—	—	—	—	—	137.7	185.9	240.9
Total revenues	—	—	—	—	—	—	77.8	120.5	149.7
W&S/current expenditures (%)	—	—	—	—	—	—	21.0	19.9	30.1
G&S/current expenditures (%)	—	—	—	—	—	—	52.8	48.5	30.8
W&S/total expenditures (%)	—	—	—	—	—	—	13.2	11.5	15.3
G&S/total expenditures (%)	—	—	—	—	—	—	33.3	27.9	15.7
Guinea-Bissau (percentage of GDP)									
Wages and salaries	16.0	14.7	13.2	12.3	11.9	8.7	5.8	5.3	—
Goods and services	6.6	8.0	7.0	6.1	6.1	5.3	5.4	6.5	—
Current expenditures	26.9	26.5	24.1	21.6	22.2	17.8	16.8	18.0	—
Total expenditures	54.6	57.1	49.5	59.2	59.0	40.7	48.1	52.3	—
Total revenues	27.2	31.4	26.3	31.5	33.4	24.4	38.1	39.0	—
W&S/current expenditures (%)	59.5	55.5	54.8	57.0	53.6	48.9	34.5	29.4	—
G&S/current expenditures (%)	24.5	30.2	29.1	28.2	27.5	29.8	32.1	36.1	—
W&S/total expenditures (%)	29.3	25.7	26.7	20.8	20.2	21.4	12.1	10.1	—
G&S/total expenditures (%)	12.1	14.0	14.1	10.3	10.3	13.0	11.2	12.4	—
Jamaica (millions of Jamaican dollars)									
Wages and salaries	—	—	967.0	1,072.0	1,083.0	1,260.0	1,335.4	1,501.5	—
Goods and services	—	—	281.4	428.5	490.5	619.2	744.9	794.5	—
Current expenditures	—	—	2,394.0	2,817.9	3,253.0	3,755.0	4,198.3	5,136.3	—
Total expenditures	—	—	2,991.0	3,335.3	3,934.0	4,719.6	5,508.8	6,855.6	—
Total revenues	—	—	1,844.4	2,334.1	2,708.3	3,700.5	—	—	—
W&S/current expenditures (%)	—	—	40.4	38.0	33.3	33.6	31.9	29.2	—
G&S/current expenditures (%)	—	—	11.8	15.2	15.1	16.5	17.8	15.5	—

150

(billions of CFA francs / %)									
W&S/total expenditures (%)	—	—	32.3	32.1	27.5	26.7	24.2	21.9	—
G&S/total expenditures (%)	—	—	9.4	12.9	12.5	13.1	13.5	11.6	—
Mali (billions of CFA francs)									
Wages and salaries	24.8	27.3	30.2	33.2	35.9	38.4	39.4	39.0	—
Materials and supplies	8.2	8.6	9.1	11.3	8.1	10.1	10.5	10.5	—
Current expenditures	40.1	42.5	45.9	51.4	56.1	62.7	62.4	62.3	—
Total expenditures	93.7	92.2	109.0	116.4	143.4	160.4	147.8	146.6	—
Total revenues	46.4	49.9	54.1	61.9	71.0	94.4	89.2	85.6	—
W&S/current expenditures (%)	61.9	64.2	65.8	64.6	64.0	61.2	63.1	62.6	—
M&S/current expenditures (%)	20.5	20.2	19.8	22.0	14.4	16.1	16.8	16.9	—
W&S/total expenditures (%)	26.5	29.6	27.7	28.5	25.0	23.9	26.7	26.6	—
M&S/total expenditures (%)	8.8	9.3	8.4	9.7	5.7	6.3	7.1	7.2	—
Niger (billions of CFA francs)									
Wages and salaries	—	—	—	—	24.9	25.8	28.3	30.3	33.8
Goods and services	—	—	—	—	42.6	46.2	47.9	49.4	51.3
Current expenditures	—	—	—	—	70.1	75.0	76.1	78.2	79.4
Total expenditures	—	—	—	—	123.6	137.9	134.8	131.8	139.4
Total revenues	—	—	—	—	69.9	74.1	75.7	68.2	70.0
W&S/current expenditures (%)	—	—	—	—	35.5	34.4	37.2	38.8	42.6
G&S/current expenditures (%)	—	—	—	—	60.8	61.6	62.9	63.2	64.6
W&S/total expenditures (%)	—	—	—	—	20.2	18.7	21.0	23.0	24.3
G&S/total expenditures (%)	—	—	—	—	34.5	33.5	35.5	37.5	36.8
Senegal (billions of CFA francs)									
Wages and salaries	78.3	83.3	92.7	100.4	106.6	111.8	119.8	122.3	125.1
Goods and services	34.8	30.3	36.9	35.4	33.5	40.9	—	—	—
Current expenditures	—	—	—	—	172.8	179.2	193.2	198.5	248.2
Total expenditures	—	—	—	—	217.1	220.5	232.6	244.6	248.2
Total revenues	125.5	151.9	175.7	189.4	203.8	218.8	251.2	251.7	273.1
W&S/current expenditures (%)	—	—	—	—	61.7	62.4	62.0	61.6	50.4
W&S/total expenditures (%)	—	—	—	—	49.1	50.7	51.5	50.0	50.4

(Table continues on the following page.)

151

Table 7.7 continued

Country	1980	1981	1982	1983	1984	1985	1986	1987	1988
Togo (billions of CFA francs)									
Wages and salaries	—	—	28.7	27.8	27.8	28.8	34.2	35.4	—
Materials and supplies	—	—	8.1	9.6	13.0	15.7	21.0	17.4	—
Current expenditures	—	—	54.4	56.1	56.2	65.2	72.0	72.0	—
W&S/current expenditures (%)	—	—	52.8	49.6	49.5	44.2	47.5	49.2	—
M&S/current expenditures (%)	—	—	14.9	17.1	23.1	24.1	29.2	24.2	—
Uganda (millions of new Ugandan shillings)									
Wages and salaries	64.0	70.0	126.0	440.2	535.0	1,159.0	3,700.0	—	—
Current expenditures	308.2	536.0	695.2	1,568.4	3,516.6	6,788.0	24,746.0	—	—
Total expenditures	535.2	720.9	1,154.3	2,397.0	4,722.0	10,931.0	42,049.0	—	—
Total revenues	243.9	526.1	929.4	1,620.9	2,845.5	5,870.4	24,870.0	—	—
W&S/current expenditures (%)	20.8	13.1	18.1	28.1	15.2	17.1	15.0	—	—
W&S/total expenditures (%)	12.0	9.7	10.9	18.4	11.3	10.6	8.8	—	—

— Not available.

Source: World Bank; Statistical Institute of Jamaica; J. Tait Davis, "Review and Evaluation of Ghana's Civil Service Reform Program, 1987–1989," unpublished mimeo, World Bank, Africa Technical Department, Washington, D.C., 1989; ministries of planning, commerce and tourism (Guinea-Bissau); Ministry of Finance and Planning (Jamaica); data provided by Niger and Gambian authorities.

data in which either the World Bank—through a SAL or a TAL—or the IMF sponsored reform, ten had wage bill increases for the last two years for which data are available. Moreover, this group included those countries in which the reform program had progressed furthest, such as the Gambia, Ghana, Guinea, and Jamaica. In only four countries did the wage bill decline in absolute terms. In six countries wages and salaries rose as a percentage of total expenditure. Moreover, the percentage of total expenditure on goods and services or materials and supplies, an indicator of the availability of necessary inputs for government staff, declined for six out of the group and rose for only five. (For Togo, the percentage of current expenditures spent on materials and supplies declined for the last year of available data.) For the other three countries, data were not available.

To repeat, these data are not very robust and it would not be wise to overgeneralize from them. Indeed, there may be any number of good reasons—perhaps completely unrelated to civil service reform programs—for wage bill increases in these countries. It is not possible to explain reliably the idiosyncratic reasons for each increase. Even for cases where it is possible to probe data more deeply, the reasons for increases in the wage bill can be ambiguous. Moreover, even at the aggregate level, the time lag between reform and impact may be longer than can be captured in the available figures. It should also be noted that personnel expenditure trends often do not show up in the aggregate wage bill figures. They can be hidden in the budget in myriad other (often nonitemized) categories. Thus, some of these wage bill figures may actually understate the total amount of personnel emoluments for a given year. Taking all these caveats into account, the data suggest that the impact of these reform programs on aggregate wage bill reduction, thus far, is negligible.

Data on wage compression are poor. Table 7.6 shows changes in only thirteen cases. Of these, three of the wage structures showed decompression and ten showed compression. Looking a bit more closely at individual reform programs, Ghana and Mozambique have made progress in decompressing the salary structure. In the Central African Republic it would appear that not much decompression has occurred. And the compression situations in the Gambia and Guinea are less encouraging still. Here, despite reform programs, wages have actually become more compressed.

Employment

In the absence of clear improvements on the fiscal side, the overall objective of employment reduction retains importance. Has this goal been

Table 7.8 Civil service employment, selected countries, 1980–89

Country	1980	1981	1982	1983	1984	1985	1986	1987	1988	1989
Cameroon	—	—	137,050	149,200	163,950	172,400	191,750	174,750	179,120	—
Central African Republic	—	—	—	—	—	—	—	—	—	—
Costa Rica	142,300	141,700	134,300	145,300	156,200	157,500	165,800	22,793	21,090	—
Congo	—	—	—	—	—	21,993	22,211	—	71,800	—
Gambia, The	—	—	—	—	—	—	73,348	14,209	12,195	12,785
Ghana	—	—	—	—	—	—	301,000	282,000	283,000	270,000
Guinea	—	—	—	—	—	—	90,000	80,000	70,000	52,000
Guinea-Bissau	—	—	—	—	—	—	—	16,625	14,665	—
Jamaica	110,100	118,000	118,800	102,000	100,500	81,100	79,900	72,800	76,000	—
Mali	—	—	—	49,116	50,924	48,455	50,970	52,553	52,608	—
Niger	—	—	—	—	—	31,924	32,680	32,465	35,342	—
Senegal	59,987	63,573	67,298	70,249	68,958	70,057	71,163	69,407	69,456	68,139
Togo	—	—	—	—	—	—	—	—	31,300	—
Uganda	—	—	—	119,000	—	29,110	—	239,528	—	—

— Not available.

Source: World Bank; Statistical Institute of Jamaica; J. Tait Davis, "Review and Evaluation of Ghana's Civil Service Reform Program, 1987–1989," unpublished mimeo, World Bank, Africa Technical Department, Washington, D.C., 1989.

achieved under these programs? Table 7.8 shows the limited data available on employment trends for selected countries that have undergone some form of employment reform. For the fourteen countries for which data are available, seven were able to reduce government employment during the recorded period. Among these, one (Ghana) reportedly experienced slippage through new recruitment in the education service, though this seems not to have affected the overall downward trend. Two—Cameroon and Jamaica—experienced significant reductions in recent years, but then reversed the trend slightly during the last year of the reform period. For the other countries, the rate of growth remained relatively constant during the period.

In general, these reductions were of small magnitude. The limited impact on the wage bill for those few cases where results have been even modestly encouraging may be a function of the very low levels of employment cuts that countries are being asked and are willing to make. Indeed, it may well be that more serious impact can only be achieved through more drastic reductions.

It is also important to note that the savings achieved through government cuts were generally not sufficient to pay for the subsequent salary increases awarded to correct previous civil service wage erosion. Indeed, preliminary evidence from the Gambia and Ghana suggests that aggregate pay increases vastly outstrip the savings gained through the retrenchment exercise. The discrepancy between the relatively small fiscal savings of retrenchment and the generous pay hikes is partially explained by the extreme wage erosion that has taken place. It is not likely that significant redress of this erosion could be achieved through anything less than massive employee layoffs, the likes of which have not been contemplated or carried out in any of the present cases. Finally, most employment reduction has taken place at the lower pay levels of the civil service. This has tended to lessen the financial impact of the redundancies.

Conclusions

Despite data constraints, the findings of this chapter suggest some lessons to guide present and future civil service reform. These can be summarized as follows:

- Most of the middle-range employment reduction mechanisms, such as voluntary departure schemes and early retirement programs, may be useful and politically astute when applied in combination with more stringent retrenchment measures. But they have not yet proved effective in reducing employment in any significant manner. Thus, they do not provide a substitute for biting the bullet and making explicit dismissals.

- Technical analysis and support activities, such as functional reviews and competency testing, for example, have been useful in providing a rational basis for cost containment measures. Their major contribution, however, may be the symbolic assurance they provide that the reform process has been undertaken with fair and equitable intentions.
- Retraining, redeployment, credit, and public works programs for redundant employees have certainly had a utility, but one that is more symbolic and political than economic. From a financial and technical perspective such programs have had limited impact and have proved administratively difficult.
- Some reform programs have promoted interim solutions to pay and employment problems through specialized incentive schemes for topping up executive-level salaries for key government posts, or, more broadly, by widely supplementing civil service salaries through donor-financed activities. Most observers familiar with the use of these mechanisms recognize their limitations and costs. The problem is that neither hard-pressed governments nor operational staff have alternative means at their disposal. Still, what must be recognized is that these salary supplement methods do not provide enduring answers to the fundamental problems of civil service incentives; indeed, they ultimately undermine the likelihood of devising a durable solution.
- The impact of programs to contain the cost and size of civil services through emergency pay and employment reforms has so far been small. Efforts in most countries to reduce the wage bill and to decrease the number of civil service employees have yielded only modest results. Attempts to correct distortions in the structure of pay and employment through the decompression of wages and the rationalization of the remuneration system have also had limited success. This record suggests that reforms to date have been insufficiently ambitious in scope to bring about the degree of change that is needed. Meaningful change is going to require more forceful reforms.
- The question of whether more aggressive reforms are feasible is partly technical but mainly political, an issue touched on in the final chapter of this volume. Nonetheless, it is possible to hypothesize from the few examples of countries where programs have been carried out that the political costs of implementing pay and employment reforms have been lower than most governments and donors anticipated. Organized opposition to reforms has not resulted in regime destabilization, and social upheaval as a result of dismissals has not occurred. In part, this may have been a function of the surprising capacity of private sector labor markets—especially in agri-

cultural and informal sectors, and particularly, but not exclusively, in Africa—to absorb surplus government workers. It may also have been a function of the unexpectedly agile handling of political factors, including the skill with which regimes generated supporting coalitions and managed contesting groups.

What this suggests is that perhaps regimes can (for political reasons) and should (for economic reasons) make deeper cuts. How far any given government can push these reforms is, of course, unknown. But the relatively mild consequences of the minimal reforms undertaken so far can, it is hoped, influence governments' perceptions of political risk and encourage them to take bolder actions in the future.

- Most activities in civil service reform have concentrated, understandably, on short-term cost containment measures, the subject of this chapter. Considerably more emphasis will have to be given to longer-term management issues if sustained improvement in government administrative capacity is to take place. More attention needs to be paid to devising a coherent, overarching strategy for civil service reform, and detailing the set of tactics by which the strategic goals will be achieved.[13]

- In light of what this chapter has reported as a mixed record on civil service reform efforts, the possibility that major donors will retreat from these activities as too difficult looms as a real and present danger. Such a retreat would, however, be tantamount to a denial of the crucial importance of government administrative capacity to implement economic and social programs. A more responsible and realistic approach is to improve such programs through a trial-and-error process. The review of experience presented here and in the case studies in this volume is intended to contribute to this process.

Notes

1. For a more comprehensive discussion of these analytical assumptions, see chapter 2 in this volume; and Barbara Nunberg and John Nellis, "Civil Service Reform and the World Bank," PRE Working Paper 422, World Bank, Washington, D.C., 1990.

2. This section draws heavily on Barbara Nunberg, *Public Sector Pay and Employment Reform: A Review of World Bank Experience*, Discussion Paper 68, World Bank, Washington, D.C., 1989.

3. Several other types of policy-based lending operations, such as Reconstruction Import Credits and Economic Recovery Credits (RICs and ERCs), were counted among the SALs. They are itemized in table 7.1.

4. Ghost workers appear on the payroll and receive a wage, but cannot be shown to exist physically. They are workers who have died, retired, or otherwise left the civil service but were never recorded as such. They are fictitious persons

whose pay is claimed by others. They are variants on a name, with one person receiving two or more salaries.

5. Data on ghost removals in Ghana are tentative and remain to be verified. Government claims that 11,000 ghosts were eliminated through head count and census exercises have not yet been validated. In Uganda about 30,000 ghost workers have been identified, but there is no evidence that these names have been removed from the payroll as yet.

6. These ongoing measures usually consist of rationalization and computerization of the payroll mechanism, generally located in the Treasury in the Ministry of Finance. (Ghana, Mauritania, Senegal, and Uganda are a few examples.) In some cases this computerization has proceeded on its own; in others, the payroll system has been linked to the improved personnel management data base discussed above. Explicit links to the budget have also been forged. The integration of the personnel data and the payroll and budgetary information is somewhat cumbersome administratively and institutionally as it involves the coordination of various organs: ministries of finance and civil service, statistical institutes, computation centers, and technical line ministries are usually all involved. But comprehensive and sustained control over personnel management functions cannot occur without a linked system. Furthermore, the greater the degree of decentralization of personnel management, the more crucial an integrated network becomes.

7. In fact, many of the mechanisms described in this section have been utilized in combination with one another, making it difficult to isolate the relative utility or impact of any single one. In Ghana, for example, voluntary departure was not stimulated through additional incentives; the "voluntary" separation package was the same as that for redundant workers, thus providing little motivation for workers to leave of their own volition. At the same time, workers theoretically had the option of early retirement, but would receive no extra payments over and above their regular pension rights. If they chose voluntary retirement, however, they would receive the lump sum separation payment in addition to their pension. Thus, there were virtually no early retirees in Ghana, but some older voluntary departees. Clearly, it was not the nature of the individual scheme, but its relation to the other parts of the staff reduction program, that determined the outcome.

8. See Richard Newfarmer, "Argentina's Progress from Insolvency to Recovery," in *Economic Insights* (Institute of International Economics) July–August 1992.

9. See Gary Reid, "Regional Study of Civil Service Reform in Latin America," World Bank, Latin America Technical Department, Washington, D.C., 1994.

10. Steen Jorgensen, Margaret Grosh, and Mark Schacter, "Easing the Poor through Economic Crisis and Adjustment: The Story of Bolivia's Emergency Social Fund," Latin American and Caribbean Technical Department Regional Studies, report 3, World Bank, Washington, D.C., May 1991, chapter 6.

11. Methodologies for determining appropriate pay levels in the civil service are only now being developed. In Jamaica a comparative pay survey was carried out through the Administrative Reform Project (ARP), the institutional counterpart for pay reform in SAL III. But the survey took so long to be completed that the ARP was terminated before the results became known. Similar sur-

veys were carried out in the Gambia, Ghana, and Thailand to determine appropriate pay levels for civil servants.

12. Attempts at parastatal–civil service pay parity tend to result in a "no-win situation." First, the equalization of state enterprise salaries with those of central government agencies is often not achievable; all that can be accomplished is to narrow the gap between the two in order to stem the flow of qualified staff from one to the other and to mitigate somewhat the resentment of civil servants at receiving relatively lower salaries. Second, even in cases where parity has been legislated, the incentives to performance of state enterprises themselves cannot help but be negatively affected. To the degree that parastatals behave more like central government agencies than private or competitive enterprises—particularly with regard to salary and personnel policies—parastatal performance is likely to suffer. See David Lindauer, "Parastatal Pay Policy in Africa," *World Development*, vol. 19, no. 7 (July 1991).

13. This agenda is increasingly being taken up through World Bank–supported development management projects that were not analyzed here. For a more comprehensive review of these activities, see Barbara Nunberg and John Nellis, "Civil Service Reform and the World Bank," PRE Working Paper 422, World Bank, Washington, D.C., 1990.

8

Implementing civil service pay and employment reform in Africa: the experiences of Ghana, the Gambia, and Guinea

Louis de Merode
with Charles S. Thomas

A number of African countries are moving to reduce overstaffing and to restore a motivating wage in the civil service. This chapter examines pathbreaking experiences in Ghana, the Gambia, and Guinea.[1] The three cases were chosen, after a review of the half dozen reform programs in Africa with the longest records,[2] for their apparent success both in achieving significant pay and employment changes in the short term and in laying the foundations for long-term improvements. Although generalizations from this small sample are exceptionally difficult, plausible hypotheses have been ventured in the belief that they may pay rich dividends for the design and implementation of other reform programs. The number of countries attempting similar reforms is growing too fast, the stakes are too high, and formal institutional feedback is too slow for implementers to wait for large samples and well-rounded reform cycles.

The study begins with a case-by-case review of the problem and the reform measures taken. This is followed by a comparative assessment of the impact of reforms in four target areas: employment, compensation, the budget, and government performance. A final section draws practical lessons for the design and implementation of reform programs.

Ghana

At the time of its Independence in 1957, Ghana—rich in natural resources and equipped with the most skilled work force in Sub-Saharan Africa—could lay claim to one of the "best organized and most efficient civil services in Africa."[3] By the early 1980s, however, the civil service's once-flattering regional reputation had become a distant memory, the victim of years of economic and political mismanagement. The public sector was overextended, overstaffed, underpaid, and underskilled. Moonlighting was commonplace and practically indispensable for economic survival. The best talent had fled in droves to the private sector or to find employment abroad. No longer an asset, the civil service had become a drain on public resources and a major impediment to the implementation of economic policy reforms designed to reverse Ghana's economic decline.

Two factors help explain the breakdown of the civil service. First, the collapse of economic activity had greatly reduced public revenues, which by 1983 had fallen to 5.3 percent of GDP, compared with 12 to 18 percent of GDP in other African countries. Second, for more than twenty years weak political regimes had used the civil service as the employer of last resort, thus swelling recruitment levels. By 1983 the work force in the civil and education services had grown to more than 300,000 strong—2.5 civil servants per 100 inhabitants—which placed Ghana at the upper end of the spectrum in Africa.[4] Squeezed by overstaffing and a dwindling treasury, civil service pay came under tremendous pressure. Although real GDP per capita was falling by an estimated 4.8 percent a year between 1975 and 1983, average government salaries were falling by more than 10 percent. Higher-level civil servants were hit hardest by the steep decline in pay, and the wage structure became extraordinarily compressed. By 1984 the equivalent of a permanent secretary at the top of the civil service earned only 2.2 times the wage of a messenger at the bottom.

The turning point for the economy was 1983, when the government launched the Economic Reform Program, an ambitious endeavor involving fiscal stabilization, radical devaluation of the currency, rehabilitation of key export sectors, and economic liberalization. This initiative was followed in 1987 by the Civil Service Reform Program. Civil service reform had become a high priority because of the serious erosion in the public sector's capacity to perform such basic functions as macroeconomic management, rehabilitation and maintenance of the country's dilapidated infrastructure, and delivery of social services. Thus, the main thrust of the Civil Service Reform Program was restoration and capacity-building rather than fiscal stabilization. Indeed, despite severe fiscal constraints, it was recognized that to improve civil service compensation, morale, and work effort the wage bill needed to grow—albeit within the limits of budgetary policy. Fiscal stabilization was to be secured by improving revenue performance, not by paring the wage bill.

The Civil Service Reform Program had three critical components: a retrenchment program that initially aimed to reduce government employment, excluding police and security forces, by 5 percent a year over a three-year period;[5] a comprehensive pay and grading reform program; and an institutional development program. Key measures taken to achieve the retrenchment targets included three civil service census exercises, a selective recruitment freeze, a job inspection and functional review program, annual retrenchment exercises, and an outplacement program to help retrenched civil servants find gainful employment in the private sector.

The first census of civil service employment in Ghana was carried out in 1986 by the Office of the Head of the Civil Service (OHCS), the central civil service management agency. The census confirmed the high proportion of civil servants at lower levels, but flaws in the census's design and implementation, compounded by manual processing of data and the absence of technical assistance, prevented it from producing an accurate picture of civil service employment. A second and third census were successfully undertaken in 1987 and 1988 with the assistance of expatriate consultants. These counts were based on the computerized payroll, drew on information supplied by payroll clerks and personnel officers, and were computer-processed.

As early as 1985 a selective recruitment freeze was put into effect, allowing recruitment in critical skill areas while preventing it in over-staffed—mostly lower-level—occupational categories. Various high-level circulars restricting recruitment were issued from time to time. These proved largely ineffective, however, and significant uncontrolled recruitment persisted, partially eroding the impact of retrenchment. This was due both to the decentralization of recruitment of lower-level staff to middle managers not firmly committed to reform and to the break-down of establishment control—constraints that received insufficient attention in the early stages of reform.

A program of job inspections and functional reviews was undertaken by the OHCS's Management Services Division, with coaching from consultants, to help implement the retrenchment exercises.[6] Between late 1987 and early 1990, job inspections covered 160 units and 18,000 positions, and seven functional reviews were completed. Findings provided objective evidence that overstaffing in the civil service was concentrated at lower levels and ranged from 25 to 50 percent, largely exceeding retrenchment targets.

The annual retrenchment exercises began in 1987. The government established the Redeployment Management Committee (RMC) under the Ministry of Labor to oversee retrenchment and outplacement activities, and various ministries created internal manpower appraisal committees to identify workers to be retrenched. Severance allowances were fixed at four months' basic pay and two additional months' pay per year of service. The OHCS set retrenchment targets for each ministry and issued instructions on the criteria to be used, such as individual performance, willingness to leave, and seniority. Job inspection findings were extrapolated to give ministries estimates of systemwide overstaffing levels by occupational category.

The first exercise faced considerable start-up difficulties. The processing of payments proved an administrative bottleneck, due mainly to the problem of determining years of effective service. Faced with the mounting frustration of retrenched workers, the government had to start paying an interim subsistence allowance. Ministries were also resisting RMC directives. After a few months, however, the administrative hurdles were surmounted and interim payments terminated; a major public relations effort was launched, and the retrenchment program gradually gained greater acceptance. Eventually, about 12,000 workers were removed from the payroll in 1987, including 8,000 retrenched and 4,000 retired; 12,400 were retrenched in 1988, 13,900 in 1989, and 12,200 in 1990. The program was extended for at least another three years through 1992 and is retaining significant momentum.

Finally, in support of the retrenchment exercises an outplacement program was developed to provide information, counseling, and placement services; vocational training and apprenticeships; assistance for agricultural settlement; and credit for self-employment. It was, however, only slowly put in place. By late 1989, more than two years after the first round of layoffs, very little outplacement support had been made available. Of 3,000 applicants for training, for instance, only 100 had received assistance. The one exception is agricultural settlement, where some 4,600 retrenched workers had been settled out of 9,600 applicants. Although the outplacement program reached only a small minority of retrenched workers, it appears to have succeeded in enabling a majority of the beneficiaries to manage their job transition successfully. About three-quarters of those surveyed "had no regrets" about their new occupation, although reports indicate that about 25 percent of those who chose redeployment in agriculture dropped out of the program in the first year. Most important, although no overall evaluation of outplacement costs and benefits is available, the program clearly played a major part in the government's effective public relations efforts to minimize the political fallout from retrenchment. If in the initial stages it was feared that the retrenchment process would become politicized, these fears subsided and little opposition lingered after start-up problems were resolved.

As the second major component of the Civil Service Reform Program, pay and grading reform had five objectives: an increase in overall real pay levels, the decompression of pay scales to improve the competitiveness of civil service pay at higher levels, a new grading system based on job evaluations, the introduction of performance-based pay, and the improvement of pay policymaking and administration. So far, reform has spanned five annual pay adjustments, from 1987 to 1991.

In February 1988 external consultants working closely with the Prices and Incomes Board (PIB) produced a quick wage survey of the modern private, parastatal, and public sectors, showing median pay levels in the civil service ranging from 28 to 41 percent of private sector and 60 to 88 percent of parastatal earnings. They also presented five alternative pay scenarios for 1988, and proposals for grading reform and the introduction of performance-based pay.

The grading reform proposals were designed to create a consistent and streamlined structure based on job evaluations, where essentially there had been none.[7] The strategy called for evaluating senior positions and regrading them in a unified structure with special pay and career provisions. A separate round of evaluations would follow for junior posts, which were to be regraded within a reduced number of occupational classes. This two-stage approach was soon discarded as too divisive for the civil service. Instead, it was decided to restructure all posts together. Furthermore, job evaluations turned out to be much more time-consuming than anticipated. By mid-1990 a team of twenty-four job analysts from the PIB and other institutions had been assembled and trained, and good progress had been made toward defining a new grade structure. Implementation of the new structure, though, was pushed back three years, from 1989 to 1992.

Work on performance-related pay has focused on creating essential preconditions identified by the consultants: the introduction of a credible individual performance appraisal process, and an increase in pay to minimum levels that relieve civil servants of the need to supplement official income. In mid-1990 a new personnel appraisal form was designed and tested successfully. Generalized use of the form was programmed for 1991, with the introduction of performance-related pay planned for 1992.

In parallel with these long-term comprehensive efforts, the government adopted two partial, short-term strategies to alleviate critical pay problems: an innovative scheme to mobilize national skills in support of key structural adjustment activities (box 8.1), and an "enclave" pay approach for key institutions (box 8.2).

The Gambia

The challenges faced by the civil service in the Gambia were clearly of a different magnitude. The economic decline had not been as steep or as long-lived as in Ghana. The severe institutional decay found in Ghana was not a major issue here. Problems of morale and performance, though, were serious and pervasive. While the Gambian economy was stagnating in the 1970s, central government employment was expanding rapidly, from a staff of about 4,000 regular and 2,000 nonpermanent employees in 1975 to 10,700 and 5,000, respectively, in 1985. The government was losing control over the wage bill, which had grown from about one-third of total farmer income from groundnut production (the mainstay of the export sector) in 1975 to twice that a decade later.

The result of this growing imbalance between the size of the public sector and the productive base was severe crowding out of budgetary outlays for operations and maintenance, which declined by 50 percent in

---

Box 8.1 The skills mobilization scheme in Ghana

This scheme aimed to maximize the use of national skills in the implementation of key structural adjustment tasks. Several mechanisms were tested, two of which were widely used: the recruitment of local consultants for discrete tasks and the payment of special duty allowances to civil servants. Under the first approach, a roster of local consultants was drawn up, along with standard rates (US$2,200–US$3,300 per month) depending on the level of qualifications. In several instances the consultants were deployed under the Civil Service Reform Program, most notably to overhaul the Civil Service Act and to produce a study on welfare provisions in the civil service.

A second mechanism provided for the payment of special duty allowances to civil servants assigned to key structural adjustment activities such as public investment programs and budget task forces. Monthly rates ran from cedis 4,000 ($25) for ancillary staff to cedis 20,000 ($125) for team leaders. Between 90 and 150 civil servants participated each year from 1987 to 1989. Although clearly the most widely used mechanism, the allowances system had its drawbacks. Allowances were paid late and partially, not because of administrative or financial constraints, but because they bred resentment within the service.

Overall, the results of the skills mobilization scheme have been modest and mixed, with some mechanisms abandoned in the face of strong resistance from within the civil service. This was the case, for example, with the proposed long-term recruitment of Ghanaians, who would enter the civil service from the private sector and nongovernmental public sector and receive salaries at their previous levels, plus a $200–$300 monthly supplement. Although the task forces have performed well in most cases, recruitment of outsiders and special treatment given to insiders may have lowered the morale and work effort of excluded civil servants. Several additional mechanisms are being explored, including an accelerated development program for promising young civil servants.

real terms between 1980 and 1985, and a similar drop of 50 percent in average real civil service compensation between 1980 and 1986. Civil service reform objectives were thus ranked differently in the Gambia than in Ghana. Reducing the high cost of the civil service to the economy became the chief objective. A second-order objective was to remove pay anomalies and, subject to budget constraints, increase pay levels so as to improve morale and work effort.

Box 8.2 Ghana's National Revenue Service

Between 1984 and 1988 the National Revenue Service (NRS), which is responsible for customs and internal revenue assessment and collection, carried out a series of major organizational changes, including deep cuts in staffing and implementation of a new remuneration scheme. Performance improvements at the NRS over the four-year period have been remarkable, even after allowing for special factors such as the adoption of a more realistic exchange rate, which had a significant effect on the valuation of imports. Over the four-year period, revenues increased from 6.6 percent to 12.3 percent of GDP. Excluding taxes on international trade, revenue from taxes on income, profits, and capital gains increased from 1.5 percent to 3.9 percent of GDP, despite a reduction in the income tax rate structure, and revenue from taxes on domestic goods and services increased from 2.1 percent to 3.7 percent of GDP.

Observers attribute at least some of these impressive achievements to the following factors:

• *Managerial and financial autonomy.* NRS was allowed to depart from civil service remuneration policies and to fund its own budget by taking a percentage off the top of tax collections. As revenue performance improved, so did NRS's funding of capital and operating requirements.

• *Incentives.* Although basic pay was identical to the civil service's, allowances—both in cash and in kind—were significantly higher. External training was also used in abundance, mostly as a reward for individual performance.

• *Skill mix.* Early in the reform program, NRS fired large numbers of supernumerary workers and generally recruited more-qualified and better-motivated staff.

• *Working conditions.* Thanks to its financial autonomy, NRS was able to provide far better working conditions (for example, work inputs and accommodations) than those generally prevailing elsewhere.

• *Information technology.* NRS developed information and tax-processing systems covering most operational areas.

• *Leadership.* The head of NRS had the full backing of the political leadership and was described as charismatic, a powerful motivator, an innovator, and a good organizer. Many observers considered this to be the most important factor.

The Gambian Civil Service Reform Program began in 1985, also in the context of an economic reform program involving devaluation, fiscal stabilization, and revitalization of the export sector. As in Ghana, the main components were retrenchment, pay and grading reform, and institutional development. But unlike the annual exercises in Ghana, retrenchment in the Gambia was conceived and implemented as a discrete, time-bound program with several stages. Among the key actions were a census, management reviews of all ministries, two overall retrenchment exercises overlapping with the restructuring of the ministries of agriculture and public works, the suppression of vacant positions and budgetary restrictions on personnel expenditures, and an outplacement program.

The target for the first round of retrenchment was wage bill savings of dalasis 5 million (US$1.3 million) out of a dalasis 50 million ($13 million) wage bill. As in Ghana, the retrenchment program was preceded by a census, in August 1985, which was also designed and managed by a government task force and processed manually. It, too, had serious design and implementation problems: census forms were not sufficiently specific to enable consistent tabulations of employment categories, no final tally was produced, and most observers agree that the results were of little value in identifying workers to be retrenched. Consequently, the scope of the first round was narrowed to nonpermanent staff, and workers subject to retrenchment were identified in a series of consultations with individual ministries directed by the Secretary-General of the Presidency. In November 1985 and extending through early 1986, some 2,600 out of 5,000 nonpermanent workers were removed from the payroll, receiving one month's salary as severance pay under existing collective bargaining agreements. Estimated annual budget savings were dalasis 2.5 million ($0.6 million).

Other measures were taken immediately to reduce personnel expenditures and tighten personnel expenditure controls. A freeze on the creation of new posts was put in place, and budgetary provisions for vacant established posts were reduced to a token amount to curtail the earlier practice of funding nonpermanent staff out of existing vacancies. The practice of reallocating funds between personnel and other expenditure categories was also abolished. These measures appear to have been effectively implemented.

In preparation for the second retrenchment round, an external management consulting firm carried out management reviews in all ministries between January and April 1986. After a survey of departmental managers and follow-up interviews, the consultants issued reports with detailed recommendations by ministry on posts to be abolished and staff to be retrenched. The recommendations were then negotiated between the Secretariat-General of the Presidency, the Personnel Management Office, and the ministries. Eventually, retrenchment notices went out, beginning in August 1986, to some 900 civil servants and 300 nonpermanent staff, representing respectively about 10 and 12 percent of total effective staff. The corresponding posts were abolished, as were 800 other vacant ones. Severance pay for most civil servants—those with more than five years' seniority—consisted of 1.2 months of salary for each year of service, plus normal pension benefits. The ministries of agriculture and public works accounted for about two-thirds of the suppressed posts. At the time, both were being reorganized around core functions, divesting themselves of peripheral activities such as building maintenance and office furniture manufacturing. This was a direct result of the management reviews, which had examined organizational priorities and objectives and identified efficiency gains to be had from alternative forms of service delivery, including privatization, management contracting, outsourcing, and public-private joint ventures.

An outplacement program and public relations efforts also featured in the retrenchment program, although to a lesser extent than in Ghana and Guinea. The Institute for Business Administration Service was given about US$200,000 in January 1987 to fund a self-employment credit scheme, and was charged with organizing counseling and training activities. The launching of the scheme appears to have been largely motivated by the proximity of presidential elections in April 1987, although the retrenchment program itself does not appear to have been a major campaign issue. Eventually, 124 loans were made and about 50 retrenched workers received training. The scheme rapidly ran out of funds in early 1988 and was not extended. Loan recovery has been extremely poor, with a repayment rate of about 30 percent compared with a 60 percent rate for traditional lines of credit managed by the same organization.

The second major component of the Civil Service Reform Program was pay and grading reform. Since 1975, the pay and grade framework had remained essentially the same. Wage erosion, however, had become a severe problem, with real wages declining 50 percent between 1980 and 1986. This put great pressure on the grade system. New job titles were allowed to proliferate for existing jobs, with better pay scales but no change in job content. In other cases, pay scales for existing job titles were expanded beyond grade ranges on an ad hoc basis, again without any change in job content. These serious anomalies were a source of dissatisfaction among service officers. Any attempt to improve pay levels could not ignore these issues.

Consultants were contracted to develop pay reform proposals. They first carried out a wage survey, which concluded that pay was on average 88 percent higher in the private and 22 percent higher in the parastatal sector than in the civil service. Using job evaluations, they recommended reducing the number of grades from nineteen to twelve, with enlarged pay bands. To keep the regrading exercise at affordable levels, they did not propose any significant wage increase beyond what was needed to implement the new system. The government eventually decided to delink grading reform from an overall pay increase. Job evaluations were completed with technical assistance from three specialists, and the changeover to the new twelve-grade structure was made in October 1988, with 2,700 posts being upgraded and another 870 downgraded. Meanwhile, a salaries commission had been established in September 1988 to look at overall pay levels. Two months later it released its report, documenting the erosion in pay since 1968, and proposing a general pay increase of 107 percent, which would have restored real compensation to 1974 levels. The cabinet revised these proposals downward to remain within budgetary parameters agreed with the International Monetary Fund and the World Bank. A pay increase averaging 67 percent was approved in January 1989. A standing commission on salaries and allowances was also set up to handle appeals and remaining pay anomalies.

Building on the new grading system, the reform program also aimed to create long-term incentives through the introduction of career development streams and a new performance appraisal process. Forty-two "Schemes of Service" covering all major occupational categories in the civil service were developed and approved. These lay out the main features of career development for each class or occupational group: entry qualifications (that is, education, training, experience) and selection procedures, pay and grade arrangements, principal functions and responsibilities of personnel at various grade levels, and criteria for promotion from one grade to the next. A revised staff appraisal system, initially covering higher-level grades, was also being introduced in the second half of 1990, although implementation was still very partial and slow.

Guinea

At the outset of Guinea's reform program in 1984, the country's civil service probably presented one of the extreme cases of institutional decay in Africa, and by far the worst of this study. Sékou Touré's tenure since Independence, characterized by brutal political repression, extreme statism, and acute economic mismanagement, left a disastrous legacy in the public sector. The single-party machinery closely duplicated public service functions and intruded in all administrative processes. Except for large-scale mining enclaves and informal sector activities, the state embraced virtually all economic activity. State employees, whether in the central government or in the many public enterprises, were lumped together as civil servants working under the same pay and grade regime. Basic skills were sorely lacking. Huge numbers of skilled and educated workers had migrated or fallen victim to repression, and the education apparatus was in total disarray. The civil service was overstaffed, underpaid, and working under appalling material conditions. Corruption and moonlighting were pervasive; productivity was practically nil.

By the most reliable accounts, public sector employment was growing by some 7 percent a year in the 1970s, largely because of the government's commitment to absorb into the civil service the entire output of the higher education system. Total employment in 1982, including state-owned enterprises and other parastatals, was estimated at around 104,000 for a population of 5.6 million. A freeze on nominal pay from 1965 through 1980 had severely eroded salaries. Although the government attempted to compensate for the decline in pay by controlling prices and giving privileged categories of civil service personnel access to scarce goods, rationing was widespread and the availability of goods largely unpredictable for a majority of those eligible.

In a complete reversal of Sékou Touré's policies, the new military regime in March 1984 sought to roll back the state and make the private sector the main engine of growth. Civil service reform objectives in Guinea thus went much further than in the Gambia and Ghana. The main objective was to achieve a radical transformation in the role and size of the public sector. A second objective was to establish, almost from scratch, a competent and motivated civil service with the capacity to manage basic public sector functions. Public expenditure objectives were linked but not central to the reforms.

The Civil Service Reform Program in Guinea was launched in 1985, and like the other two cases, it had three focal points: downsizing—an initial target called for 25,000 staff to be removed from civil service payrolls, mostly by eliminating jobs but also by removing parastatal employees from the civil service proper;[8] implementing pay and grading reform; and strengthening of the personnel function. It was also part of a broader Economic and Financial Reform Program supported by several donors.

Of the three cases, the employment reduction measures in Guinea were the most varied and complex, featuring two nationwide censuses and one local census in Conakry, the nation's capital; early retirement and voluntary departure programs; a competency testing program for most of the civil service; retrenchment of those who failed the tests; and outplacement support. The first census, taken between December 1985 and May 1986, estimated total civil service employment at about 71,000, excluding parastatals. However, payroll and personnel information systems proved unable to maintain accurate census information. Indeed, in 1987 a verification exercise in Conakry revealed considerable slack in the payroll: 5 percent of the entries in existing rolls were spurious. The results of this census proved equally ephemeral. It was not until late 1988 that the lack of institutional capacity for manpower monitoring and control began to be addressed. Administrative and financial affairs divisions were established in all ministries and improved information systems were developed.

A second general census, carried out between December 1989 and July 1990, validated about 93 percent of nominal rolls in the regions and 73 percent in Conakry, again illustrating the rapid erosion of payroll information since the 1987 exercise. Provisional results placed total civil service employment at about 51,000 in late-1990. The new census information was to be loaded onto newly developed payroll and personnel information systems, which were expected to come on line in early 1991.

Although it is not possible to account fully for the change in employment between the first and second overall censuses, it is clear that the first round of significant staff reductions came immediately after the completion of the first census. Some 4,000 staff above the statutory retirement age of 55 were forced into retirement, and about 6,100 civil servants with thirty-plus years of service were given early retirement. A voluntary departure program was also established for those not eligible for normal or early retirement. At first open only to parastatal staff, the program was later extended to central government employees, but only about 1,700 of the latter availed themselves of it. Severance benefits included a flat sum, which was equal to about five years' base salary,[9] and access to an outplacement program.

To ease the severance process, a special personnel pool was created in December 1985. Employees slated for retrenchment, or whose status was uncertain, were transferred temporarily to this pool. They were to receive regular salary payments (frozen at current levels) for six months. Under severe political pressure the payments were extended for three years, with a cutoff date of December 1988. The personnel pool, however, was later reactivated to accommodate civil servants who had failed competency tests.

The centerpiece of the staff reduction effort was a competency testing program to screen civil servants and retrench those lacking the requisite skills (box 8.3). By the end of 1990 some 23,000 civil servants had been tested, of whom 53 percent passed, 21 percent failed and were transferred to the personnel pool to be retrenched, and the rest were placed in the personnel pool as well, but with the possibility of being selected back into the civil service following retraining. In support of the testing program, the Commissariat for Administrative Reform initiated a restructuring program involving all ministries. Organization and staffing charts and job descriptions were prepared both to provide a framework for the selection of qualified civil servants and to facilitate future manpower control and staff development. The exercise was supposed to precede the testing program, but implementation was slow and eventually lagged behind the testing. Thus, problems arose when in several large ministries, such as agriculture and health, the number of staff remaining after testing and other reduction measures still exceeded organizational requirements by a wide margin. In late 1990 this issue was holding up staffing decisions for restructured organizations and slowing the implementation of new organizational arrangements, which was very uneven.

Support for outplacement was provided by the Bureau d'Aide à la Reconversion des Agents de la Fonction Publique (BARAF), a self-

---

Box 8.3 Competency testing in Guinea

At the outset of the reform program, it was widely perceived that skill levels in the civil service were very low and poorly matched with job requirements. This understanding informed the decision to subject a large majority of civil servants to formal tests as a condition for employment in the new civil service.

An interministerial committee was established to oversee the testing program. With limited exceptions on the basis of seniority and education (no more than 10 percent per ministry), all civil servants were to be tested, even though testing of health and education personnel was deferred to a second phase. The process initially involved three stages: aptitude and knowledge tests customized by occupational category and by level, a competitive selection process, and a probation period. Examinees were to be classified as either pass, fail, or to be tested again following training.

At first, ministries were given complete latitude to organize their tests within this framework, and they hired various consulting firms. Early testing was poorly organized and administered, unit costs and standards varied widely, and test results had limited credibility. As a result, the government decided to centralize the contracting process in the Commissariat for Administrative Reform (CGRA).

With much tighter management of the testing program, a number of improvements were made: generic terms of reference were developed for test consulting services, target groups were tested by occupational category rather than by ministerial affiliation, trial tests were carried out to determine the suitability of various testing instruments and to calibrate them, testing supervision and processing were strengthened, and

employment advisory service backed by a credit program. With BARAF's assistance, retrenched civil servants or parastatal employees were eligible, pending approval of their project proposals, for credit lines up to the equivalent of thirty years' salary. The credit was provided by the banking system and fully guaranteed by donors (80 percent) and government (20 percent). By the end of 1988 some 1,800 applications had been received out of roughly 10,000 eligible workers and about 400 loans had been extended by the banks. Aside from modest success in helping civil service leavers establish themselves in recently privatized activities (for example, pharmaceutical retailing), the program was experiencing severe problems, most of all in loan recovery. About 80 percent of the loans were delinquent, and this threatened to undermine the emerging national credit system. As a result, the banks were withdrawing their support for the program in mid-1990, and the outplacement scheme was in abeyance.

Although retrenchment was the dominant element in the Guinean Civil Service Reform Program, the government also moved to improve

CGRA administered tests directly for such core interministerial skills as accounting, budgeting, and personnel administration. These measures and a vigorous media campaign made it possible for the testing program to proceed.

Observer reactions were mixed. On the one hand, more than 23,000 employees were successfully tested over the period 1986–90. On the other hand, more than 26,000, mostly in health and education, had yet to be tested and there were no specific plans to proceed. Moreover, the competitive selection process did not take place immediately after the testing phase as planned. Staff who had passed the tests had not yet been formally selected many months afterward. Conversely, some staff who had failed were still on the payroll and sometimes still working. High unit costs (between US$50 and several hundred dollars per capita) came under criticism. Several other criticisms were leveled at the testing concept and its implementation. These included the inability of the tests to measure experience, integrity, work attitudes, and other important factors; possible ethnic bias; and the suspicion that results had been manipulated for a few occupational categories. Other observers, however, argued that competency tests were less susceptible to ethnic bias than more personalized processes such as interviews, and thus a valid technique in an ethnically diverse country where other screening methods such as performance evaluations were not available.

In the final analysis, the concept of competency testing has retained some support given the special circumstances in Guinea, but few observers believe that the Guinean process, with its large technical assistance requirements and assignment of major responsibilities to expatriate personnel, would be widely replicable.

civil service pay. At year-end 1985 the average civil service salary was about US$16 a month, not including numerous but poorly documented in-kind benefits. Following the initial devaluation and dramatic increase in the prices of rice and petroleum products, the government increased base salaries by 80 percent in May 1986 and introduced cost of living and transport allowances. Average civil service pay, inclusive of allowances, rose to $43 a month. In 1988, base salaries were again boosted by 80 percent, along with large increases in allowances and premiums, resulting in an average monthly remuneration of about $94. Following these ad hoc pay adjustments, a new pay and benefit framework was introduced in April 1988 under the reform program. Largely a unique system, it was based neither on wage surveys nor on job evaluations, and it departed in other important respects from standard civil service models. A comprehensive set of new allowances—notably for housing, transportation, risk, hardship, and responsibility—replaced the old ones and was expected to represent a large proportion of individual pay packages, especially at higher grade levels. The new structure raised average remuneration to about $111 a month.

Impact of reform

Comparative analysis of reform results focused on how well the three country cases matched up in four target areas: employment, pay, the budget, and government performance. To assess and compare results, differences in country definitions of civil service employment had to be reconciled.[10] Extensive fieldwork was also required to compensate for the poor availability and quality of data and the fact that little was done in the three reform programs to establish baseline information and a monitoring framework.

Employment reductions

Reductions in civil service employment, the first of the four reform target areas, were made in all three cases, with downsizing ranging from 21 percent of prereform staff levels in Guinea to 4 percent in the Gambia (table 8.1). This ranking should be tempered, however, by recalling that the Gambia made sizable reductions in nonpermanent staff (not included in table 8.1) and started from a relatively smaller civil service. More important, despite gains in all three countries, the final impact of retrenchment on employment, has been undercut by rates of recruitment that have continued to exceed those of natural attrition. In the Gambia, where this erosion of downsizing gains was most severe, the government chose to maintain relatively high rates of recruitment. In Ghana, however, the erosion was not the product of policy; rather, it was caused by weak controls on recruitment. Although "uncontrolled recruitment" is difficult to evaluate in Ghana, rough estimates put it as high as 25 percent of the number of retrenched civil servants.[11] Moreover, there is evidence that a non-negligible proportion of the Ghanaian recruits were from the same occupational categories as those retrenched, and that some of those recruited had been retrenched earlier, thus pointing to slippage in the retrenchment program.

The composition of civil service employment also changed under the reform programs. Despite incomplete recruitment data for Ghana, there is strong evidence that recruitment of higher-level skilled staff rose considerably over the reform period, at a time when the retrenchment program made large reductions in the share of lower-level staff in overall civil service employment, both desirable outcomes. In the Gambia most of the reductions were made, mainly through divestiture, in two sector ministries—agriculture and public works—while other ministries, particularly in the social sectors, continued to grow. All of the countries exempted the education sector from employment cuts, with the exception of nonteaching staff in Ghana and Guinea and uncertified teachers in the Gambia. The health sector was also off limits to retrenchment in the Gambia and Guinea, and in Ghana it suffered hardly any cuts despite strong evidence of high levels of overstaffing.

Table 8.1 Impact of civil service downsizing in Ghana, the Gambia, and Guinea, various periods

Indicator	Ghana[a]	Gambia, The	Guinea[b]
Civil servants per 1,000 inhabitants			
Initial period	23	12	15
Latest period	18	10	8
Number of civil servants retrenched as a percentage of initial employment level[c]	16	10	23
Impact of retrenchment on employment, after recruitment and natural attrition (percent)[d]	15	4	21
Reference period	1986–90	1985/86–89/90	1985–89

Note: All employment figures exclude nonpermanent staff and military personnel.
a. Employment figures for Ghana include the civil service, the education service, and district assemblies, but exclude public service organizations that are not part of the civil service.
b. Employment figures for Guinea exclude parastatal civil servants.
c. Retrenchment is defined broadly to include all mechanisms used to remove civil servants from the payroll, including voluntary departure and early retirement programs and forced retirement and firings.
d. In each case the recruitment rate exceeded that of natural attrition. This accounts for the difference between retrenchment and final impact figures. The young age structure of the civil service in the three countries contributed to low rates of natural attrition—about 1 percent a year in each case, compared with roughly 5 percent in industrial countries.
Source: World Bank.

Pay reform

The impact on civil service pay, the second target area of reform, can be seen in table 8.2, which reviews pay conditions before and after the reforms. A robust pattern emerges in which pay outcomes are consistent with prereform country conditions. Real pay appears to have improved spectacularly in Guinea (118 percent), which had the smallest wage bill before the reforms (2.7 percent of GDP), and only slightly in Ghana (8.7 percent). The magnitude of the pay increase in Guinea, however, is probably overstated by a wide margin, as there were substantial but poorly documented in-kind benefits at the outset of reform. In Ghana the average increase also somewhat overstates the rise in individual wages, because 1.5 to 2.0 percent of the 2.1 percent average annual wage growth was due to increased recruitment of higher-skilled staff, which left little scope for an overall increase in individual wages. In the Gambia, the country with the largest wage bill (8.1 percent of GDP) and the highest pay at the outset of reform, real pay decreased by 12 percent.

Table 8.2 Outcomes of civil service pay reform in Ghana, the Gambia, and Guinea, various periods

Item	Ghana	Gambia, The	Guinea
Compression ratio[a]			
Initial period	4	10	4
Latest period	5	10	4
Average pay (US$ per month)			
Initial period	57	114	16
Latest period	61	100	128
Total average real pay increase (percent)	8.7	−12.0	118.0
Average annual real pay increase (percent)	2.1	−3.1	30.0
Average annual growth of GDP per capita (percent)	1.9	2.1	1.6
Ratio of average pay to GDP per capita			
Initial period	1.9	7.4	1.6
Latest period	2.0	6.8	3.7
Reference period	1986–90	1985/86–89/90	1986–89

Note: With the exception of compression ratios, pay data include allowances. Nominal pay has been deflated using the consumer price index.

a. The compression ratio is the ratio of the base pay of the top civil servant (for example, permanent secretary equivalent in the Gambia) to the base pay of the lowest civil servant (for example, messenger, watchman). In Ghana the fifty highest pay scales were excluded because they cover an odd assortment of positions that are graded above the level of the permanent secretary equivalent and capture only 0.1 percent of the civil service. This explains the apparent discrepancy between the widely cited ratio of 9:1 for Ghana in 1991 and the 5:1 reported here. Some analysts may also be factoring in generous housing allowances received by senior civil servants.

Source: World Bank.

No clear cross-country pattern, on the other hand, can be discerned in the compression ratios, which measure the highest to lowest base pay salaries. The ratios proved unsatisfactory indicators for making comparisons of wage differentials between higher- and lower-skilled staff, because of marked differences in the countries' pay and grade structures and the importance of nonwage allowances, especially in-kind benefits for which there is little information. Nonetheless, they do show that Ghana made limited progress in improving the relative pay of higher-level staff, an important pay reform objective in that country. Ghana actually did better than table 8.2 suggests. As a result of several changes in its income tax structure, Ghana's "take-home" pay compression ratio improved from 3:1 in 1986 to 5:1 in 1991.[12] In Guinea the gross pay scales remained very compressed, although if allowances had been taken into account, the compression ratio would probably have improved, since substantial nonwage allowances, representing a larger share of the compensation packages of higher-level staff, had been introduced into the pay structure in 1988.

Restructuring of the grade system featured in the pay reform programs of all the study countries. Grading reform was introduced fairly rapidly in the Gambia and Guinea, taking less than two years in each instance, even though the Gambian program involved the use of systematic job evaluations. In the Gambia grading reform was undertaken separately from pay increases and thus its impact can be measured. Out of a total of some 9,000 posts, 2,700 were upgraded and 870 were downgraded (and grandfathered), at a total cost of about 12 percent of the wage bill. This cost was expected to decline in succeeding years, because the pay of grandfathered staff was to remain frozen until servicewide pay adjustments brought it back in line with the new grade structure. In Ghana, where a more elaborate and participative approach was used and more radical changes were contemplated, the development of a new grade structure will have taken more than four years, assuming it is implemented as planned in early 1992.

With the exception of Guinea, pay reform did not affect nonwage benefit policies, although several ad hoc adjustments were made.[13] Indeed, it proved extremely difficult in all three cases to document and value nonwage benefits. Reform in this area was felt to be extremely complex and fraught with implementation difficulties. In Guinea numerous allowances were scrapped and a comprehensive set of new allowances was introduced along with the new grade structure. Implementation went smoothly, with the changes accompanied by a large overall wage increase. The new structure, however, was introduced without much prior analysis, and the potential impact on productivity, staff deployment, pay competitiveness, and career development is not clear.

Budget reform

The budgetary impact of reform, the third area targeted by the Civil
Service Reform Programs, is presented in table 8.3, which shows
changes in the wage bill in relation to economic output and the budget.
The Gambia and Ghana reduced some of the pressure from the wage bill
on the budget. Although improvements in the relative size of operations
and maintenance outlays were small in both countries, the change was
greater in the Gambia, where preventing wages from crowding out
operations and maintenance expenditures had been a key reform objective. At the same time, zero real annual growth in Ghana's wage bill is
disappointing; the government had counted on modest growth,
financed partly by rising revenues, to restore a motivating wage. By contrast, the wage bill's share in the budget grew in Guinea, where the

**Table 8.3 Impact of reform on the budget in Ghana, the Gambia, and
Guinea, various periods**
(percent)

Indicator	Ghana	Gambia, The[a]	Guinea
Wage bill as a share of GDP			
Initial period	5.1	8.1	2.7
Latest period	4.3	7.8	3.8
Wage bill as a share of total expenditures			
Initial period	27	29	13
Latest period	24	20	18
Wage bill as a share of current expenditures			
Initial period	43	48	21
Latest period	42	32	35
Wage bill as a share of operations and maintenance			
Initial period	210	178	40
Latest period	205	157	106
Annual real growth			
Wage bill	0.0	4.5	16.3
GDP	4.6	5.4	4.4
Total revenues	2.4	9.4	7.4
Total expenditures	2.9	14.7	5.0
Current expenditures	0.8	15.1	−1.0
Operations and maintenance	3.3	7.8	−15.6
Reference period	1986–90	1985/86–1989/90	1986–89

Note: Expenditures on military staff have been excluded. Aggregates have been deflated by the GDP deflator. The only notable difference in budgetary coverage among the countries is the cost-sharing arrangement in Ghana for district assembly staff, half of whose basic salaries are funded under assembly budgets.
a. The large difference in the Gambia between the GDP deflator and the consumer price index, which
was used to deflate pay in table 8.2, accounts for the apparent discrepancy between the growth rates of
the wage bill and average civil service pay.
Source: World Bank.

wage bill and pay levels were initially the lowest, and where pay improved the most. Guinea's wage bill benefited from budgetary wind-falls, as the rollback in the state's role produced significant one-time savings in operations and maintenance requirements. It is therefore unlikely that pay levels in Guinea will continue to increase at recent rates, even if economic growth is maintained.

Another important budgetary consideration affecting the state's ability to improve civil service pay is the net effect of retrenchment on personnel expenditures. Two important questions emerge: How long does it take for salary savings from retrenchment to offset severance pay costs? Are the savings significant? To answer the first question, cost-savings streams are estimated for the downsizing programs in the Gambia and Ghana (table 8.4). Costs are based on estimated severance outlays, excluding pension benefits for which no reliable data could be obtained. They reflect the actual number of retrenched workers each year times the average severance pay package, which was reconstructed from the approximate length of service and grade level of the workers. Savings are estimates of base salary that government no longer pays retrenched workers, and they include extrapolations of future salary trends. The cost-savings streams in table 8.4 show that savings offset costs in a rela-

Table 8.4 Estimating downsizing costs and savings in Ghana, 1987–92, and the Gambia, 1985/86–1989/90

Ghana (millions of cedis)	1987	1988	1989	1990	1991	1992
Severance pay[a]	138.2	257.9	406.1	424.0	517.7	569.0
End-of-service award[b]	712.4	1,882.9	3,279.8	2,544.0	3,106.1	3,414.2
Total cost	850.6	2,140.8	3,685.9	2,968.0	3,623.8	3,983.3
Compensation savings	280.7	1,320.9	3,301.0	5,845.3	8,868.2	11,430.5
Net savings (costs)	(569.9)	(819.9)	(384.9)	2,877.3	5,244.4	7,447.2
Real net savings (costs)	(409.5)	(442.3)	(161.7)	914.5	1,392.5	1,835.0
Cumulative real net savings (costs)	(409.5)	(851.8)	(1,013.5)	(99.0)	1,293.6	3,128.6
Discounted cumulative real net savings (costs)	(409.5)	(778.1)	(890.4)	(361.1)	310.4	1,047.9

Gambia, The (millions of dalasis)	1985/86	1986/87	1987/88	1988/89	1989/90
Severance pay[c]	0.8	3.0	0.4	0.4	0.4
Compensation savings	2.0	9.9	12.3	12.3	12.3
Net savings (costs)	1.2	6.9	11.9	11.9	11.9
Real net savings (costs)	1.8	8.6	13.5	11.9	10.5
Cumulative real net savings (costs)	1.8	10.4	24.0	35.9	46.3

Note: Costs exclude pension benefits, for which no reliable information was available.
a. Severance pay consisted of four months' base pay.
b. The end-of-service award consisted of two months' base pay per year of service.
c. Nonpermanent staff received one month's salary, and civil servants with more than five years' seniority received 1.2 months' salary per year of service.
Source: Author's estimates, based on World Bank data.

tively short period: less than one year in the Gambia and about five years in Ghana. The quick "payback period" in the Gambia reflects the preponderance of nonpermanent staff in a retrenchment program that consisted of just two rounds, as well as the relatively low severance payments for civil servants. By contrast, Ghana's retrenchment program focused on established staff and consisted of a series of annual exercises with relatively high severance benefits.

A notable finding of the analysis, however, is the limited ability of downsizing to fund pay increases. In Ghana savings from retrenchment were low since most retrenched workers came from the lower tiers of the salary structure. At the same time, Ghana faced the relatively high cost of recruiting larger numbers of higher-skilled staff. In Guinea and to a lesser extent in Ghana, the cost of retrenchment and other employment reduction measures absorbed substantial resources. A further claim on resources was the young age structure of all three civil services, which translated into low natural attrition levels—about 1 percent a year as against roughly 5 percent in industrial countries—and hence into costly grade drift.[14] In Ghana, where the wage bill remained roughly constant in real terms, savings from retrenchment were sufficient to offset retrenchment costs and grade drift over the reform period, but hardly enough to finance a significant increase in average real pay. Only in the Gambia, where retrenchment costs were much lower, would savings from downsizing have paid for a modest increase in average compensation if the real wage bill had remained constant.

Severance and other payments thus represent a substantial initial drain on the budget, often exceeding the short-term savings from downsizing. Grade drift makes a further claim on savings. At the same time, increasing the wage bill at the expense of other discretionary expenditure categories is not a viable option. This would be difficult to justify in the three countries, as indeed it would be in most African countries, in view of inadequate levels of operations and maintenance, not to mention capital expenditures. In sum, although two of the three pay and employment reform programs have clearly halted the downward pay spiral, they offer little prospect for a rapid return to earlier remuneration levels.

Government performance

The ultimate target of pay and employment reform, improved government performance, proved the most elusive of the reform goals. Policy changes insinuate themselves slowly into organizational cultures. With the three programs still under way and only five to six years behind them, changes in individual and organizational behavior may not have shown up yet. Some tentative conclusions can be ventured, however. On the macroeconomic side, it is clear that the reform programs have been fairly successful in treating critical systemic disorders that have had pernicious effects on organizational performance. Where pay was extremely low, it was increased (substantially in Guinea and slightly in Ghana); where the wage bill's share in the budget was large, its growth was halted and the share marginally reduced (the Gambia, Ghana); and where overstaffing was manifest, it was cut back (all three). In Ghana the skill mix in government has also improved. At the same time, there is some anecdotal evidence on the microeconomic side that government workers do respond with much-improved performance to a combination of better pay, better working conditions, more satisfying work, and good leadership. Cases in point are the strong performance in Ghana of some of the Economic Reform Program task forces, the Management Services Division, and a handful of organizations outside the civil service proper, such as the National Revenue Service.

Although improved pay and streamlined staffing featured in almost all of the successful organizations, no conclusive evidence was found of better pay and leaner staffing alone leading to major productivity gains. Indeed, many observers believe that performance gains have been meager in the Guinean civil service, where pay improvements have been the greatest. Civil service moonlighting, rent-seeking, and absenteeism, for instance, do not appear to have been curbed. This suggests that pay and employment reforms, although important determinants of performance, need to be supplemented with other measures. Macroeconomic policy reform cannot by itself foster the major changes in work attitudes, ethics, and organizational culture that are needed if significant performance improvements are to be realized. A more focused effort in nurturing behavioral change is likely to be a major challenge faced by second-generation reforms.

Finally, the analysis of reform results requires some assessment of their sustainability. Are the gains being preserved? Are civil service management institutions internalizing capabilities for continuous change and adaptation? On each count, the study cases measure up very differently. Having met its initial employment reduction targets and cut the size of the wage bill, the Gambia is pursuing neither retrenchment nor other reform measures that could significantly improve performance. Its relatively effective system of establishment controls sufficiently safeguards against the rapid reversal of recent manpower efficiency gains. The reform program has also gone far to build up the institutional infrastructure of the central personnel function. This work has included a revised legal framework (the Public Service Act, general orders, and Public Service Commission regulations); an improved payroll system processed on the Ministry of Finance's mainframe computer;

the piloting of a computerized personnel information system in the Personnel Management Office, with direct links to payroll in the Ministry of Finance; and the development of a personnel procedures manual and a staff information handbook. Notwithstanding these accomplishments, prospects for future gains, and the continuing adequacy of existing pay and employment policy frameworks, are uncertain. The Personnel Management Office is having trouble graduating from an essentially reactive policy role to a proactive one, overall civil service staffing levels have begun creeping upward again, pay has continued to fall, and institutional processes and capabilities have not been built in to ensure continuing policy adaptation.

In contrast, Guinea is still struggling to establish the basic building blocks of routine civil service management functions. Reform accomplishments are thus vulnerable to rapid erosion as happened with early census actions. Major efforts are under way to establish viable manpower control and information systems, including the computerization of payroll and the development in the Ministry of Civil Service of a personnel data base that is linked to the Ministry of Finance's payroll system. If successful and internalized, these measures will help secure reform gains and lay the foundation for sustained performance of routine functions. The fruits of these labors are several years off, however.

Of the three cases, Ghana has made the most progress in developing civil service management institutions. After an early period of training and coaching from external consultants, the OHCS's Management Services Division, whose staff has grown from eight to fifty-two, can now carry out job inspections independently. The focus of coaching has turned to more complex management reviews. The Personnel Policy Development Division has established a basic personnel information system tied to payroll, which will greatly improve its capacity for manpower planning and analysis. Payroll management has also been strengthened. Together, these developments have made it possible for Ghana to reestablish manpower budgeting and control procedures and to integrate them fully into the overall budgeting process. The country now possesses the essential tools to lock in reform gains. With further strengthening of the Management Services and Personnel Policy Divisions, Ghana will have internalized the capacity for continuous productivity improvement and institutional adaptation. Still, this outcome is clearly several years away. Furthermore, even in Ghana the reform process is still dependent on top-down direction and external stimuli. The ultimate challenge is to build grass-roots constituencies for reform, within the civil service and the public at large, that will allow the process to survive both changes in political leadership and the phasing out of external finance for policy reform.

Lessons of reform: the elements of success

Many African countries have launched, and others are preparing, similar programs to put government pay and employment back on an even keel. The early implementation experiences of Ghana, the Gambia, and Guinea offer an opportunity to shorten the learning curve. This section weighs the merits of the strategies chosen and tries to pinpoint the elements of success and failure in implementation.

Reform strategy and design

In Ghana the reform strategy combined short- and long-term policy and institutional reform objectives. Short-term policy actions centered on the design, preparation, and implementation requirements of retrenchment and pay reform. Institutional activities encompassed a review of the personnel function, strengthening of the Management Services Division, introduction of a new grade structure, and improvements in civil service training. With the exception of the general training component, institutional and policy components were tightly integrated. In retrospect, the analysis of retrenchment results shows that cross-functional institutional issues, such as manpower budgeting and control, payroll, and manpower information systems, did not receive enough attention in the early stages of reform. The institutional development component would have had more effect had it been broadened to include selected budgeting and accounting functions in the Ministry of Finance and the Controller and Accountant-General's Office. It may also have been premature to insert a general training component without clear linkages to policy reform. Finally, a distinguishing feature of Ghana's program was the relatively intensive involvement of civil servants in preparing and implementing reform measures. Although the high degree of national participation slowed the implementation of some components, it generated a strong sense of reform ownership and helped make Ghana's Civil Service Reform Program by far the most proactively managed of the three study cases.

Driven by fiscal concerns, the Gambia's strategy put a premium in the early stages on the speedy execution of employment reductions, with pay and grade adjustments to follow shortly thereafter. A second phase was expected to address longer-term institutional development issues. The short-term nature of the initial phase was reinforced by the use of external consultants operating under a lump sum, time-bound contract. Working under budget and time constraints, the consultants could not mobilize much local participation at the technical level. The objectives of the first phase were attained rapidly in the Gambia in comparison with the other two study cases, although at some cost in lost opportunities for internalizing reform and training local staff. In some instances, short-term actions also undermined long-term objectives. By way of example, in the 1989–90 budget hearings the Personnel Management Office's request for job inspector positions was denied by the Ministry of Finance on the grounds of staffing restrictions, thus effectively preventing the personnel office from auditing manpower levels.

Under the second phase of the Gambia's reform, the emphasis shifted away from short-term employment and pay issues to a longer-term institutional development program, for which resident advisers were deemed more suitable than short-term consultants. The shift in focus appears to have been problematic. The former Secretary-General to the Presidency, the initial "champion of reform," was no longer associated with the program. The leverage provided by the first phase's close integration with the structural adjustment program diminished as reform moved away from cost-cutting issues and no longer figured explicitly in lending conditions for policy reform. No internal constituency for reform emerged to substitute for this loss, and government commitment slackened. Despite active donor involvement and supervision, the second phase was losing momentum.

The distinctive features of Guinea's reform strategy were its long-term perspective and focus on capacity-building, and its comprehensiveness and complexity. The complexity of the reform program strained implementation capabilities, as illustrated by the problems in implementing census follow-up, staff reductions, and ministerial restructuring. Guinea's highly integrated approach led to sequencing problems when some actions (for example, ministerial restructuring and staffing) lagged behind, and were in turn delayed by the outcome of other actions (for example, competency testing). In retrospect, a more selective and sequential approach to reform with an earlier emphasis on civil service "maintenance" functions—payroll management, personnel information systems, ministry-level personnel administration—might have paid greater dividends and averted, for instance, costly repeats of the initial census.

Several lessons can be distilled from the three reform strategies. The Ghanaian strategy illustrates the need for systematic analytic and institutional sector work prior to the design phase. Such an analysis would have highlighted and helped specify institutional actions that should have accompanied the policy reforms—in this instance, measures to strengthen controls over manpower, especially recruitment. In contrast, the Gambian strategy points to the inability of good technical design and support to compensate for shallow commitment, and it demonstrates the need for cost-cutting to be ingrained in the organizational culture as a long-term concern. Finally, the Guinean strategy shows the limits to reform imposed by weak initial administrative capacity. These limits cannot be entirely overridden through large infusions of technical assistance, without compromising reform ownership and internalization.

These lessons have important implications for program design. At the program identification stage, analytic work should lay out the main features and trends of pay and employment policy and relate them to current and future budgetary and macroeconomic conditions. An important product of this work would be a financial model for generating alternative pay and employment reform scenarios that highlight the tradeoffs between pay and employment reforms, and between the reforms and macroeconomic policies. A second essential step is an institutional assessment of personnel management systems and procedures that at a minimum identifies the main shortcomings of establishment control. Together, the analytic work and institutional assessment will help frame a reform strategy in which short-term measures are explicitly designed to support long-term objectives; policy and institutional reform actions are closely integrated; and the scope of reform is tailored to administrative capacity. Strategy development will also provide an early test of the commitment to reform at the political and technical levels. In some cases, high-level seminars or workshops may prove valuable at this stage in eliciting an awareness of the strategic implications of short-term civil service reform measures in a structural adjustment context. The rest of the preparatory work would consist of engaging local stakeholders and their consultants in the process of sorting and fleshing out specific reform options and implementation requirements.

Reform sequencing

The retrenchment experience also offers lessons on the sequencing of targeting techniques. When the reform programs began, overstaffing had reached such chronic and visible levels that it would have been overkill to engage in extensive analysis to identify redundant staff. Where overstaffing has reached similar proportions, early work should ideally focus on establishing a fair and objective process for laying off staff, ensuring that manpower controls—especially those on recruitment—are reliable, and improving information systems as rapidly as possible. As overstaffing is cut back, more sophisticated targeting tools, such as management and functional reviews and job inspections, would be required.

Although overall strategy, design, and sequencing weighed heavily in the outcomes of the three programs, the key elements of success at the implementation stage were technical assistance strategies, country ownership and commitment, and reform management structures.

Technical assistance. It is hardly surprising that technical assistance played a critical role in all three countries. Civil service censuses have not been implemented successfully without some form of technical assistance, and the complexity of pay and employment reform tasks calls for an array of professional skills (for example, organizational analysis and design, policy analysis, compensation expertise) that are in short supply in developing countries. Faced with these requirements, the three countries used technical assistance in different ways. In Ghana consulting services were provided throughout the program by a joint venture combining a management consulting firm and a public administration training institute. The staffing strategy involved the use of a resident coordinator and specialists who made periodic visits. In the Gambia an initial short-term management consultancy involving a team of consultants was followed by the assignment of three resident advisers. In Guinea assistance was provided all along by long-term resident advisers, with relatively small inputs from visiting specialists.

The approach followed in Ghana appears to hold the most promise, despite the higher costs in the short run. The generalist resident coordinator provided the needed continuity and element of coordination. At the same time, the use of visiting specialists provided the needed flexibility to adjust to local decisionmaking uncertainties, to capitalize on unforeseen opportunities, and to produce combinations of professional skills and roles well suited to the specific tasks. The approach also produced incentives for counterpart training and thus capacity-building. Visiting consultants in a long-term relationship were under pressure to train their counterparts to ensure that reform implementation continued apace between their periodic visits, while at the same time the progress of the reform program was opening up new areas for the consultancy. Equivalent pressure does not exist with resident technical advisers, whose comparable skill advantage is more rapidly exhausted and who may not be needed at the next stage of reform.

Another especially useful feature of Ghana's technical assistance arrangement was the production, early in the consultancy assignment, of detailed reform component strategies for pay and grading, personnel management, management services, and training. This helped produce action programs, organize counterpart staff, and program specialist inputs, and thus served to structure the assignment and reduce task uncertainty. The main risk of such an arrangement is for the consultancy to become excessively supply-driven, a risk that can only be minimized when the implementing agency plays a leading role in managing the consultancy, with backstopping, if necessary, from aid management specialists.

In contrast, the Gambian experience shows that although short-term, time-bound, lump sum consultancy contracts can help produce a

quick payoff, they are not likely to generate enduring institutional benefits. The decision to use resident advisers in the second stage also had its
drawbacks. Such personnel can lack accountability and a sense of
urgency, and their cost advantage is partly offset by the greater flexibility of consulting firms whose inputs can be timed for maximum impact,
whose "downtime" can be minimized, and whose specialists can bring
deeper expertise to bear on technical issues. In addition, the deployment
of resident advisers does not reduce the risk of supply-driven technical
assistance, since they have less flexible professional alternatives than
their consultant counterparts.

Country ownership and commitment. The level of technical assistance
inputs and the way in which they were used also contributed to varying
degrees of reform ownership, another important element of success.
Country ownership of the reform program and commitment at the technical level were highest in Ghana, where consultants were used mainly
for methodological and training inputs, while national staff contributed
the bulk of preparation and implementation work. Although the initial
cost of greater participation was slower implementation, this was offset
by improved chances of sustainability. This was a deliberate choice, and
in a few explicit instances decisions were made to forsake desirable
design features and rapid implementation in order to generate greater
participation and reform ownership (see box 8.1). In the Gambia, mainly
on account of the emphasis on short-term results, the involvement of
national staff in design, decisionmaking, and implementation was lower,
and so was ownership. In Guinea the role of external consultants and
donors was greatest, if only because of the imbalance between the high
complexity of reform measures and the scarcity of local skills. At the
same time, commitment to reform in the three countries varied considerably by line ministry. In the Gambia two sector ministries, initially representing some 30 percent of total government employment, accounted
for two-thirds of the civil service staff reductions. Likewise in Ghana
and Guinea, some ministries contributed disproportionately to reform
outcomes while others contributed little or nothing and, in some cases,
significantly delayed reform implementation.

This suggests the potential attractiveness of an alternative reform
strategy in place of the top-down, across-the-board approaches adopted
by the three countries: in the first phase, pilot self-selected sector organizations would be given incentives to downsize and restructure; systemwide reforms would follow in a second phase. Similarly, the potential of "enclave" approaches for treating critical pay problems should
not be overlooked as an interim step toward servicewide reform. As
noted earlier, selected institutions of varying strategic importance in

Ghana have been allowed to depart from civil service pay and employment policies (see box 8.2 for the exceptionally successful case of the National Revenue Service). The overall experience, however, has been mixed. Resentment was generated among excluded agencies, which created pressure to expand the privileges of the few. Thus, although enclave approaches hold some promise, they should be used cautiously and selectively. Success appears to hinge on the presence of certain stringent enabling conditions, including the recognized strategic character of the institution, clear accountability for performance, high-quality leadership, and the existence of a credible long-term strategy to improve overall civil service pay. Apart from the National Revenue Service, these conditions could be found in only a handful of other institutions.

Reform management structures. A third element of successful implementation was the institutional setup for managing reform. In the Gambia and Ghana reform management structures consisted of interministerial oversight committees, led by the head of the personnel function or by the Secretary to the Cabinet. The committees received technical support from the central personnel function. In Ghana a separate interministerial working group with overlapping membership—the Redeployment Management Committee—was created to manage the retrenchment process. This was a useful arrangement because it allowed the general oversight committee to distance itself somewhat from the cost-cutting aspects of reform and to focus more on capacity-building. Guinea followed a different approach altogether and established first a Commissariat for Administrative Reform, then a Ministry for Administrative Reform and the Civil Service. Several problems emerged. In the absence of a systematic process for interministerial consultations, line ministries failed to buy into several reform activities such as the restructuring program. Moreover, the attempt to develop simultaneously reform and civil service management capabilities within the same ministry diluted both efforts.

Lessons of reform: recurring problems

The poor record of civil service censuses in generating lasting reforms is a conclusive finding of this study (box 8.4). Even when they produced reliable results, they frequently failed to produce significant budgetary savings or to bring about durable improvements in personnel or payroll information systems. Where censuses led to personnel actions, the final but necessary step of correcting payroll data for the personnel actions was often not taken. Thus, greater discrimination is warranted in the use of censuses, and closer monitoring is necessary, especially in the final

Box 8.4 Lessons from civil service censuses

The main benefits of improved manpower information are an improved
analytic basis for policymaking, including better targeting of employment
reduction programs and pay decisions, and improved manpower-plan-
ning capabilities. Typical census exercises, whose purpose is to help build
or strengthen this essential information base, can be divided in six phases:
design, preparation, fieldwork, processing, validation, and a concurrent
systems implementation phase. An essential requirement is a detailed
design that is carefully reviewed before launching the census. Critical
design elements are the forms or questionnaires, which must be field-test-
ed and precoded; the enumeration strategy; census logistics, particularly
staffing; external or local technical assistance, which is almost always
needed; data-processing requirements; an information strategy (use of the
media will normally be required); postprocessing validation in which census findings yielding personnel actions are verified and individual appeals
are heard; and planning of systems improvements downstream of the processing phase.

Seven censuses were carried out under the three Civil Service Reform
Programs, three each in Ghana and Guinea and one in the Gambia. Two
failed to produce reliable results altogether, largely because they were carried out without technical assistance and were processed manually; three
produced better information, although only two of these generated short-
term budgetary savings; and only two hold promise for generating
durable budgetary and information gains. Where censuses led to estimates of short-term savings, the level of estimated budgetary savings
ranged from 2 percent to 5 percent of the wage bill. The two censuses with
the best prospects of achieving durable results had been carried out within
a program to improve institutional manpower information systems as
well as manpower budgeting. Thus, census data were being used to load a
new payroll system (Guinea) or, alternatively, to enhance data on the
existing system and to revitalize manpower budgeting and control
(Ghana). In the absence of specific measures to ensure the sustainability of
census results, the rate of erosion of payroll data can be significant: the last
census in Conakry, carried out less than two years after the previous one,
found that 23 percent of the entries in existing rolls were spurious.

Costs, implementation time, and technical assistance support varied
widely: censuses were relatively cheap in the Gambia and Ghana, but cost
US$5 to $25 per civil servant in Guinea; the duration of the exercises varied from six to twelve months; and technical inputs ranged from none to
about sixty staff-months. Costs and time varied according to the existence
of computerized manpower information systems such as the payroll, the
availability and degree of utilization of local skills, and the thoroughness
of the field validation process, where managers may simply verify data
generated by personnel and budget officers, or mobile census teams may
be sent out to conduct work site interviews of individual civil servants.

phase. Wherever there is no immediate prospect of correcting the systemic weaknesses that have made the census necessary, costly general censuses should be avoided. In many cases this means taking actions, without preamble, to strengthen controls on payroll and personnel and to improve information systems. Lighter, cheaper census exercises, like those in Ghana that stopped short of sending out field teams to interview civil servants, might also be used as interim measures.

The experience of formal outplacement schemes is equally poor. These schemes are exceptionally difficult to design, given both the poor match between the skills of redundant state workers and the main sources of demand for labor—agriculture and the informal sector—and the poor understanding of how jobs are created in the informal sector. Experience suggests that a majority of civil servants do not require structured outplacement assistance beyond severance benefits and orientation information (for example, feedback from workers already redeployed), as evidenced by the small fraction of retrenched workers who applied for assistance; and that formal self-employment credit programs should be avoided altogether. Such credit programs have consistently had a very poor credit recovery record and an equally dubious record in establishing viable private ventures. Credit recovery rates in the Gambia and Guinea were about 30 percent or less. This compares with 60 percent for traditional credit schemes administered by the same self-employment organization in the Gambia. Credits also proved extremely costly on a per capita basis and often had to be rationed, thus leading to perceptions of inequity.

With the qualified exception of Guinea, the reforms also failed to improve overall pay levels significantly, in spite of favorable economic conditions over the reform periods. Various combinations of methods were used to estimate desirable pay levels and policies, but with mixed results. Ghana, for instance, used both a comparative wage survey and minimum household budgets constructed from discussions with focus groups. Each method led to pay recommendations that far exceeded the government's budgetary constraints.[15] A more modest pay reform objective in the Gambia—the restoration of real pay to earlier levels that were deemed adequate—was also shelved indefinitely because it could not be afforded. Thus, until budget constraints are eased, it may be more fruitful for governments to pursue the less costly alternative of increasing pay differentials. In addition, although Guinea has acted to restore some balance between nonwage benefits and pay by monetizing pay and increasing average pay sharply, the Gambia and Ghana have not yet tackled the problem of in-kind benefits, particularly housing; still, these benefits do not yet appear to have reached the alarming proportions found in other countries such as Angola or Zambia.[16]

Finally, the three study cases underscore the need to weigh the relative costs and benefits of different employment reduction mechanisms. By far the most cost-effective measure is the imposition of a recruitment ceiling and the avoidance of unplanned recruitment. In terms of financial returns to the budget, the second most effective mechanism is retrenchment, with payback periods ranging from less than one to about five years. Early retirement is next on the scale, since the savings stream is short and inducements are relatively high. By far the most costly measures are voluntary departure schemes. Early retirement and voluntary departure programs are also the least desirable from a performance standpoint, unless they are structured to prevent skilled staff from leaving key occupations and sectors. Such cost-benefit considerations raise doubts about Guinea's decision to use the two most costly mechanisms, and about the appropriateness of the sequencing of staff reduction measures in Ghana, where an earlier focus on strengthening recruitment controls would have minimized the erosion of retrenchment gains.

Conclusions

Several broad lessons have emerged from the study cases. First, successful reform begins with the development of a strategic framework that harnesses cost-cutting objectives to the overarching goal of performance improvement over the long haul. Second, reform programs need to be tailored to country conditions including, for example, the financial and economic weight of the country's civil service, the level of pay, the degree of pay compression, and initial administrative capacity. Third, although commitment of the core political leadership is sufficient to achieve most pay and employment reforms in the short run, sustained results and capacity-building require a broader base of support that extends to sector institutions and middle management.

Fourth, most reform scenarios will call for up-front institutional actions (for example, appraisal and strengthening of manpower controls, if necessary), which must be closely integrated with policy actions (censuses, retrenchment) if the benefits are to be sustained. Fifth, the underlying premises of outplacement programs must be reconsidered: that some outplacement support is needed is not disputed, but the accumulating evidence from the study cases and other experiences indicates that scarce resources would be better spent on severance allowances and employment information services. Sixth, upstream sector work needs to be improved. Better analysis of pay and employment issues and their links to the macroeconomic framework would inject more realism into reform design; and more systematic institutional assessments would identify the critical institutional weaknesses that, if uncorrected, imperil implementation and sustainability.

In the end, new ground was broken by the retrenchment experiences. The three countries have helped dispel unhelpful preconceptions about the behavior of retrenched civil servants. Governments had assumed that civil servants would lack the skills and will to seize employment opportunities in rural areas and in the informal sector. Downsizing was put off in the fear of higher unemployment and political unrest. But evidence from the Gambia and Ghana should allay those concerns. Many of those laid off chose redeployment in agricultural activities; many others made the leap to the informal sector. The Ghanaian authorities even received a significant number of unsolicited applications for the retrenchment program. Other countries preparing similar reforms can also take heart from the findings that retrenchment is susceptible to good technical and political management, and that it need not have long-term adverse consequences on morale and performance.

Notes

1. The chapter is based on extensive field work by consultants and World Bank staff, and it draws on a large volume of government and project documents, as well as numerous interviews with the key reform actors: government officials, donors, consultants, and technical assistance providers.

2. Other cases with established records of comparable length—about five to seven years—include the Central African Republic, Mauritania, and Senegal.

3. A. L. Adu, *The Civil Service in New African States* (London: Allen & Unwin, 1965), p. 8.

4. In 1983 the number of civil servants per 100 inhabitants in English-speaking countries ranged between 0.7 (Malawi) and 2.1 (Zambia), and in French-speaking countries between 0.5 (Burkina Faso, Niger) and 1.8 (Cameroon). For data on civil service employment in Sub-Saharan Africa, see David Lindauer, Oey Astra Meesook, and Parita Suebsaeng, "Government Wage Policy in Africa: Some Findings and Policy Issues," *World Bank Research Observer*, vol. 3, no. 1 (January 1988), p. 6; and World Bank, "Mozambique: Public Sector Pay and Employment Review," Report No. 9815-MOZ, Washington, D.C., December 1991, p. 13.

5. Although nurses in the civil service and teachers in the education service were exempted from the retrenchment program, both personnel groups were included in the base from which the 5 percent retrenchment target was calculated. Together these groups represented more than a third of total employment in the combined government services.

6. Job inspections assess the work needs of an organization in relation to organizational objectives and the adequacy of staffing, grading levels, and reporting relationships. Functional reviews, as the term is used in Ghana, review common functions or services (for example, catering, building maintenance, sup-

ply management) performed throughout the administration with the aim of establishing objective staffing, service level, and productivity standards.

7. The existing pay system merely lays out pay points and ranges, but individual grades for a given occupational grouping or class overlap several pay ranges and there is no consistency among grades of different classes.

8. The share of public enterprise employees in the target could not be determined. Their separation from the civil service was, however, an important early reform since they had been employed on the same terms as civil servants. In a related reform, the government was carrying out a sweeping privatization program in which many public enterprise employees were being removed entirely from public sector employment.

9. Thirty percent of this sum was paid up front, and the balance in monthly installments over twenty months. At first, severance payments were based on length of service, but the formula was abandoned after it proved difficult to administer because of the poor state of personnel records.

10. In Ghana, for example, the education service and district assemblies are separate from the civil service, although pay and employment conditions in the education service are only slightly different from those in the civil service, and in the district assemblies they are virtually the same. A more serious problem is that many public service organizations in Ghana (such as national revenue, highways, and universities) operate outside the civil service, while their equivalents in the Gambia and Guinea are part of the civil service. Although staff in the education service and the district assemblies have been included in the employment figures for Ghana (see table 8.1), data were unavailable for staff in public sector organizations. This may slightly affect intercountry comparisons, but it is unlikely to invalidate them. Finally, incomplete data for the three countries prevented the author from including nonpermanent staff in the comparative analysis, even though this group was greatly reduced in the Gambian retrenchment program.

11. Insufficient data prevented an assessment of the effects of "uncontrolled recruitment" in Guinea.

12. Take-home pay ratios, although more meaningful than gross pay ratios, were not available for the Gambia and Guinea. See notes to table 8.2 for an explanation of the apparent discrepancy between reports that put Ghana's compression ratio at 9:1 in 1991 and our figure of 5:1 in 1990.

13. In July 1991, several months after this study was completed, Ghana began consolidating fringe benefits into base salaries. The reform encompasses both the civil service and public servants outside the civil service. Implementation is generally well advanced. Base pay now incorporates housing benefits—including an imputed sum for free housing—and transportation, lunch, and leave allowances. Income tax brackets and the formula for employees' social security and pension contributions—but not for employers' contributions—were adjusted downward to neutralize the effect on take-home pay. Although only partially implemented, the reform would end the practice of providing senior officials with cars, and the existing fleet would be sold off at preferential rates to users. The reform has not been free of controversy. Some civil servants erred in believing they would receive a higher salary. Others were upset when they real-

ized just how badly paid they were relative to public servants outside the civil service who had been receiving large, "hidden" allowances.

14. Grade drift occurs when recruitment, career progression, and attrition change the distribution of civil servants in the grade structure. In a steady state with little variation in recruitment patterns, the grade distribution can be designed so that career progression is offset by young recruits joining at the bottom of grade ranges and replacing retirees leaving at the top.

15. Efforts by the three countries to determine appropriate levels of pay were also plagued by a number of technical problems, including the choice of a suitable reference period, the small size of the modern private sector, insufficient disaggregation of available household survey data, and the difficulty of measuring nonwage allowances, especially in-kind benefits.

16. See note 13 above.

9

Dealing with redundancies in government employment in Ghana

Peter Gregory

In 1957 Ghana became the first Sub-Saharan African nation to achieve independence. Compared with other countries in the region, Ghana boasted the highest per capita income and endowment of human capital. As the world's largest producer of cocoa and endowed with ample land and natural resources, Ghana's economic prospects seemed bright.

Origins of overstaffing in the civil service

The country's first government after Independence departed little from the policies of the colonial administration and favored private investment and production. The gross domestic product responded favorably, with growth averaging about 5 percent a year between 1955 and 1959. By the end of the decade, however, the orientation of government shifted radically toward an increasing role for the state. Although small-scale private investment was tolerated, all major investment projects were reserved for the public sector. Considerable investment was made in improving infrastructure as well as in establishing large-scale, capital-intensive industrial establishments and mechanized state farms. At the same time, other forms of government intervention in the economy increased substantially as direct controls were introduced over prices, exchange rates, imports, and allocations of foreign exchange. Ghana came to be characterized quite appropriately as a "command economy."

The results of the economic program proved severely disappointing. In spite of a doubling of the capital stock during the 1960s, per capita income declined by more than 10 percent.[1] Conditions did not improve in the 1970s. Rather, the economy continued to deteriorate as economic policies destroyed incentives for production for domestic markets and exports. As the tax base shrank and inflation accelerated, the government resorted increasingly to monetary expansion to finance expenditures. Gross domestic product declined on average by half a percent a year, and by 1982 per capita income had fallen by 30 percent from the 1970 level, according to official data.[2]

Despite the economic decline and the dwindling resources available to the government, the civil service expanded steadily. By the mid-1980s the core civil service numbered almost 144,000, while the educational establishment and other governmental services employed an additional 161,700 persons (excluding military, police, and parastatal personnel). As employment expanded, the real wage bill shrank by 15 percent a year and government real expenditures on goods and services by 13 percent. Obviously, these changes implied a sharp decline in the volume of expenditures on goods and services each government employee had to work with.

Simultaneously, real wages of civil servants fell precipitously, especially for the upper ranks since salary increases heavily favored the less skilled occupational groups that accounted for the bulk of public employment. In 1982 the salary of a messenger was the equivalent of 47 percent of his 1977 wage while that of a senior civil servant, such as a permanent secretary, had plunged to 12 percent of the 1977 level. Much of the decline in real earnings occurred in 1977–80, when only small adjustments were made in nominal wages though the price level quadrupled.[3] With wage adjustment policies that favored the lower grades, a sharp compression of the wage structure was inevitable. Between 1977 and 1983 the salary ratio of the most to the least skilled civil servant tumbled from about 10.8:1 to only 2.2:1 and declined further to 1.9:1 in early 1985. This compared to an estimated ratio in the private sector of 10:1.[4]

By the early 1980s it was obvious that the effectiveness of public administration had been so weakened that it served as a major constraint to the implementation of an economic reform program. Shortages of skilled professional and technical personnel were endemic, while considerable overstaffing was evident in the junior levels. Nonlabor inputs, such as paper, office machinery, pharmaceutical supplies, and tools, had become extremely scarce. Productivity was acknowledged to be extremely low in all of the basic functions of government, a condition exacerbated by absenteeism, moonlighting, poor morale, lack of supervision, and an absence of pride in work and rewards for good performance. Contributing to this state of affairs were the inadequate level of remuneration, political instability, and the erosion of checks and balances designed to limit expansion in staff, enforce discipline, and control corruption.[5]

The combination of a badly deteriorated economy and an ineffective public sector finally forced the government to seek a change in direction. Part of this new direction involved the retrenchment of large numbers of redundant civil servants. In the discussion that follows, the concerns of government leaders over the consequences of the redeployment exercise are considered and the merits of these concerns evaluated.

Feasibility of retrenchment

In 1983 the government embarked on a broad program of economic and structural reforms to reverse the deteriorating state of the economy. Among the problems to be tackled were an overstaffed civil service and inadequate and compressed pay scales. By late 1985 the government had committed itself to an overhaul of the salary structure and to a phased program of retrenchment. It proposed a 4 to 5 percent reduction in employment in each of three years beginning in 1987. Since total central government employment exclusive of the army and police force numbered more than 300,000, this implied a reduction of nearly 12,000 government employees each year. Adding reductions contemplated in the parastatal sector and autonomous agencies meant that public sector employment could shrink by more than 50,000 within a three-year period.

Although government officials were convinced of the necessity of reducing public sector employment, they were also apprehensive about the political fallout. In particular, they were fearful that the dismissals would add to increased urban unemployment and political unrest. Their fears reflected a belief that rigidities in labor markets would inhibit adjustment to changing conditions. For example, it was assumed that former agricultural workers, having experienced employment outside the agricultural sector, would prefer to remain unemployed rather than return to agriculture. On the evidence of the tiny share of private sector wage employment (less than 6 percent in 1984) in the total labor force, the absorption of released government workers into urban wage employment was expected to be slight. Furthermore, the private sector had its own burden of redundant workers as a result of a 1972 decree barring staffing reductions of more than ten employees without government permission,[6] as well as generous severance allowances negotiated in collective bargaining agreements during more affluent times.

Although these concerns were understandable, they seem to have been unduly pessimistic. We draw this conclusion based on three independent sets of information. First, previous layoffs of large numbers of workers in Ghana, including government retrenchment in the 1960s and repatriation of Ghanaian workers from Nigeria in the 1980s, do not appear to have been associated with marked increases in open unem-

ployment or political destabilization. Second, surveys showed that government employees who were candidates for separation had characteristics and employment intentions consistent with available labor market
opportunities. And third, analysis of the aggregate employment effects
of the structural adjustment program suggests that redeployment of civil
servants would be more than matched by employment generated by
increased investments and other expenditures.

Previous retrenchment programs

The literature on Ghana identifies other occasions on which governments discharged large numbers of civil servants. From the limited statistical information available, there is no evidence that these moves led
to equivalent increases in measures of open unemployment. Following
the deposition of President Nkrumah by the National Liberation Council
in 1966, many statist policies of the previous government were reversed.
Some government firms were privatized, state farms were closed down,
and measures were taken to improve the economic performance of the
remaining state enterprises. In the process, redundant workers in organizations such as the Workers' Brigade and a state construction company were laid off. In spite of a belief that open unemployment was
increasing in the stagnant economy, the government and private
employers resorted to layoffs estimated to have affected some 59,000
workers between July 1966 and August 1967.[7]

A comparison of the 1960 and 1970 population censuses reveals no
change in the unemployment rate of 6 percent.[8] Among the reasons
unemployment failed to increase as expected was a realistic appraisal of
job opportunities by school leavers. Contrary to the common perception,
they were not reluctant to accept manual work; moreover, "potential
job-seekers were relatively well-informed about their prospects and realistic in their aspirations."[9] Furthermore, urban unemployment was
eased by a return to agriculture, a move that was encouraged by an
improvement in the barter terms of trade of food farmers. As we will see
below, these observations appear to be apt for the 1980s as well.

Massive return migration

A far greater challenge to the economy was the expulsion of foreign
workers in Nigeria. During the petroleum boom of the late 1970s and
early 1980s, Nigeria averted labor shortages by hosting a large number
of foreign workers who were employed in a wide spectrum of occupations. Ghanaians were the most numerous contingent of foreign workers
in Nigeria, a consequence of the depressed Ghanaian economy and their

relatively advanced educational attainment. As oil prices collapsed and Nigeria plunged into economic crisis, all foreign workers without proper papers were suddenly ordered to leave the country within a two-week period early in 1983. Although the number of people expelled is unknown, estimates range between 700,000 and 1 million Ghanaians. Even if this number includes some nonworking family members, it would still represent a very substantial influx into Ghana's labor force.

Press reports at the time reflect the concern of Ghanaian officials about the possible threat to internal stability presented by this massive population return. Many feared that the returnees would flock to urban areas and swell the ranks of the unemployed. According to dispatches to the *New York Times*, the government sought to ensure that the returnees were dispersed throughout the country as quickly as possible to avoid the formation of "a volatile mass in Accra."[10] Village chiefs were urged to allocate land to the returnees in order to ease their integration into productive employment, a viable course for a country with substantial amounts of uncultivated but arable land. Interviews with returned workers found them ready to till the land, although many viewed it as a transitory activity to be pursued only until employment opportunities appeared that better matched their skills.[11] Integrating these migrants appears to have caused no major disruption in the urban labor market. Had the returnees held out for urban employment, this preference would have been captured by the 1984 population census in the form of high open unemployment. The census reported an unemployment rate of only 2.8 percent.[12]

The same scenario was repeated, on a smaller scale, in May 1985 when Nigeria again expelled its foreign workers. This time a lesser although still substantial number of Ghanaians were among the expelled —some 300,000 workers. As had happened in 1983, these returnees appear to have been integrated into the rural labor force rather than seeking jobs in urban areas, where employment opportunities were scarce. These huge repatriations of Ghanaians from Nigeria in 1983 and 1985, accomplished without massive increases in open unemployment, suggest a much greater absorptive capacity of the economy than government officials presumed to exist.[13]

Characteristics of redeployed workers

The number of Ghanaians who returned from Nigeria and were reabsorbed into the domestic economy dwarfs the number of government workers expected to be redeployed and provides some perspective on the potential aggregate employment problems of retrenchment. In addition, the characteristics of those likely to be redeployed suggests that the magnitude of the problem is more manageable than had been perceived.

Consider the first year of redeployment, during which 12,500 persons were successfully separated from government service. Of these, 3,400 were over 60 years old and thus eligible for normal retirement benefits. Because of their age, this group was less likely than younger retrenched workers to become job seekers.[14] Another 5,000 of the redeployed were nonteaching personnel in schools scattered throughout the country, mainly outside the larger urban centers. Because of their rural ties, these people were likely to be absorbed in agriculture or other rural-based activities. The roughly 4,000 remaining separations were of civil servants located primarily in urban centers. Virtually all of these had only modest educational qualifications and were employed in the lowest categories of the occupational pyramid. This class of workers would constitute the bulk of the redeployed and cause the greatest concern about their future labor force status.

However, in the first year of the redeployment exercise, the net infusion of workers into the urban labor market proved less than the 4,000 noted above. Partially offsetting the separations were roughly 3,000 new hires. Some of these hires were to replace retirees; others filled civil service vacancies at higher levels perennially difficult to staff because of inadequate compensation levels.[15] Although those released may not have been perfect substitutes for the new hires, particularly if the latter came from the more highly educated segment of the labor force, a net influx of only about 1,000 workers into the urban labor market is unlikely to have had a noticeable effect on employment conditions.

In fact, relative to a total labor force of about 6.4 million in 1986 or a nonagricultural labor force of more than 2.0 million, even a full release of 15,000 workers into the market would be expected to have only a small impact. Certainly, relative to the natural increase in the labor force of roughly 180,000 a year, the scheduled releases formed a small proportion.

Another factor that might have lessened the impact of the redeployment on the labor market was the sex and marital status of those released. A substantial proportion of these were women, almost all married.[16] To the extent that some of these women were secondary wage earners, some may have chosen to retire from active labor force participation, at least temporarily, particularly in light of the generous separation allowances. This might explain the failure of a substantial number of workers scheduled for redeployment to indicate employment plans or preferences.

Job preferences of the redeployed

The pace of retrenchment set in 1987 extended into 1988, when some 12,800 employees were separated. Officials administering the program noted that many of these separations were voluntary, suggesting that employees either found the termination payments attractive, considered alternative employment prospects favorable, or both. (Severance allowances amounted to four months' basic pay plus two additional months' pay for each year of service.)

To encourage voluntary retirement, the government also offered employees occupational training or, for independent producers, start-up resources. Information obtained from people seeking such assistance provides evidence on job preferences and suggests that the majority of retrenched government workers should not face open unemployment.

Although a substantial number of workers had registered for assistance at the start of the program, only a few of those separated to date—just 3,713 out of some 18,500—had actually availed themselves of the offered help. It is unclear why so few sought assistance. Possible inferences are that most of the redeployed decided to withdraw from the labor force or found satisfactory alternative productive employment. Alternatively, they may not have had much faith in the government's ability to deliver on its offers of assistance.[17]

Not all who registered for assistance indicated an occupational preference—only 2,898 of the 3,713 registrants did so. Fifty-seven percent of those expressing a preference selected agriculture (table 9.1). This proportion is only moderately smaller than the proportion of the total labor force employed in the agricultural sector, 61 percent in the census year of 1984. Significantly, even in the greater Accra region a majority of the redeployed men expressing an occupational preference chose agriculture. No other occupational preference came close to rivaling agriculture. Some 250 respondents, almost all women, chose dressmaking and tailoring. Cooking and catering and carpentry were the only other choices indicated by more than 100 registrants.

The revealed preference for agriculture might surprise many people in government circles who believed that the agricultural sector would hold little attraction for redeployed civil servants, particularly those located in urban areas. Indeed, it was this conviction that provoked the fear that redeployment might result in serious urban unemployment. Apparently, ties to the rural community proved stronger than anticipated. But the expressed preferences represent a rational choice for many of those displaced from the public sector. A substantial minority of the redeployed reported no formal education, and of the remainder, few had more than some primary education. Particularly among men with no education at all, agriculture was an overwhelming choice.

That so many of the redeployed opted for agriculture should have been taken as an encouraging phenomenon, for it was clearly the sector with the greatest absorptive capacity. It also would appear to have been a calculated response to market signals. Although economic decline had pushed real wages down sharply, rural incomes are unlikely to have declined as much because these generally have a large in-kind component. In fact, reports of labor shortages were commonly heard during peak periods of agricultural activity and although it was difficult to find agreement among various sources of information on rural wage rates, all of the daily rates cited in mid-1988 were well above prevailing urban wages for unskilled labor. Furthermore, the structural reforms the government was undertaking included the gradual elimination of price controls on agricultural produce and an improvement in the price to farmers of the principal export crop, cocoa. As a declining import constraint improved farmers' access to purchased inputs, the prospects of further relative gains must have appeared good. In addition, many communities still had uncultivated land at their disposal that could be made available for assignment to members upon their return.

The redeployed revealed an acute awareness of the nature of the labor market in another way. In response to a question about the employment status they would prefer (table 9.2), few opted for wage employment in the private sector: of those indicating a preference, only

Table 9.1 Occupational preferences of redeployed civil servants, Ghana, 1988

Occupational preference	Number	Percentage
Agriculture	1,662	57
Industrial	602	21
Automobile repair	51	2
Carpentry	117	4
Electrical installation	70	2
Maintenance fitting	82	3
Masonry	82	3
Other manual trades	200	7
Personal services	555	19
Cooking and catering	120	4
Dressmaking and tailoring	256	9
Hairdressing	90	3
Other nonmanual trades	89	3
Commerce	79	3
Petty trading	45	2
Storekeeping	34	1
Subtotal	2,898	100
No preference indicated	815	n.a.
Total sample	3,713	n.a.
Number redeployed	18,500[a]	n.a.

n.a. Not applicable.
Note: Sample refers only to those redeployed workers who applied for economic assistance. This group is a minority of all the redeployed and cannot be assumed to be a random sample.
a. Approximate number of redeployed as of mid-1988.
Source: Government of Ghana, Ministry of Mobilization and Productivity.

184, or 7 percent, elected private wage employment. Again, this matches closely the proportion of the total labor force employed in a wage-earning capacity in the private sector. Sixty-nine percent expressed a preference for self-employment, a proportion that is identical to that prevailing in the labor force as a whole. The only departure from the existing structure of the labor force was manifested in the preference expressed for cooperative ventures; almost a quarter of the respondents indicated such a choice, although less than 1 percent of the nation's work force is so employed.

Thus, the preferences expressed by this sample of the redeployed largely parallel the existing pattern of employment. This sense of realism—reminiscent of that demonstrated by the Ghanaians who returned home after expulsion from Nigeria—should have been reassuring to government officials because it suggested that absorption of the redeployed could be more easily achieved than had been expected.

Summary

In summary, the past experience of Ghana in absorbing unplanned infusions of workers into the labor market—whether as a result of government retrenchments or massive migration—should have mitigated government officials' concern about the consequences of the current modest releases of workers into the market. If memories were short, then the responses of the redeployed to the questionnaires should have been reassuring.

Of course, we are not suggesting that all the redeployed could be assured of "good" jobs at high wages. But what is relevant is the opportunity cost of their government job. In view of the sharp deterioration in

Table 9.2 Preferred employment status of redeployed civil servants, Ghana, 1988

Employment status	Agriculture		Nonagriculture		Total	
	Number	Percent	Number	Percent	Number	Percent
Self-employment	1,124	72	782	65	1,906	69
Cooperative	420	27	260	21	680	24
Private wage employment	20	1	164	14	184	7
Government	2	0	6	0	8	0
Subtotal	1,566	100	1,212	100	2,778	100
No preference indicated	95	n.a.	837	n.a.	932	n.a.
Total sample	1,661	n.a.	2,049	n.a.	3,710	n.a.

n.a. Not applicable.
Note: Sample refers only to those redeployed workers who applied for economic assistance. This group is a minority of all the redeployed and cannot be assumed to be a random sample.
Source: Government of Ghana, Ministry of Mobilization and Productivity.

real government wage levels, those at the lower end of the civil service pay structure received monthly gross basic wages in 1987 of between US$19 and $25 valued at the average auction exchange rate, or between $31 and $39 with all allowances included. This was significantly less than wages paid to agricultural labor and exceeded the country's per capita income by only 19 to 50 percent.

In view of the low level to which real wages had fallen in the public sector, it is unlikely that alternative employments could imply a serious deterioration in income flows from amounts officially earned in the civil service. Unofficial income stemming from government employment, including all types of illicit income and preferential access, might be harder to replicate in private sector activity. However, although we do not minimize the potential gains to some individuals from such activities, we doubt that the many unskilled workers slated for redeployment were primary recipients.

The point we emphasize is that neither large-scale, open urban unemployment nor radical losses in already meager earnings is likely to be a consequence of redeployment. The redeployed will seek out ways to earn income, and their ingenuity should never be underestimated. Indeed, even while they were still government employees, many had already developed side activities that supplemented their civil service salaries. A greater dedication to these activities may have proved a viable course for many of the redeployed.

Employment effects of other public policy initiatives

We noted earlier that rather than speculating exclusively on the labor market impact of redeployment, the government might have been well advised to consider the net employment effects of its other activities. Had it done so, it might not have been as fearful of the unemployment stemming from retrenchment.

Employment is a function of the aggregate demand for goods and services. To the extent that retrenchment reduced public sector spending, and that this was not offset by increased private spending, employment could be expected to drop not only by the number redeployed but by an additional number of workers, victims of reduced expenditures by idled public sector employees. However, in Ghana this was not the case. Although the number of government workers was reduced, wage increases for remaining civil service employees were being planned to improve compensation levels and, particularly, to restore larger wage differentials between the lower and higher ranks. Thus, the aggregate purchasing power of public servants would be maintained as would the private sector employment that is a function of their expenditures.[18]

Public investment

Of greater significance than the impact on employment of the government's payroll were the increases in government investment that would be financed largely by external sources. The central government's budget for 1988 foresaw a real increase in investment expenditures of 4.3 percent in 1988 over 1987.[19] A substantial proportion of these expenditures was to be devoted to improvements and additions to infrastructure that would require substantial labor inputs.

It was possible to estimate the labor requirements of the government's investment programs for each of three years beginning with 1988, based on a detailed description of each project approved for implementation as of mid-1988. The totals in table 9.3, however, are not all-inclusive. Rather, they represent only the employment that will be created by projects involving substantial labor inputs. Neither, of course, do the figures include employment that will be generated by investment projects not yet approved. Thus, the totals represent a minimum number of man-years of employment that will be generated directly by the government's investment expenditures.[20]

Table 9.3 also records only the direct employment effects of the investment program, that is, the number of workers hired to execute the projects. In addition to these jobs, others will be created in the domestic industries that supply material inputs for the investment projects. And finally, the earnings received by newly employed workers will be spent on purchases of domestically produced goods and services. This injection of additional spending into the economy will thus be reflected in increased employment in other sectors. A conservative estimate of the "second round" employment generated by each direct job was on the order of 0.5. That is, for each two net additions to employment attributable to the government's investment program, one additional job would be created elsewhere in the economy.

Table 9.3 Direct employment generation projected for public investment, Ghana, 1988–90
(man-years)

Program	1988	1989	1990
Public investment program	29,850	53,360	43,975
PAMSCAD[a]	4,720	8,795	2,240
Priority works projects	1,080	2,150	0
Total	35,650	64,305	46,215

a. Program of Action to Mitigate the Social Costs of Adjustment and Development.
Source: Republic of Ghana, *Public Investment Program 1988–90*, vol. 1, *Main Report* (Ministry of Finance and Economic Planning, Accra, April 1988).

In addition to the employment-generating activities of the central government's investment program, there is the Program of Action to Mitigate the Social Costs of Adjustment and Development (PAM-SCAD), which would undertake public works and housing projects employing labor-intensive methods of production. Also, there are food-for-work programs organized and administered by private welfare agencies in particularly depressed regions of the country. Combined, these programs should provide thousands of jobs at the same time that the economy loses employment because of redeployment from the central government. In sum, the net effect of government activities on employment appears positive, notwithstanding the redeployment program.

Box 9.1 Estimating employment growth

The employment consequences of continued growth are based on sectoral growth rate projections available from the Ghanaian government and from the World Bank (box table 1). (The overall growth rates forecast by these two sources diverged for 1988—5.5 percent according to the government and 6.0 percent by World Bank accounting.) For purposes of estimating employment effects (box table 2), it is assumed that over the 1988–90 period only modest improvements in sectoral productivity would be achieved. For purposes of this exercise, no productivity increases are assumed in agriculture, construction, and commerce. An annual rate of increase of 2 percent was estimated for mining, manufacturing, and transportation and communications since these were the likely beneficiaries of planned investment expenditures or, in the case of the first two sectors, also enjoyed large excess capacity. A 0.5 per-

Table 1 Projected sectoral growth rates, Ghana, 1988–90
(percentage of GDP)

Sector	Government of Ghana projections 1988	World Bank projections 1988	1989	1990
Agriculture	3.7	-0.1	2.9	2.9
Mining	9.8	22.5	16.7	14.1
Manufacturing	13.4	14.0	10.0	10.0
Construction	10.5	15.0	8.0	8.0
Transport, communication	8.9	8.9	5.4	5.4
Commerce	5.0	14.0	7.0	7.0
Financial services	7.0	7.0	5.5	5.5
Nongovernment services	5.5	15.0	7.0	7.0
Total	5.5	6.0	5.0	5.0

Source: 1. Republic of Ghana, *The P.N.D.C. Budget Statement and Economic Policy for 1988* (Accra, January 16, 1988), p. 6; World Bank, "Ghana: Structural Adjustment for Growth," Report 9475-GH (Washington, D.C., January 23, 1989), p. i and p. 84.

Employment consequences of continued growth

Continuation of the dynamic economic growth of the previous three years should also expand and improve employment opportunities for the Ghanaian labor force. On the basis of then-available projections of GDP growth and assumptions about the rate of increase in productivity, it was possible to estimate employment levels for the economy as a whole (box 9.1). If sectoral growth rates conform to expectations and if increases in productivity approximate those assumed here, minimum estimates of employment growth of 3.1, 3.9, and 4.1 percent are projected for 1988, 1989, and 1990, respectively. As long as the rate of increase in aggregate labor requirements exceeds the rate of increase in the labor

cent annual increase was forecast for the private service sector. Government employment was estimated from current levels, making allowances for reductions stemming from redeployment.

Because the projected sectoral growth rates for 1988 prepared by the Government of Ghana and the World Bank diverged, two sets of employment estimates for the three-year period are computed. Base year employment levels are those estimated as prevailing at the end of 1987 and are based on a household survey conducted during late 1987 and early 1988. The estimates for 1988 based on World Bank projections are less optimistic than the government's, largely because the Bank forecast an absolute decline in agricultural output while the government forecast an increase of 3.7 percent. Considering the generally favorable weather conditions prevailing during the 1988 growing season, the Bank's forecast seems unduly pessimistic.

Table 2 Estimated employment by sector, Ghana, 1988–90

(thousands of employees)

Sector	Government of Ghana projections			World Bank projections		
	1988	1989	1990	1988	1989	1990
Agriculture	4,359	4,485	4,615	4,203	4,325	4,450
Mining	74	85	95	83	94	106
Manufacturing	485	523	564	487	525	567
Construction	88	95	103	92	99	107
Transport, communication	141	149	157	141	149	157
Commerce	900	963	1,031	978	1,046	1,119
Financial services	25	26	28	25	26	28
Nongovernment services	270	287	306	260	277	295
Central government	285	270	270	285	270	270
Total	6,626	6,884	7,167	6,553	6,812	7,097
Annual increase (percent)	4.3	3.9	4.1	3.1	4.0	4.2

Note: Employment numbers may not add up to totals because of rounding.
Source: Author's estimates.

force—about 3.3 percent—an improvement in the quality of employment can be expected. Labor market adjustments will then most likely take the form of a movement of workers from employments with low productivities and low earnings to those that are more productive and remunerative. With employment projections for 1989 and 1990 exceeding growth in the labor force by comfortable margins, the prospects for improved employment opportunities appear favorable over the 1988–90 period and beyond.

Conclusion

The main objective of this evaluation of Ghana's program to redeploy redundant civil servants was to address, before the fact, Ghanaian officials' concerns about the consequences of laying off large numbers of civil servants. Specifically, we have tried to assess the employment implications of redeployment both at an aggregate and an individual level, and to counter the presumption that such a program would yield significant increases in open unemployment and a reduction in welfare of the redeployed.

Although we recognize that the employment situation in Ghana is already poor, there is little evidence that redeployment of 50,000 or more civil servants will lead to substantial changes in unemployment, especially open unemployment, in Accra and other urban areas. We draw this conclusion based, first, on the magnitudes involved. The number of redeployed is small relative to the labor force, the number of new entrants to the work force, and the cumulative net change in employment opportunities resulting from all government programs and policy changes. Second, historical precedent, especially the apparent absorption of far larger numbers of Ghanaian workers expelled from Nigeria in the mid-1980s, bodes well for the economy's capacity to absorb retrenched government workers. Third, the redeployed possess characteristics and reveal preferences consistent with the structure of the economy, all of which suggests informed responses to prevailing opportunities.

If these arguments are correct, it is difficult to conclude that the redeployment program will, in the aggregate, have a marked effect on either open unemployment or poverty levels. However, what of the plight of the redeployed? Will a majority of them suffer a reduction in welfare as a result of losing their government positions? As always, predictions concerning individuals are less accurate than those pertaining to the aggregate, but we do speculate that, on average, the redeployed will not experience a sharp decline in living standards. This conclusion is based on earlier redeployees' demonstrated realism about employment opportunities, as well as on our assessment of the current opportunity cost of government employment. Considering the dramatic declines over the past decade in the real earnings of Ghanaian civil servants, the economic value of a government position may, in fact, be limited.

Although we predict that the majority of the redeployed will be reabsorbed into the economy, including agricultural pursuits, we are by no means suggesting that Ghana's economy offers large numbers of productive and remunerative employment opportunities. On the contrary, average returns to labor, especially to the unskilled, remain low, whether employment is available in the public or private sector, in agriculture, industry, or the services. Our point is simply that the redeployment of 50,000 government workers should not be thought of as a program that will send 50,000 households with very modest incomes into dire poverty.

The predictions in this chapter concerning the impact of redeployment require verification. Chapter 10 takes a step in that direction. However, it must also be emphasized that even if some, and perhaps many, of the redeployed suffer further economic hardships as a result of retrenchments, government action to reduce redundancy remains necessary. If the Ghanaian government is to once more play a meaningful and supportive role in national development, it must rebuild the civil service to a point where public goods and services are delivered and where government employment makes a far more productive contribution to social welfare.

Notes

1. Tony Killick, *Development Economics in Action: A Study of Economic Policies in Ghana* (London: Heinemenn, 1978), p. 69.

2. World Bank, "Ghana: Toward Structural Adjustment," vol. 1, Report 5854-GH (Washington, D.C., October 7, 1985), pp. i–ii.

3. Ibid., pp. 138–40.

4. Ibid., pp. 139 and 154.

5. Ibid.

6. The degree to which these regulations governing dismissals in the private sector were actually enforced remains an open question.

7. Killick, op. cit., p. 55.

8. Kodwo Ewusi, "The Size of the Labour Force and Structure of Employment in Ghana," Technical Publications Series no. 37, Institute of Social, Statistical, and Economic Research, Legon, Ghana, 1978, p. 91. Nor did an increase in registrations of the unemployed with the government employment office even approach the number estimated to have been laid off. Registrations in 1967 rose to 16,700 from 11,500 in 1969. (These measures are only suggestive and should not be taken as representing the actual volume of open unemployment.)

9. Killick, op. cit., p. 77.

10. *New York Times*, February 7, 1983, p. A-4.

11. *New York Times,* February 10, 1983, p. A-2.

12. The low levels of unemployment reported by the census and a 1987 household survey—about 1.9 percent—are derived by applying the conventional concepts of labor force and unemployment (either employed or actively seeking employment) with a reference period of the week preceding the survey. These low values should not be interpreted in the same way as a similar statistic drawn from surveys in industrial countries or even in dynamic newly industrialized countries like Korea and Taiwan. The low values for Ghana reflect the heavy concentration of the Ghanaian labor force in agriculture where a concept of unemployment is difficult to apply. Thus, although open unemployment measures are very low, it should be kept in mind that many of those counted as employed may only be working intermittently or at very low levels of productivity and earnings, or both.

13. Although the apparent absorption into the domestic economy of Ghanaians returning from Nigeria bodes well for the successful redeployment of civil servants, differences may distinguish these two groups of job seekers. Specifically, are the human as well as physical capital endowments of both groups the same? Who is likely to be better educated, the returning Ghanaian or a redeployed government employee? Did those returning from Nigeria bring with them savings that facilitated their creation of productive self-employment and were such savings in excess of severance packages awarded the redeployed? Unfortunately, these and other questions about the absorptive capacity of Ghana's labor market cannot be readily answered because the "natural experiment" of returning migrants has not been subjected to data collection or analysis.

14. Of course, the number of those retrenched because they are at or above retirement age would fall in subsequent years of the redeployment program.

15. A substantial number of the new hires, however, reflected an absence of effective control over the hiring of low-skill workers by government units, a problem that persisted for some time and complicated the attainment of the government's employment goals.

16. According to estimates by Alderman, Canagarajah, and Younger (chapter 10, this volume), 35 percent of all redeployees were women as compared with their substantially lower 21 percent share in overall civil service employment.

17. Long delays were experienced in making training programs generally operational so that as of July 1988, only forty persons had been enrolled.

18. It was expected that the real wage bill of the government would increase in 1988 by 10 percent over 1987. Although a 5 percent decrease in the wage bill was forecast for 1989, it was expected that by 1990 the wage bill would be restored to 1988 levels. It also should be recalled that the purchasing power of those redeployed was being maintained for at least a year, a factor that would reinforce the employment effects of expenditures of those remaining on the payroll.

19. Republic of Ghana, *The P.N.D.C. Budget Statement and Economic Policy for 1988* (Accra, 1988), p. 34.

20. The estimated employment generated in 1988 does not represent a net addition to employment over 1987, for this cannot be calculated in the absence of information regarding the employment generated by public investment in 1987. However, since the total investment for 1988 represented an increase over that for 1987, it may be presumed that the net change in employment was also positive.

10

Consequences of permanent layoff from the civil service: results from a survey of retrenched workers in Ghana

Harold Alderman, Sudharshan Canagarajah, Stephen D. Younger

Ghana's economic problems and its response to those problems have been similar to those of many other African countries in the past decade, but they have been experienced more intensely. Civil service reform is no exception. Although it is difficult to establish precise numbers for the growth of public sector employment in Ghana, it is clear that by 1983, when the current round of economic reforms began, employment in the civil service and state-owned enterprises had grown dramatically. The 1984 population census indicates that 2.5 percent of the entire population of Ghana was employed in the civil service, one of the highest ratios in Africa.[1] Public enterprises and boards employed another 2.0 percent. Yet at the same time that the number of civil servants was expanding rapidly, the government's ability to pay them was declining. Government revenues fell from about 15 percent of GDP in the early 1970s to only 6 percent of GDP in 1982, forcing public sector wages to decline precipitously. De Merode (chapter 8, this volume) reports that between 1975 and 1983, average civil service pay declined by 10 percent a year in real terms. In addition, the salary structure became so compressed that in 1983 the highest civil service salary was only 2.2 times the lowest. As in many other countries, moonlighting (and "daylighting") became necessary for survival. Moreover, many qualified employees left the civil service to pursue better options elsewhere, often abroad.

To rectify this situation it was clearly necessary that the government lay off a large number of employees (or as the government prefers to say, "redeploy" them to the private sector), especially at the lower echelons of the civil service, where overstaffing was most severe. Nonetheless, the government was loath to undertake such a program. Civil servants are concentrated in urban areas and were thus perceived to be able to mount forceful opposition to any attempt to lay them off. In addition, senior government officials feared that the economic and social consequences for laid-off workers would represent too severe a burden for one sector of the population to bear.

Despite these reservations, the government did proceed with a redeployment program. The political fallout was subdued, with little organized opposition to civil service layoffs. Less is known about the social consequences of the program. The purpose of this study is to begin to fill that gap. During the eight months beginning in May 1991, the Cornell Food and Nutrition Policy Program conducted a survey of redeployed civil servants to find out how redeployment has affected their incomes, consumption, migration patterns, and so on. This chapter offers a first report on the findings of that survey.

The redeployment program

Just as the disintegration of the Ghanaian civil service is striking, so too is the reform program the government initiated in 1986. The program has concentrated on reducing the number of public sector employees and, at the same time, on improving their compensation, especially at the higher levels. Preliminary audits of the payrolls for the civil service and some state-owned enterprises disclosed about 10,000 "ghost workers" in the civil service and some 30,000 elsewhere, mostly at the Cocoa Marketing Board.[2] These names were removed from the payrolls in 1986, and the government moved to a system of payment through bank drafts—rather than direct cash disbursement by payroll officers—to reduce further payroll fraud. At the same time, the government began plans for a more careful census of public sector employment, with the goal of eliminating redundant employees.

The redeployment program has proceeded aggressively in the civil service, including the Ghana Education Service and the district assemblies. Between 1987 and 1990, 47,439 civil servants were redeployed— roughly 12,000 a year, or 4 to 5 percent of the total civil service roster per year. This stands in contrast to the experience in the state-owned enterprises, which have made very little progress on redeployment, apparently because collectively bargained agreements provide for end-of-service benefits so generous that the enterprises (and the government behind them) cannot afford to pay the stipulated severance pay.[3]

Operationally, the government established a Redeployment Management Committee, chaired by the Ministry of Mobilization and Social Welfare (formerly, the Ministry of Labor). The committee set annual redeployment targets for the civil service and guidelines for selecting redeployees, including, in order of priority:

1. Employees with falsified qualifications or whose work and conduct have persistently been below par.
2. Employees older than 60, the mandatory retirement age.
3. Employees with physical infirmities that seriously handicap their performance.
4. Employees who volunteer to be redeployed, on the condition that their employment is not critical to the performance of their ministry or office.
5. Employees who were most recently hired.

Except for a few ministries that the government explicitly exempted (the Ministry of Health, teaching staff in the Ghana Education Service), these rules were applied across the civil service. Although the first criterion leaves open the possibility of using redeployment for personal or political ends, this does not appear to have happened to any significant extent. After the release in 1987 of a large number of nonteaching (and apparently nonworking) education service staff, redeployment appears to have followed the more objective criteria 2 through 5.

Except for civil servants older than the mandatory retirement age and those with serious physical handicaps, each redeployee is entitled to a severance package equal to four months' pay plus two additional months' for each year of uninterrupted service. (Those older than 60 are entitled only to their regular pension benefits. We are not aware of any disability benefits in Ghana.) In addition, the government announced its intention to provide employment counseling, retraining, and courses in entrepreneurial development as well as land, tools, and inputs for potential farmers. In practice, these programs were slow to emerge. Before 1991 the vast majority of redeployees neither applied for nor received any benefits other than severance pay. Nonetheless, a few programs were initiated as part of the Program of Action to Mitigate the Social Costs of Adjustment and Development, most notably food-for-work schemes for redeployees returning to rural areas.

In looking at the pattern of redeployment in the civil service from 1987 to 1990, two trends are noteworthy (table 10.1). First, after an initial flourish in 1987, forced retirements account for few of the redeployments. This is probably due to the fact that few employees older than 60 remained in the civil service after 1987. Second, after declining substantially in 1988 and 1989, redeployment from the Ghana Education Service again surged in 1990, probably because of uncontrolled new hiring in the service in the late 1980s. With the prevailing "last-in-first-out" rule for redeployment, it seems likely that many of the education service employees who were redeployed in 1990 were recently hired, a point corroborated by the relatively low severance compensation for education service employees in 1989 and 1990.

Although the Controller and Accountant General's Office has automated controls to prevent rehiring of redeployed civil servants, controls on new hires have not been as tight as they should be. Thus, Gregory (chapter 9, this volume) estimates that as much as 25 percent of the staffing reductions from redeployment was offset by new hires in the early stages of the retrenchment program. Many of those hired were skilled employees that the government needed, but a significant proportion of the new hires filled the same low-skill posts the redeployees had vacated.

Nonetheless, the civil service has shrunk overall during the course of the redeployment program. The 1984 population census found 310,658 civil service employees. A 1986 census of the civil service found roughly 317,000 employees. By January of 1989 this number fell to 280,788, and the number of civil servants (excluding the Ghana Education Service) fell another 12,100 by January 1991. After eliminating about 10,000 ghost workers in 1986, the redeployment program between 1987 and 1990 reduced overall staff levels by around 12 percent.

Most redeployees have come from the lower echelons of the civil service. Of the posts that the Ministry of Mobilization and Social Welfare could classify, more than 80 percent of redeployees held unskilled jobs. This is consistent with formal staff appraisals that show that overstaffing is most acute in unskilled posts, while many skilled positions remain difficult to fill because government salaries are not competitive. Because

Table 10.1 Civil service redeployments, Ghana, 1987–90

Year	Sector	Redeployed	Redeployees over age 60	Total severance (millions of cedis)	Severance as a share of government expenditure (percent)	Severance per worker (U.S. dollars)
1987	Civil service	4,574	657	492		430
	Education service	4,307	224	359		333
	Subtotal	8,881	881	851	0.8	383
1988	Civil service	11,310	330	1,967		556
	Education service	1,062	7	174		523
	Subtotal	12,372	337	2,141	1.5	553
1989	Civil service	12,127	30	3,403		821
	Education service	1,810	13	283		457
	Subtotal	13,937	43	3,686	1.9	661
1990	Civil service	5,891	14	1,879		925
	Education service	6,358	51	1,289		588
	Subtotal	12,249	65	3,168	1.2	750
Total		47,439	1,326	9,846		

Note: U.S. dollar figures are calculated using the end-of-period bureau exchange rate.
Source: Government of Ghana, Ministry of Mobilization and Social Welfare; authors' calculations.

most redeployees held low-paying jobs, the budgetary savings of the redeployment exercise are not great. De Merode (chapter 8, this volume) estimates the budgetary savings of reduced compensation at cedis 8.9 billion in 1991, about 8 percent of the civil service wage bill for 1991, or 2.5 percent of total government expenditure.[4] After netting out the costs of end-of-service benefits for redeployees, little has been left to augment the salaries of skilled and senior officers and, thus, decompress the civil service wage structure. But this situation will improve considerably in the coming years. As with any investment, the costs of redeployment (severance payments) are incurred in the early years of the program, while the benefits (reduced wage bills) will accrue for many years into the future.

The Cornell survey

In 1990 the Ministry of Mobilization and Social Welfare (MMSW) agreed to give the Cornell Food and Nutrition Policy Program a list of all civil servants redeployed between 1987 and 1990. However, because of data entry difficulties, the population that we draw from is not complete.[5] Furthermore, for financial reasons we limited our sample to redeployees in three regions that are easily accessible from the nation's capital—the Greater Accra, Ashanti, and Central regions.[6] Within these regions we drew a random sample of 811 redeployees. Finally, note that the sample includes only civil servants (including the Ghana Education Service and the district assemblies). We could not locate comparable records for employees redeployed from the state-owned enterprises. We conducted the survey from late May 1991 to February 1992. By the middle of January we were finding only one or two additional redeployees per week per region, and therefore cut off our search.

The MMSW records included each redeployee's former place of employment, but no addresses. For that reason, we had to go to the former place of employment to inquire about the redeployee's address, relying on either personnel records or other employees' recollections. This limited our ability to locate redeployees, although the difficulty reflects limitations of the records rather than characteristics of the workers. Of the 811 names in our draw, we were able to locate 540, or 67 percent (table 10.2). Of those, we did not interview twenty-four people who were still at their posts (usually because their redeployment paperwork had been delayed).[7] In addition, six people refused to be interviewed. Thus, we actually interviewed a sample of 510 redeployees.

Of the several reasons for not locating redeployees (table 10.2), migration abroad or to a remote part of Ghana (10 percent of redeployees) might present the most problems for generalizing from our sample. Since migration is an important economic decision, our results could suffer from the bias of excluding migrants. In tracing redeployees, however, we did try to reach those who had moved within or among the three regions our sample covers (plus an additional region, the Eastern region, if that was a destination).

Survey results

In this section we describe the redeployees in terms of general socioeconomic characteristics and address more specific questions about their fate since redeployment. For much of the discussion it is useful to compare our sample of redeployees to the population at large or a random sample of civil servants. To do so, we make use of the Ghana Living Standards Survey, an integrated household survey carried out in 1987–88.[8] The Living Standards Survey covered 3,200 households drawn randomly from the entire country. Of those households, roughly half are in the three regions in which we surveyed redeployees. Because there are marked regional differences in many socioeconomic characteristics, we compare our sample to the Living Standards Survey households from our three regions rather than the entire country.

Many of the issues we raise address concerns of African policymakers and the donor community. For example, although it was generally agreed that the Ghanaian civil service was badly overstaffed, government officials argued that laid-off civil servants would not be able to find work in the cities, since formal sector employment opportunities were quite rare in the wake of the Economic Recovery Program. At the same time, they argued that civil servants who had lived in a city for some time would be unlikely to return to a rural area or work as a farmer. Thus, a policy of massive layoffs risked leaving many former civil servants without work and destitute. To evaluate this risk, we examine the types of work that redeployees are doing, if they are working at all, and we compare their incomes to the general population sur-

Table 10.2 Responses to survey of redeployment in Ghana

Number and share of respondents	Total	Response	Deceased	Abroad	Unreach-able in Ghana	Cannot trace	Unknown	Still at post	Refusal
Number	811	510	27	18	68	90	68	24	6
Proportion	n.a.	0.629	0.033	0.022	0.084	0.111	0.084	0.030	0.007

n.a. Not applicable.

Note: "Unreachable in Ghana" are redeployees that we know have moved within the country, but to a destination too remote for us to reach economically; "cannot trace" applies to civil servants who have a staff record or are known to someone at their former employer, but for whom there is insufficient information to find an address; "unknown" applies to civil servants who were unknown and unrecorded at their former place of employment and might include "ghost workers."

Source: Cornell Food and Nutrition Policy Program (CFNPP) redeployee survey, 1991–92.

veyed in the Living Standards Survey. We also consider the number of redeployees who might be considered "poor." Finally, we examine redeployees' decision to migrate and the types of work recent migrants are doing.

Another set of concerns, both for policymakers and donors, is that the administrators of a redeployment program may discriminate against certain groups of the population for political or social reasons.[9] A further worry is that a disproportionate number of women will lose their jobs in a redeployment program—that decisionmakers might favor laying off a woman because she is viewed as providing a "second" income for her family while the man of the household is seen as the "bread winner." Although we have not collected information on redeployees' ethnic group or political affiliation, informal reports suggest that the Ghanaian government carried out the program in a balanced, unbiased manner. We do have information on the gender composition of redeployees, which we will compare to civil servants interviewed in the Living Standards Survey.

The last issue we discuss is the effectiveness of government programs aimed at assisting redeployees. Even though the government hoped to implement a variety of programs for redeployees, the programs either have not materialized or have been slow to get going. For example, despite the government's intention to provide transitional employment opportunities and to help redeployees make a start in new small-scale enterprises (including agriculture), only 8.4 percent of our respondents had participated in a food-for-work program since redeployment, and a mere 1.4 percent had received tools. A government report[10] claims that as of mid-1990, only 4 percent of redeployees had participated in a retraining program. Thus, it appears that at least until recent years, organized attempts to assist redeployees have had little impact.[11] The one important exception is the severance package redeployees receive. Although severances were small in the first years of the program, redeployees have recently received sizable payments, reflecting both an increase in real civil service wages and the consolidation in 1991 of all allowances into the base salary.[12] We look at the payment amounts and the way redeployees spent them—on daily consumption of basic needs or on investments to improve their incomes after redeployment.

Socioeconomic characteristics of redeployees

When we compare the age and gender composition of redeployees' families to that of the households in the Living Standards Survey, we find them quite similar. The redeployee sample, however, has significantly more people in the 46–60 and over-60 age groups than the Living Standards Survey sample, and many fewer in the 17–25 group. The large number of 17–25 year-olds in the Living Standards Survey sample is probably due to the inclusion of military personnel in the civil service employment category.[13]

Considering the provision for forced retirement, it is not surprising that the redeployee sample has more people older than 60; but one might think that the last-in-first-out criterion should have protected people in the 46–60 age group. Yet this pattern is similar for volunteer and nonvolunteer redeployees alike. Nor can the difference be explained by work experience; 46–60 year-olds have an average of eight more years experience in the civil service than 25–45 year-olds. It appears, then, that criteria other than last-in-first-out were applied in a significant number of cases.

Women constitute a significantly larger percentage of redeployees (35 percent) than they do of civil servants in general (21 percent), which is consistent with one of the reservations that some analysts have had about retrenchment programs. The higher proportion of female redeployees in Ghana probably does not represent explicit discrimination, however. Women are more vulnerable to the last-in-first-out rule (which is widely perceived as a fair rule in layoff decisions) because widespread hiring of women in the civil service is a relatively recent phenomenon. Among nonvoluntary redeployees, females had fewer years of service than males, contrary to what one would expect to see if women were being unfairly discriminated against (table 10.3). In addition, the marital status of the women in our sample is quite close to that of the female civil servants in the Living Standards Survey: 92 percent of female redeployees are or have been married,[14] while the corresponding Living Standards Survey figure for female civil servants is 93 percent. This also runs counter to what we should see if married women were discriminated against because they provide only a "second income" to their household. Thus, there does not seem to have been a greater effort to redeploy married women than other civil servants.

Turning to education, the highest completed level of schooling for redeployees is significantly lower than that for civil servants in the Living Standards Survey. Thirty-eight percent of redeployees completed only primary school or less (including Koranic education as primary), while only 26 percent of the civil servants in the Living Standards

Table 10.3 Length of service, by voluntary or involuntary redeployment and by gender, Ghana

Redeployed	Gender	Number	Average years in civil service
Voluntarily	Male	116	17.4
	Female	58	14.4
Involuntarily	Male	217	13.2
	Female	119	10.6

Source: CFNPP survey, 1991–92.

Survey were at the primary level or lower. On the other hand, redeployees are significantly better educated than the population as a whole in the three regions we sampled; fully 68 percent of that group had not completed more than primary school. Very few civil servants with secondary and postsecondary education have been redeployed, as one would expect from the structure of the program. Both male and female redeployees have significantly lower probabilities of having completed secondary education than the general pool of government workers in the Living Standards Survey.

Volunteers for redeployment

Civil servants whose continued presence was not considered crucial to the functioning of their ministry or agency were allowed to volunteer for redeployment, with the same severance benefits as involuntary redeployees. In general, the socioeconomic characteristics of volunteers, including gender, education, type of work, and postredeployment spells without work, are quite similar to those who did not volunteer. Civil servants in the 46–60 age group were somewhat more likely to volunteer (44 percent of volunteers came from this age group, compared with 35 percent of nonvolunteers). This is probably explained by the fact that end-of-service benefits from the redeployment program are tied to years of experience, and thus, more experienced workers receive higher benefits. As long as the redeployment program is viewed as temporary, older workers have a strong incentive to volunteer. With only a limited period in which to volunteer, employees nearing the age of 60 know that they will be forced into retirement without the redeployment benefits, so they have a particularly strong incentive to elect redeployment.

A comparison of the median severance pay of volunteers and nonvolunteers reveals that redeployees who volunteered received considerably higher severance benefits than nonvolunteers (table 10.4). Civil service salaries have been rising in recent years, and it appears that a rush of volunteers followed each pay raise.[15] That civil servants respond to increased termination benefits suggests that a government could base its redeployment program entirely on volunteers if it were willing to pay high enough termination benefits.

Labor force participation

We compared redeployees' labor force participation at the time of our survey with that of Living Standards Survey respondents living in our three regions and over the age of 16 (table 10.5). The data reveal identical participation rates for the two groups. In addition, redeployees' post–government service labor force participation is quite close to that of the entire population of the Living Standards Survey,[16] as well as to rates found in earlier studies.[17] While our study does not enable us to easily distinguish the unemployed from people who are not in the labor force, the proportion of people who are neither working nor studying is quite close to Living Standards Survey results, suggesting that unemployment rates among redeployees may also be similar to those of the population in general.

Table 10.4 Redeployee severance pay, by voluntary or involuntary redeployment and by year of redeployment, Ghana

Redeployed	Number of redeployees	Median severance pay (thousands of 1984 cedis)
Voluntarily	169	72.6
Involuntarily	316	47.8
Total	485	n.r.
Year of redeployment		
1987	111	42.6
1988	74	50.3
1989	111	62.6
1990	148	65.5
1991	41	71.2
Total	485	n.r.

n.r. Not reported.
Source: CFNPP survey, 1991–92.

Table 10.5 Labor force participation status of redeployees and Ghana Living Standards Survey respondents in three regions, Ghana

Survey/ respondent	Working	Unemployed	Other inactive	Student	Total
Redeployees					
Male	289	11	23	10	333
Percentage of total	87	3	7	3	
Female	134	6	18	19	177
Percentage of total	76	3	10	11	
Total male and female	423	17	41	29	510
Percentage of total	83	3	8	6	
Ghana Living Standards Survey					
Male	1,100	46	75	99	1,320
Percentage of total	83	3	6	8	
Female	1,287	45	174	54	1,560
Percentage of total	83	3	11	3	
Total male and female	2,387	91	249	153	2,880
Percentage of total	83	3	9	5	

Note: Because the redeployee survey does not distinguish between "out of labor force" and "unemployed" people, we have grouped everyone who is not working or is ill or in school under "unemployed," which clearly exaggerates the unemployment rate for redeployees.
Source: CFNPP survey, 1991–92; and Ghana Living Standards Survey, 1987–88.

We also looked at unemployment spells the redeployees suffered immediately after being redeployed. Contrary to some policymakers' fears, most redeployees had found new jobs, and their spells without work after redeployment were reasonably short. Sixty-three percent of the 510 redeployees had no spell without work after redeployment (table 10.6), a figure exactly equal to the proportion of Living Standards Survey respondents who had no spell without work in the year before they were surveyed. Many redeployees simply continued to work at other jobs they had been working while they were in the civil service. In addition, some redeployees knew about their eventual redeployment well before the fact and so could look for another job before leaving government service.

We now turn our attention to the length of redeployees' spells without work. To make our data set and the Living Standards Survey comparable with respect to information on spells without work, we truncate the redeployees' spells at one year, as was done with the Living Standards Survey respondents. We also base our calculations on only those respondents who had a nonzero spell, to avoid pulling the averages down close to zero. Even though female redeployees are more likely to have had a spell without work (table 10.6), there is no significant

Table 10.6 Spells without work for redeployees and Ghana Living Standards Survey respondents in three regions, by gender, Ghana

| Category | Redeployees (since redeployment) | | | | | |
	Male	Percentage of males surveyed	Female	Percentage of females surveyed	Total	Percentage of total survey sample
Sample size	333		177		510	
Share in sample (%)	65		35			
Continuously employed	236	71	87	49	323	63
Share in sample (%)	73		27			
Without work[a]	97	29	90	51	187	37
Share in sample (%)	52		48			

| Category | Ghana Living Standards Survey (past year) | | | | | |
	Male	Percentage of males surveyed	Female	Percentage of females surveyed	Total	Percentage of total survey sample
Sample size	1,320		1,560		2,880	
Share in sample (%)	46		54			
Continuously employed	903	68	916	59	1,819	63
Share in sample (%)	50		50			
Without work[a]	417	32	644	41	1,061	37
Share in sample (%)	39		61			

a. Without work for at least a week in the past year or since redeployment.
Source: CFNPP survey, 1991–92; and Ghana Living Standards Survey, 1987–88.

difference between males and females for the average length of those spells: the 29 percent of males who had a spell without work waited twenty-two weeks on average between jobs, while for the 51 percent of women who had nonzero spells, the average waiting period was twenty-four weeks. In addition, there is no significant difference between the average spells of workers from the Living Standards Survey and the redeployees, for either men or women. In general, it does not appear that the incidence or the duration of redeployees' spells without work was any worse than the norm for the population at large.

For the redeployees themselves, it is interesting to note that the civil servants who were laid off had longer spells without work than volunteers: twenty-six weeks on average as opposed to seventeen. In addition, although the average length of unemployment of redeployees who migrated after redeployment is not very different from that of nonmigrants, 75 percent of the migrants had no spell without work compared with 60 percent of the nonmigrants, suggesting that migration helps reduce the occurrence of unemployment in the wake of redeployment.

For the 83 percent of redeployees and Living Standards Survey respondents who are working (see table 10.5), redeployees are more likely than survey respondents to be self-employed, with correspondingly lower likelihoods of either farming or working for wages (table 10.7). This probably reflects a postadjustment labor market in which few formal sector jobs are being created.[18] But it also suggests that, despite the

Table 10.7 Type of work for redeployees and Ghana Living Standards Survey respondents in three regions, by gender, Ghana

Survey/respondent	Farming	Self-employed	Wage work	Unknown work	Total
Redeployees					
Male	125	87	77	n.a.	289
Percentage of total	43	30	27	n.a.	
Female	42	80	12	n.a.	134
Percentage of total	31	60	9	n.a.	
Total male and female	167	167	89	n.a.	423
Percentage of total	39	39	21	n.a.	
Ghana Living Standards Survey					
Male	455	145	496	4	1,100
Percentage of total	41	13	45	0	
Female	629	515	139	4	1,287
Percentage of total	49	40	11	0	
Total male and female	1,084	660	635	8	2,387
Percentage of total	45	28	27	0	

n.a. Not applicable.
Source: CFNPP survey, 1991–92; and Ghana Living Standards Survey, 1987–88.

fact that the formal sector is not hiring new workers, many redeployees are able to find gainful self-employment.

Incomes

Because incomes are typically shared within a household, it is preferable to examine household incomes rather than the incomes of redeployees alone when making judgments about the welfare of redeployees. A look at the monthly household incomes for our sample of redeployees and for households in the Living Standards Survey[19] reveals that overall, the median income of redeployee households is about equal to that of the population at large, although it is less than the median household expenditure from the Living Standards Survey respondents (table 10.8).[20] What's more, because redeployee households are somewhat larger, their median per capita income is 21 percent lower than that of the households in the Living Standards Survey. Although precise comparisons are not possible because of differences in the two surveys, it would appear that the incomes of redeployee households are somewhat lower than those of the population in general in the three regions we sampled.

In addition to comparing redeployee households with the population at large, we can also compare the earnings (wages and self-employment income, including agriculture) of redeployees at the time of their

Table 10.8 Income of redeployees and Ghana Living Standards Survey respondents in three regions, Ghana
(1991 cedis per month)

	Redeployees		Ghana Living Standards Survey	
Expenditure/income	Median	Number of households	Median	Number of households
Household expenditure	—	—	46,443	1,346
Household expenditure per capita	—	n.a.	13,087	n.a
Household income	20,000	510	19,524	1,346
Of which:				
Wages	16,433	207	6,951	429
Agriculture	5,333	227	14,474	672
Self-employment	12,000	363	12,616	733
Other	7,340	82	1,185	771
Household income per capita	4,247	n.a.	5,344	n.a
Remittances	4,000	127	2,370	472

— Not available.
n.a. Not applicable.
Note: The medians are the middle value of only the households that have some of the particular type of income reported. Remittances are not included in household income.
Source: CFNPP survey, 1991–92; Ghana Living Standards Survey, 1987–88; and authors' calculations.

redeployment and at the time of the survey. For all redeployees, average earnings fell by 28 percent from the month before they were redeployed to the survey period, but this includes several redeployees who have zero earnings. However, if we exclude all redeployees who have no current earnings because they are unemployed or have withdrawn from the labor force, average earnings still fell by 20 percent. To some extent, these earnings reductions are offset by the receipt of a severance package. If we add to earnings the interest income from investing the redeployees' severance pay at a 10 percent real rate of return,[21] then the average loss of earnings plus interest is 16 percent of preredeployment earnings for all redeployees (including those with no earnings).

These income declines suggest there is reason to be concerned about the poverty implications of the redeployment program. Indeed, a more careful look at the distribution of redeployee households' incomes suggests that a nontrivial proportion of these families are living in poverty. Poverty lines are usually defined in terms of expenditures or consumption rather than incomes. Since our survey does not collect this information, and because defining poverty lines based on income is likely to exaggerate the extent of poverty, we chose to report a slightly different statistic. First, we calculated the income deciles from the Living Standards Survey households in our three regions. We then calculated the number of redeployee households that fall into each of these deciles. If redeployee households had exactly the same income distribution as the survey households, there would be 10 percent in each decile. But this is not the case (table 10.9).[22] There is a disproportionately large number of redeployee households in the lower income deciles, which suggests that the proportion of these households falling below the poverty line is probably higher than it is for families in the Living Standards Survey.[23]

Table 10.9 Distribution of redeployee household per capita income over Ghana Living Standards Survey per capita income deciles, Ghana

Ghana Living Standards Survey per capita income decile (three regions)	Redeployee households in each decile	
	Frequency	Percentage
1	58	11.4
2	77	15.1
3	73	14.3
4	59	11.6
5	54	10.6
6	44	8.6
7	37	7.3
8	40	7.8
9	38	7.5
10	30	5.9

Source: CFNPP survey, 1991–92; Ghana Living Standards Survey, 1987–88; and authors' calculations.

Which redeployees are likely to be poor? Although there is no statistically significant relationship between either the redeployees' age or gender and their household income, there is a strong relationship between their type of work and their income bracket. We compared income quintiles for redeployee households by type of employment (table 10.10). Not surprisingly, given the results in table 10.8, redeployees who are farming are far more likely to be in the lower quintiles than those in other types of work (including those who are not working): 70 percent fall in the lowest two quintiles, while only 3 percent are in the highest.

· Why are agricultural incomes so low among redeployees? Examining the agricultural data more carefully, we find that small plots and poor yields are to blame. While 44 percent of farmers in general have plots larger than 10 acres, only 3 percent of redeployees do. More than half of redeployees are working plots smaller than 2 acres, compared with only 22 percent of farmers in the Living Standards Survey. In addition, yields per acre for redeployees are far below average. Table 10.11 shows yields per acre for several crops in our sample, along with reference yields that we obtained from the Ministry of Agriculture. To some extent, these differences may be attributable to relatively poor rains in 1990, the year for which many of our households reported agricultural information. The dramatic differences in pepper yields are probably due in part to comparing dry and wet weights. Nonetheless, these differences are remarkable.

We can think of three possible interpretations for these results. First, many redeployees are new to farming and may not be very good at it. Second, our sample of redeployees may include a larger than usual number of part-time farmers—people who farm small plots as a second

Table 10.10 Number of redeployee households in Ghana Living Standards Survey income quintiles, by redeployees' main employment, Ghana

Quintile	No work	Column %	Farming	Column %	Self-employed	Column %	Wage work	Column %	All re-deployees	Column %
Lowest	19	32	66	38	33	19	17	17	135	26
Row %	14		49		24		13			
Second	11	19	56	32	44	25	21	21	132	26
Row %	8		42		33		16			
Third	8	14	30	17	33	19	27	27	98	19
Row %	8		31		34		28			
Fourth	9	15	17	10	31	18	20	20	77	15
Row %	12		22		40		26			
Highest	12	20	6	3	34	19	16	16	68	13
Row %	18		9		50		24			
Total	59		175		175		101		510	
Row %	12		34		34		20			

Source: CFNPP survey, 1991–92; Ghana Living Standards Survey, 1987–88; and authors' calculations.

Table 10.11 Yields for redeployees and average yields, Ghana
(kilograms per acre)

Crop	Redeployees	Redeployees whose main work is farming	Ghana average
Maize	278	305	510
Cassava	436	409	3,239
Cocoyam	291	305	2,347
Pepper	45	51	1,158
Tomato	636	320	1,905

Note: Average yield figures are national totals for 1989.
Source: Government of Ghana, *Quarterly Digest of Statistics* (September 1991); and authors' calculations.

job. These "weekend farmers" would lower the average farm income for all families reporting farm income. Finally, redeployees may put less effort and resources into farming because they view it as a temporary occupation—a fallback option that they do to survive while they look for a better job elsewhere. This would discourage them from making longer-term investments (for example, land clearing and improvement) in farming, which would be an especially important consideration if, as recent returnees to their village, redeployees received marginal or unimproved land to work.[24]

If the first hypothesis were true, we should expect to see differences in the farming income of redeployees who began farming after redeployment and the income of those who were farming before redeployment and continued to do so afterward.[25] Our data, however, offer little support for this idea. The average household agricultural incomes for new and continuing farmers are virtually identical. To examine the second hypothesis, we compared total household incomes for households whose main work (that which occupied the majority of the household's time in the past month) was farming, self-employment, and wage work. Under this hypothesis, the abundance of part-time farmers would pull the average household agricultural income down, but the overall incomes of households whose main occupation is farming should be similar to those of other households. This, too, is inconsistent with our data. Even though farming households do have higher agricultural income than households whose main work is either self-employment or wage work, their total incomes are much lower. Moreover, households whose main work is farming still have a considerably lower median agricultural income than the Living Standards Survey sample. It is difficult to cite evidence supporting or contradicting the third hypothesis—that redeployees expend less effort and resources on farming—but it is the explanation most consistent with our conversations with redeployees and with other observers in Ghana.

Beyond agricultural incomes, it is interesting to note the contrasts in the incomes of wage workers, farmers, and the self-employed.[26] Fifty-one percent of redeployee household income comes from self-employment, mostly because a large number of redeployees and their families are involved in self-employed activities. Thirty percent of redeployee household income comes from wages. Considering that only 21 percent of redeployees have wage or salaried work, the results in table 10.8 suggest that many redeployees have family members working in relatively high-paying wage jobs. Indeed, 41 percent of redeployee households have wage income. Finally, we note that redeployee households are receiving larger remittances than Living Standards Survey households. If we accept the notion that remittances are part of an informal insurance network among relatives, the larger remittances to redeployee households would suggest that their extended family views them as having fallen on hard times and thus meriting larger "insurance payments" in the form of remittances to redeployees.

Migration

Ghanaians are a very mobile population. Seventy-seven percent of the Living Standards Survey respondents older than 16 indicated they had lived in at least two different places for a period of more than three months. Twenty-six percent had moved at least three times. In net terms, this migration is generally toward the cities, but there are significant gross flows in the opposite direction.

Among redeployees, 19 percent have moved since they were redeployed. Although this is a much smaller proportion than for the Living Standards Survey sample, that sample refers to the respondent's entire lifetime while our survey asks only about migration since redeployment. Checking the Living Standards Survey responses for the date of the most recent change in residence, we find that 22 percent of the sample had migrated within four years of the survey date (roughly the lag between the start of the redeployment program and our survey), a figure quite close to our migration numbers. Our survey, however, does not include eighty-six redeployees who migrated beyond our reach. So it appears that redeployees are about twice as likely to have migrated as the population at large.

The difference between the migration pattern revealed by the Living Standards Survey and the survey of redeployees is striking: while the net flow of the Living Standards Survey respondents is from rural to urban areas, 82 percent of redeployees who changed residence since redeployment moved to a rural area from an urban.[27] Thus, redeployment seems to have caused a significant amount of "reverse" migration to rural areas. There are two possible explanations for this, with quite different implications for any evaluation of the social and economic impact of the redeployment program and the government's reform program in general. On the one hand, one could argue that widespread price liberalization has shifted the internal terms of trade in favor of agriculture so that migrants now have a greater incentive to move into farming than into other occupations. In this view, the reverse migration is a positive consequence of the general program of policy reforms in Ghana. On the other hand, traditional land tenure practices allow farming to serve as a fallback occupation for those who cannot find work elsewhere. In most of Ghana, people have a right to use land in the village of their birth (or nearby), even if they have been away for some time. Thus, it is always possible to farm when all else fails. In this view, redeployee farming represents underemployment, and the reverse migration is a sign of people entering a low-productivity occupation that serves either as a last-resort job or as a way of marking time until a better opportunity comes along.

The household income data for migrant and nonmigrant redeployees (table 10.12) support the second hypothesis. As discussed earlier, agricultural incomes are very low in this sample, so those who are farming are likely to be poor. The vast majority of redeployees' migration is toward rural areas, and most of those migrants are farming. Not surprisingly, the household incomes of urban-to-rural migrants are only about two-thirds those of redeployees who stayed in urban areas. Although it is possible that other factors explain this income difference, statistical tests show no relationship between the migration categories in table 10.12 and variables (such as age, gender, and education level) that might predict a redeployees' income.

At the same time, a significant number of migrants to rural areas are not farming. Twenty-nine percent of urban-to-rural migrants have a nonagricultural occupation as their main work. Among this group, the median

Table 10.12 Average household per capita income of redeployees by change in residence, Ghana
(1991 cedis per month)

Change in residence	Income per capita	Number of households
Never moved		
Urban	6,161	350
Rural	3,460	61
Urban to:		
Urban	6,636	17
Rural	4,286	79
Rural to:		
Urban	1,547	1
Rural	1,615	2

Source: CFNPP survey, 1991–92.

income for households whose redeployee is self-employed is 60 percent higher than the median for households that are farming, although the level is still not as high as that of households that remained in urban areas. Nonetheless, it appears that concerns about low incomes among redeployees should be focused on farmers rather than on migrants.

Allocation of severance pay

Ninety-five percent of redeployees received severance pay.[28] Economic theory suggests that people receiving a one-time payment will save most of it, unless their income is so low that they must spend their assets (the severance pay in this case) to survive. A review of the pattern of savings and expenditures out of severance pay (table 10.13) shows that at the time of the survey, which could be from one month to four years after redeployment, total savings out of severance pay were more than half the total amount received. The accumulation of net financial assets is rather small, 21 percent of total severance pay, and one-third of that amount (8 percent) was allocated to canceling debts. This is not too surprising, however, in view of the poor state of Ghana's banking system and the riskiness of holding cash.

On the other hand, expenditures on items that are traditionally considered to be investment—land, housing, business equipment, and education—are relatively high, amounting to 34 percent of total severance pay. The largest expenditure in this category is for nonfarm equipment, the basis for much of the self-employed income observed in the sample. If we also include consumer durables and medical expenses as "investment" (in the sense that they provide a flow of services over time or develop human capital), then redeployees saved 68 percent of their severance pay in the broadest sense. This is comparatively large, especially considering that the drawdown of the lump sum severance payment has occurred over several years for many of the households in our sample.

Examining the breakdown of severance pay allocations by socioeconomic characteristics of the redeployees yields some insights and some surprises. There is no significant difference in the proportion different age groups save out of their severance, even though the life-cycle hypothesis would predict that the middle-aged should save more.[29] There are, however, differences in the patterns of saving, with older redeployees investing mostly in real estate and liquid assets, while the younger groups allocate a larger proportion (18 to 23 percent) of their severance to equipment for their businesses.

Women saved a significantly larger proportion of their severance pay compared with men—62 percent as against 51 percent—despite the fact that women generally received smaller amounts. Most of the difference is accounted for by greater liquid assets, although women also purchased more business equipment than men.

The most striking set of differences in savings behavior was that self-employed redeployees saved 65 percent of their severance pay, significantly more than redeployees with other occupations (table 10.14). Farmers have the next highest savings rate, 59 percent. Most of the difference between the self-employed's saving and that of other redeployees is in the purchase of business equipment, which is sensible. The

Table 10.13 Allocation of redeployees' severance pay, by expenditure and savings type, Ghana
(nominal cedis)

Use of severance pay	Mean	Percentage of total
Liquid assets	28,030	13
Of which:		
Bank savings account	27,261	
Bank checking account	465	
Savings with Susu[a]	0	
Foreign exchange	0	
Savings in cash	304	
Repayment of debts	18,065	8
Real estate	25,820	12
Of which:		
Urban land purchase	2,655	
Farm land purchase	2,381	
Construction	20,784	
Business equipment	41,570	19
Of which:		
Tractor, car, motorcycle	8,258	
Farm equipment	9,105	
Nonfarm equipment	24,207	
Education	7,490	3
Subtotal: Financial and real savings	120,975	56
Consumer durables	17,321	8
Of which:		
TV, furniture, radio, and so on	5,365	
Clothing	11,956	
Consumer nondurables	77,332	36
Of which:		
Daily food and transport	47,648	
Medical expenses	8,288	
Gifts to relatives	15,251	
Other	6,145	
Total: Severance pay	215,628	100

a. Susu is rotating savings.
Source: CFNPP survey, 1991–92.

lower savings out of severance for wage workers and those not working are also consistent with our survey results. Wage workers have high average incomes (see table 10.8) and probably the steadiest source of income, leaving them with a lower precautionary motive for savings. In addition, redeployees who currently have wage jobs had longer spells without work after redeployment, and probably lived on their severance while they searched for work. Redeployees who are not working obviously have a need to consume their severance pay, since they are without income. In addition, many are older and likely to be out of the labor force, with a correspondingly lower incentive to invest in physical assets. Note, however, that those who are not working generally hold larger liquid assets than other redeployees.

Finally, the pattern of savings behavior over the course of the redeployment program is interesting. Civil servants who were redeployed in 1987 saved only 35 percent of their severance, but the rate rose to 49 percent in 1988 and 1989, and 63 percent in 1990.[30] We have already noted that severance pay per redeployee increased over time (see table 10.4), and the larger amounts may have allowed redeployees to save more. At the same time, there is general agreement in Ghana that early redeployees did not really understand what was happening to them and may not have believed that their layoff was permanent. Beginning in 1988 the government made an effort to explain the program more clearly to redeployees, both individually and through the media. If this helped convince redeployees that they would not regain their government post, it may have induced them to save a larger amount of their severance pay.

Table 10.14 Allocation of severance pay, by redeployee's main work, Ghana

(percentage of total severance pay)

Use of severance pay	No work	Farming	Self-employed	Wage work	Training/student
Liquid assets	19	12	12	12	12
Repayment of debts	10	8	9	8	7
Real estate	3	18	13	5	16
Business equipment	13	17	28	10	16
Education	3	4	2	5	3
Subtotal: Financial and real savings	47	59	65	40	54
Consumer durables	5	9	6	11	16
Consumer nondurables	48	32	29	50	30
Total: Severance per redeployee (in nominal cedis)	258,048	207,465	235,070	197,418	121,713

Note: Numbers may not add exactly to subtotal or total because of rounding.
Source: CFNPP survey, 1991–92.

Conclusions

While recognizing the serious consequences of overstaffing in the civil service, the Government of Ghana expressed two main reservations about redeploying a sizable number of government employees: redeployed workers would present political problems, and they would add significantly to the ranks of the unemployed. The first concern has proved unfounded. The Cornell survey results provide evidence that the latter fear was also exaggerated. The majority of redeployed workers had no spell without work after leaving government service, in part because they continued occupations undertaken side by side with government service. What's more, despite the skeptics' prediction that redeployed civil servants would not return to their villages, a significant number of redeployees chose to migrate from urban to rural areas, and most of them are now farming. This is the good news regarding civil servants' employment response to redeployment.

The bad news is that redeployees' household income is somewhat lower than the general population, with a significant proportion probably poor by any standard definition. In particular, households whose redeployee is engaged in agriculture often have very low incomes. Although it is difficult to pinpoint the reasons for this, it is plausible that redeployed civil servants view farming either as a last-resort employment option or as a way to mark time until other, more remunerative opportunities arise. In either case, if the government wants to mitigate the impact of redeployment on those who are hardest hit, it should look to support those who are farming.

Even though we are concerned about the low incomes of redeployees engaged in agriculture, it is important to remember that they constitute a minority of the redeployees and that others are generally doing about as well as other households in Ghana. Nonfarm income is higher for former government workers than for the general population, reflecting, in part, their higher-than-average education. It is particularly interesting to note that the self-employed redeployees are earning average incomes despite the fact that few received any training or assistance (except for their severance pay). When the redeployment program began, much was made of the need to provide credit, "entrepreneurial training," and so on to help redeployees start productive small-scale enterprises. In the end, these programs either did not develop or came on the scene too late to benefit the redeployees that we interviewed. Training and credit programs for redeployees have not done well in other countries,[31] and Ghana's self-employed redeployees seem to have managed well enough without them.

One aspect of the redeployment program that has promoted a significant amount of investment, albeit unintentionally, is the severance package. Redeployed workers have devoted a significant share of their severance pay to savings (broadly defined) and much of that has gone to physical investments for self-employed enterprises. It is interesting to note that although the government was able to get donors to finance certain other aspects of the redeployment program that were supposed to promote investment, no donor would finance severance pay. Yet most of the donor-financed programs have been very slow to produce results. Considering that effective means of promoting private sector, small-scale investment are often sought and rarely found, it is worth considering severance packages as a policy option to promote investment. This is in addition to evaluating severance payments in terms of how effectively they reduce the wage obligations of the central government and how effectively they ease the burden of redeployment for affected civil servants.

The redeployment program in Ghana is widely viewed as a success in a field where other governments have failed, mostly because it succeeded in reducing the size of the civil service and did not generate strong political opposition. The one lingering question has been the impact of the program on the redeployees. This study begins to address that question, finding that the answer is mixed. Redeployees did find gainful employment soon after they left the civil service, sometimes migrating to a rural area to find it. Another positive result is that many redeployees saved or invested a significant proportion of their severance pay. Finally, with the exception of the earliest redeployees (who generally received the smallest severance pay), we have not noticed much bitterness or resentment among the redeployees we interviewed.

At the same time, however, redeployees' incomes are somewhat low relative to the population at large, and a nontrivial proportion are probably poor by any definition. Although the government has planned a variety of programs to aid this group, difficulties with both financing and administration have slowed or prevented their realization. In view of this gap, and noting the generally positive effects of the severance package, the most straightforward policy option would be to increase the severance package, perhaps with some provision to cap the total payments to avoid paying very high amounts to a few civil servants with high base pay, long experience, or both. Going beyond this straightforward and administratively costless change presents a host of problems that the Ghanaian government and its donors have not always handled well. Nonetheless, from a social welfare perspective, it seems clear that any further policy aimed at benefiting redeployees should focus on the problems of those who are farming. Although we still do not know enough about the problems and interests of this group, it is clearly the poorest among the redeployees and as such, merits whatever extra attention the government wishes to give its former employees.

Notes

The authors gratefully acknowledge the support of the United States Agency for International Development under its Cooperative Agreement AFR-000-A-0-8045-00 with the Cornell Food and Nutrition Policy Program. We also want to thank S. A. Laryea-Brown for diligent assistance in field work.

1. Lindauer and others (David Lindauer, Oey Astra Meesook, and Parita Suebsaeng, "Government Wage Policy in Africa: Some Findings and Policy Issues," *World Bank Research Observer*, vol. 3, no. 1, January 1988) report civil servant–population ratios between 0.7 percent and 1.9 percent in Liberia, Malawi, Nigeria, Senegal, Sierra Leone, Sudan, and Zambia. De Merode (chapter 8, this volume) reports ratios between 0.5 percent and 1.8 percent for several French-speaking African countries.

2. A "ghost worker" is a fictitious name on the payroll whose salary is collected by someone else.

3. Labor contracts in Ghana's state-owned enterprises stipulate up to ten months' base pay for each year of service for workers who are dismissed because they are redundant.

4. This calculation assumes that the retrenched workers are never replaced, that is, that their post really does disappear when they are laid off.

5. For part of 1989 and 1990, the data were available at the Prices and Incomes Board (PIB) in computer-readable files. For 1987 and 1988, the data were recorded on hard copy at MMSW. We arranged for the ministry to enter those data on PCs. That process yielded a number of records significantly lower than the number of redeployees for those years, probably because hard copy records were misplaced or mistakenly not entered. For 1987, the MMSW reports that 5,577 civil servants were redeployed in the three regions we sampled (Government of Ghana, "Labour Redeployment Programme: Achievements, Problems, and Prospects," report issued by the Labour Redeployment Programme's Management Committee, 1990), while we have 3,965 records, or 71 percent of the ministry's total. For 1988, we have 87 percent of the ministry's total. In addition to these shortfalls, we have no data for the first half of 1989—the PIB data begin about August of 1989. Those data, however, are quite close to the number of redeployees reported for late 1989 and 1990. Ex post, our sample is fairly evenly distributed across the four years.

6. Ghana has ten regions. The three regions covered in the Cornell survey accounted for 54 percent of redeployees.

7. Civil servants are allowed to continue working until they receive their severance pay.

8. See, for example, Boateng and others (E. Oti Boateng, Kodwo Ewusi, Ravi Kankur, and Andrew McKay, "A Poverty Profile for Ghana," Social Dimensions of Adjustment Working Paper 5, World Bank, Washington, D.C., 1989) for a description of the survey.

9. David S. Kingsbury ("Compensatory Social Programs and Structural Adjustment: A Review of Experience," Development Alternatives, Inc., Bethesda, Md., 1992) reports that such a redevelopment program in Senegal suffered due to political manipulation.

10. Government of Ghana, op. cit.

11. Kingsbury (op. cit.) finds that the same is true of redeployment programs in Mali and Senegal.

12. Severance benefits are based on the base salary, which increased substantially with the unification even though total compensation did not change very much.

13. It is also true that the youngest redeployee is 22. We chose the 17–25 age group following the categories of P. Beaudry and N. K. Sowa ("Labour Markets in an Era of Adjustment: A Case Study of Ghana," University of Montreal, Department of Economics, 1990) in order to compare our results with theirs. Nonetheless, this choice implies that our lowest age group will always be underrepresented.

14. This figure does not correspond exactly to the concept we would like, since women who are divorced, separated, or widowed don't live with a "bread winner." Unfortunately, our survey does not explicitly ask respondents their marital status, although we do ask the relationship of each person in the household to the redeployee. We have assumed that a woman who lives with either her husband or her children is married, while one who does not is "single." For consistency, we compare married, divorced, separated, and widowed respondents in the Living Standards Survey to our respondents.

15. Recall that the amount of severance pay is based on a civil servant's salary at termination. As a result, each pay raise increases the end-of-service benefit, almost proportionally. Also note that pay raises generally come at the same time for all civil servants, which accounts for the surge in volunteers.

16. Beaudry and Sowa, op. cit.

17. See Kodwo Ewusi, "The Size of the Labour Force and Structure of Employment in Ghana," Technical Publication Series no. 37, Institute of Social, Statistical, and Economic Research, Legon, Ghana, 1978.

18. This is obviously true of the civil service and, to a lesser extent, the parastatal enterprises. We have the impression that it is also true of larger private firms, some of which are being forced to retrench in the face of renewed competition from imports. Note also that many of the redeployees who migrated beyond our reach in Ghana (and are therefore excluded from our sample) went to regions where farming is the overwhelmingly dominant occupation, so our data on the proportion of redeployees who are farming are probably too low. On the other hand, the eighteen redeployees who went abroad are almost certainly not farming.

19. Since the Living Standards Survey took place between October 1987 and April 1988, we have "inflated" the GLSS figures to prices consistent with the timing of our survey. We did this by first deseasonalizing the national consumer price index series, then using the ratio of the midpoint of the Living Standards Survey, January 1988, over the midpoint of our sample, September 1991, to inflate the GLSS data.

20. There is a significant discrepancy between incomes and expenditures in the Living Standards Survey. If we assume that our survey has a similar degree of income under-reporting, then the appropriate comparison is with incomes in the Living Standards Survey. However, the discrepancy in the Living Standards

Survey is unusually large, with household expenditures roughly double household income, so we might expect a better comparison to be somewhere between the GLSS income and expenditure figures. We report both, as lower and upper bounds.

21. Because it is likely that any capital income earned from productive assets that redeployees purchased with their severance pay is already included in their earnings, we calculated the 10 percent return based on total severance pay minus severance pay that redeployees used to purchase productive assets. This avoids double-counting that capital income.

22. An x^2 test rejects the null hypothesis that each decile contains 10 percent of the redeployee households. Note that because our concern here is poverty rather than earnings, we include remittances in both the GLSS and redeployee income data in this table. We also note that these results may be biased by the unusually low household sizes reported in the Living Standards Survey. This would yield per capita incomes that are too high, and thus make the redeployees appear poorer relative to the general population than is actually the case. In addition, to account for the fact that some redeployees have recently received a substantial sum of money in the form of severance pay, we added 0.1/12 of the amount of the redeployees' severance pay reported as held in liquid assets. This assumes a 10 percent real rate of return per year, divided by 12 to get an implied monthly income.

23. Using data on household expenditures, Boateng and others (op. cit.) find that 35 percent of GLSS households are "poor" and 7 percent are "extremely poor," where "poor" is defined as any household falling below two-thirds of mean household expenditures and "extremely poor" as those falling below one-third.

24. We have also considered the possibility of nonsample error in our data. Household surveys generally find that respondents under-report their incomes. As mentioned, the Living Standards Survey has average household income equal to only 60 percent of household expenditures. In that survey, however, the main source of under-reporting appears to be self-employed income, not agriculture. Moreover, our survey asks for production data as well as sales and prices. For the most part, the ratio of reported sales receipts to reported quantities sold is close to market prices in our survey. Thus, to under-report sales, a farmer would first have to under-report production before we asked about sales. It seems more likely that intentional under-reporting would occur on the sales question, in which case yield data would be accurate but the ratio of sales to quantity would be lower than market prices.

25. One hundred sixty-eight redeployees (33 percent) reported that they farmed as a second job while they were employed in the civil service and continued to farm until the survey date.

26. Earnings by sector are studied in Harold Alderman, Sudharshan Canagarajah, and Stephen Younger, "A Comparison of Ghanaian Civil Servants' Earnings before and after Retrenchment," World Bank, Policy Research Department, Poverty and Human Resources Division, Washington, D.C., 1994.

27. We consider an urban area to be any regional or district capital. Although some district capitals are not very large, results for a more precise breakdown of urban, semiurban, and rural areas are quite similar to those we present here.

28. Most of those that did not receive severance pay were either older than 60 or discharged for medical reasons or misconduct. A few were redeployed so recently that they had not yet received their check.

29. For the purposes of this discussion, "saving" consists of accumulating liquid assets in bank accounts or cash; paying off debts; purchasing land, housing, or business equipment; and paying for education.

30. The rate for 1991 is even higher, 68 percent, but that is probably because recent redeployees simply have not decided what to do with their severance yet, as evidenced by the fact that 36 percent of their severance remains in liquid assets.

31. See Kingsbury, op. cit.

11

Conclusion: The political economy of civil service pay and employment reform

Barbara Nunberg and David L. Lindauer

In assessing the state of the art of civil service pay and employment reform, the ascent up the learning curve remains a steep and hilly climb. Many analytic gaps persist, and reform outcomes so far have been less than fully satisfactory. Nonetheless, the essays in this collection stand as testament to the ample body of knowledge accumulated on this topic over a fairly short period. Many aspects that ten years ago were either unknown or misconceived are now better understood. Where government wages were once perceived as too high, research has shown that in many developing countries the opposite is true, especially for more skilled occupations. Fiscal, labor market, and civil service wage and employment policies, once treated as separate phenomena, are now more readily viewed as fundamentally related. Indeed, the perception of the basic civil service pay and employment syndrome—high aggregate wage bills, low average salaries, compressed remuneration structures, and surplus employment—is now widespread. Moreover, the negative effects of this typical scenario on government performance are also widely understood.

As part I of this volume illustrates, we have learned a great deal about how to diagnose civil service pay and employment problems in concrete settings. The essays indicate how to conduct fieldwork on this subject and demonstrate ways in which apparently insurmountable data obstacles are in fact overcome. In addition, the analyses provide an empirical assessment of the redundancy problem, moving beyond vague notions of overstaffing to more precise appraisals of how much and where overstaffing occurs. The diagnoses also impart some creative and practical techniques for framing problems and weighing options for reform.

Turning to attempts at reform in part II, the account is decidedly mixed. On the bright side, there is increasing evidence of a technical package for implementing reforms. These essays document the development through trial and error of a range of policy instruments and pragmatic techniques to reduce employment numbers, restructure pay, and install ongoing capacity to manage a cleaned-up personnel system. Although considerably more research is needed to refine these techniques and develop methodologies for more sophisticated prescriptions for, say, estimating redundancy or designing severance packages, it is still the case that we know much more about what works and what does not than when these activities first began.

The overall picture of the impact of reforms, in terms of both fiscal consequences and improved civil service performance, is less rosy. In some cases, wage compression and redundancy were partially combated. In others, reforms succeeded only in arresting declines that had been occurring over a period of many years—no mean feat, but neither a dramatic triumph. In the worst scenarios, reforms had negligible impact or were reversed after initial progress. No systematic analysis of the impact of reforms on performance has taken place, but anecdotal reports do not suggest significantly more efficient civil services, even in the most successful reform cases.

Even with all these difficulties, civil service pay and employment programs are probably moving in the right direction. These programs do not offer a panacea for performance improvements; other institutional reforms such as career development, training, recruitment strategies, and performance evaluation are also critical. But reforming government pay and employment is still essential to meaningful civil service reform. This is argued despite the limited institutional and fiscal impact of some reform programs. We submit that the failure of such reforms to have greater positive effect was due in part to the lack of adequate attention to some of the aforementioned institutional dimensions. But it was also due to what may have been overly modest aims with regard to employment reduction and pay adjustment. Indeed, in a number of countries, 5 or 10 percent rightsizing cannot begin to address the problem; government employment will have to be reduced more drastically to effect real savings. Pay will need to be decompressed further and some salaries raised much higher to have a chance of resolving the recruitment difficulties, absenteeism, moonlighting, and other related problems that now cripple government.

Are deeper reforms feasible?

Could reforms be pushed further, faster, and deeper to greater effect? Although it seems clear that the technical capacity exists to execute more radical reforms, greater uncertainty arises with regard to the political economy implications of bolder actions. Governments have generally resisted sweeping employment and wage decompression reforms, particularly on grounds of political infeasibility. And, taking such calculations of political risk at face value, international donors have not pressed countries to undertake reforms beyond these perceived limits.

Without the benefit of in-depth research on the political economy of pay and employment, we may at least assemble anecdotal evidence to assess past reform experience and to speculate about the prospects for more daring restructuring policies in the future. Experience so far supports the view that, in the main, the political risks incurred by regimes undertaking civil service pay and employment reforms have been overestimated. Indeed, predicted dire consequences of reform—ranging from increased open unemployment to regime destabilization to social upheaval—have not come to pass. Nor did less dramatic forms of political opposition materialize: strikes did not occur; where relevant, incumbent regimes were not defeated in elections; neither, where pertinent, did by-election results reflect discontent with civil service reform outcomes.

In building the argument for political feasibility, it is important to stress that most reform programs analyzed so far have taken place in (mainly African) countries where democratic opposition may have been thwarted by the threat of retaliation from authoritarian regimes, where de facto or de jure one-party systems operate, or where collective organizations such as labor unions, particularly those with strong links to political parties, are weak. It is worth noting too that most of the reforming countries were largely agricultural, and legal obstacles to reforms were minimal. We recognize that the case for politically easy reforms cannot be extended automatically to middle-income, urbanized countries with strong labor movements and political opposition parties and more complex legal institutions. Countries such as Brazil, for example, fit the latter description. Efforts to downsize the Brazilian civil service have run into formidable opposition and have been constrained by constitutionally guaranteed employee rights that have been upheld by the courts when challenged through litigation. Speculation about the prospects for significant reforms in such environments in the near term is risky. But it is also important to note that Argentina, which conformed to a virtual caricature of the middle-income "hard case," has undertaken perhaps the most ambitious downsizing exercise. The 20 percent reduction in civil service employment has occurred despite the country's long history of labor strife and political instability.

What, then, explains the relatively mild political response to civil service reforms taken to date, especially in contrast to the major social and political disruptions caused by other economic reforms such as devaluations or the elimination of food or energy subsidies?

The scope of reforms

The relative lack of political disruption associated with civil service pay and employment reforms to date may be due, simply, to the shallowness of reforms undertaken so far. Reforms have not been carried out on a sufficiently dramatic scale to test the political limits, since the number of people directly affected by reform has been comparatively small. However, even if pay and employment reforms were to become more far-reaching, the numbers directly affected would be far smaller than when, for example, bread prices or bus fares are raised. Even in those instances where public employees represent a majority of all wage workers, they will still amount to small percentages of the total labor force or urban households—relevant groups when food or energy subsidies are reduced. Because of the relative numbers of people affected, civil service reforms may enjoy greater political feasibility than do other attempts at liberalization.

How much is left to lose?

If we assume that resistance to reform is greatest when what is to be taken away is of value, then it is worth looking more closely at the real value of a civil service job. Measured in terms of compensation, including wage and nonwage benefits, the value of civil service employment has already fallen precipitously in those countries in need of policy reform. The less the job is worth, the reasoning goes, the less fierce the opposition to reform, since the costs of adjustment have, by and large, already been borne. Thus, even modest severance pay solutions may be adequate to compensate for large-scale retrenchments.

It is also fairly clear that pressure has been relieved through the absorption of redundant government workers into agriculture and the informal sector to a degree perhaps not anticipated at the outset of the reform process. Civil servants' daylighting and moonlighting activities in other economic activities before downsizing occurred may have contributed to the smooth transition after retrenchment. Indeed, many workers were involved in agricultural pursuits or informal economic activity that simply expanded when they left government. However, to the extent that civil service positions provided access to transportation, telephones, personal contacts, and the like, such extracurricular activities may have been more difficult to engage in or less profitable after retrenchment.

Although increased open unemployment, with all its potential for political unrest, has not followed retrenchment exercises to the extent once feared, the financial fortunes of retrenched workers remain precarious. It would appear, however, that many are no worse off than if they had remained in government employment. Considerably more empirical work needs to be done to follow the fate of laid-off civil servants, but early accounts suggest that the transition is not as onerous as originally feared. Severance payments appear to have eased the journey from public to private spheres, frequently by bankrolling entrepreneurial activity. All of the above mitigating factors would logically act to defuse potential discontent with reforms.

Profile of the retrenched

The lack of strong, organized opposition to reforms may also be related to the profile of the typical civil servant targeted for retrenchment. Most redundancies come from the lower ranks of the civil service, where the main surplus tends to be located. These retrenchments are sometimes combined with layoffs of daily paid or casual labor. Although some governments have argued that urban, unskilled government workers constitute an essential part of their political constituency, which can be penalized only at great cost, the contrary appears to be true. These employees—at least in the modest numbers so far dismissed—have not mounted particularly powerful or vociferous opposition to the reform program; regime stability and civil peace have not been disrupted. Evidence suggests instead that these workers are fundamentally powerless in the face of reforms and insufficiently organized into labor unions or party structures to mount a viable protest to proposed cuts. The exception that proves the rule is that of the teachers in Côte d'Ivoire. Threatened layoffs there sparked considerable protests, possibly because education employees tend to be better educated and wield significant influence in the political system.

Lower-echelon workers were also the main losers from pay decompression reforms. For the most part, decompression did not meet with overt opposition, although in the Jamaican case, a strong civil service union successfully opposed pay restructuring that threatened to reward upper tiers at the expense of lower ones. In general, though, decompression was effectively used as a payoff to a smaller but more empowered group of civil servants—higher-level bureaucrats. The political acceptability of reforms seems to have depended more on co-opting this group than on deflecting what turned out to be only minimal opposition from lower-ranked employees. The question of whether to promise improved civil service pay before or after retrenchment thus hinges on whose pay is to be raised. Reducing the number of lower-level civil servants is facilitated by eroded compensation, as suggested earlier, arguing for postretrenchment pay hikes. But decompression and the associated salary spurt co-opts higher civil servants into supporting the reform. In sum, selective targeting of potential reform beneficiaries seems required.

Implementation

Reform timing may have been a factor in quieting political protest. Reforms were generally implemented with a big bang through initial employment cuts and then smaller adjustments over a span of a few years. Indeed, a cursory look at other reform experiences suggests that only Chile, under rigid authoritarian rule, took a long period (nine years) to carry out systematic employment cuts. Swift rather than slow, deliberate actions may work better at preventing opposing coalitions from mounting timely and effective opposition.

The application of certain policy and technical instruments may also have lessened the political and social pain of reforms. The degree to which transparency of policy intentions helps or hinders reform implementation is still open to debate, but some experiences suggest that public information campaigns were useful in allaying anxiety among to-be-dismissed workers by assuring them of their legal and financial rights, and informing them of transition support services available to them. Such services, including worker retraining programs and small business credit schemes, appear to have been more important as a political tool to placate disgruntled civil servants than as a technical mechanism to ease redeployment. Similarly, the technical impact of functional reviews to identify redundant employees seems to have been of secondary importance; their real value was in assuring civil servants that arbitrary dismissal, based on political or ethnic criteria, would not occur.

Finally, international donors are often accused of imposing politically explosive reform programs on sovereign governments. But it may be that civil service pay and employment reforms were actually facilitated by the availability of a villainous international partner that could be blamed for the painful aspects of reforms. The direct political risk for regimes was thus reduced.

Why, then, are reforms opposed?

Given our hypothesis on the political feasibility of reform, it is worth posing the question: Why do governments, including those administering some of the worst cases of wage erosion and compression and staffing redundancies, strenuously resist far-reaching reforms? There are several possible answers. Regimes may suffer from a kind of "policy illusion," underestimating the operation of labor markets and their absorptive capacity, or seriously miscalculating the power resources or expectations of key players in the bureaucratic-political game. Alternatively, among the countries that have elected not to pursue civil service pay and employment reforms, there may be those that have accurately calculated the political costs of such initiatives. Resistance may also stem from the perhaps well-founded belief that the value of civil service employment is related not to direct compensation—pay and nonwage benefits—but to indirect access to a variety of rents, including income from graft, and to rationed goods.

Initial government commitment to reform may be undermined as well by behavior within government elite circles. At the political level and among higher civil servants, reducing redundant employment defies classic bureaucratic politics, the object of which is to build empires and grab power and resources by amassing large staffs. There may be considerably more reform intransigence among these actors than among rank-and-file civil servants who can be more easily detached from an increasingly worthless job.

Final arguments

Clearly, political economy variables will need to be examined in rigorous detail on a cross-national comparative basis to yield robust findings that go beyond the speculations laid out in this chapter. For the moment, the limited evidence argues that the assumptions of high political risk that informed most civil service pay and employment reforms in the past decade need to be reconsidered. Such a recalculation might lead governments to undertake more penetrating reforms at lower-than-expected political costs and for higher economic gains.

Although the political constraints to reforms may turn out to be less binding than was initially perceived, we also advocate deeper reforms on the basis of their fundamental objective—to improve the performance of the government sector. As has been argued throughout this volume, correcting existing distortions in civil service pay and employment is crucial for rehabilitating government. Other institutional reforms directed at improving civil service management are also essential to strengthen government performance. But if civil servants are not adequately paid and if a more appropriate balance between staffing levels and nonlabor inputs is not achieved, improvements in the delivery of public goods and services will not be realized. Without a sustained and far-reaching reform effort we can expect the wage bill to continue to drain public revenues while offering little in return. Worldwide, there is a need to have governments do what they do better. Broader and deeper civil service pay and employment reforms are vital to achieving this end.